Pantelis Tsoucas

AF713583

# Macroeconomic Information and Financial Trading

**Advances in Theoretical and Applied Economics**
A series from the European Economics and Financial Centre
*Edited by Dr Homa Scobie*

*The Economics of Oligopolistic Competition*
*Price and Nonprice Rivalry*
Robert E. Kuenne

*Informal Financial Markets in Developing Countries*
*A Macroeconomic Analysis*
Peter J. Montiel, Pierre-Richard Agénor and Nadeem Ul Haque

*Macroeconomic Information and Financial Trading*
Robert I. Webb

# Macroeconomic Information and Financial Trading

Robert I. Webb

BLACKWELL
Oxford UK & Cambridge USA

Copyright © Robert I. Webb 1994

The right of Robert I. Webb to be identified as author of this work has been asserted in accordance with the Copyright, Designs and Patents Act 1988.

First published 1994

Blackwell Publishers
108 Cowley Road
Oxford OX4 1JF
UK

238 Main Street
Cambridge
Massachusetts 02142
USA

All rights reserved. Except for the quotation of short passages for the purposes of criticism and review, no part of this publication may be reproduced, stored in a retrieval system, or transmitted, in any form or by any means, electronic, mechanical, photocopying, recording or otherwise, without the prior permission of the publisher.

Except in the United States of America, this book is sold subject to the condition that it shall not, by way of trade or otherwise, be lent, resold, hired out, or otherwise circulated without the publisher's prior consent in any form of binding or cover other than that in which it is published and without a similar condition including this condition being imposed on the subsequent purchaser.

*British Library Cataloguing in Publication Data*

A CIP catalogue record for this book is available from the British Library.

*Library of Congress Cataloging-in-Publication Data*

Webb, Robert Ivory, 1952–
Macroeconomic information and financial trading/Robert I. Webb.
p. cm. – (Advances in theoretical and applied economics)
Includes bibliographical references and index.
ISBN 1–55786–325–3
1. Securities – Prices – United States. 2. Stock-exchange – United States.
3. Speculation – United States. I. Title. II. Series.
HG4915.W4 1994
339.4'3–dc20 93-37355 CIP

Typeset in 11 on 13 pt Times by Scientifik Graphics (Singapore) Pte. Ltd.
Printed in Great Britain by T.J. Press (Padstow) Ltd., Padstow, Cornwall

This book is printed on acid-free paper

# Contents

# Figures

# Tables

# Series Editor's Preface

The Advances in Theoretical and Applied Economics series, which stems from the European Economics and Financial Centre, is designed to capture recent advances in both theoretical and applied economics. The theme of the series has deliberately been kept broad to portray new developments in a wide range of subjects covering both macroeconomics and microeconomics.

It is intended that the series will act as a forum for new developments in various areas of economics – finance, trade, industry, labour, etc. as well as specific topics such as general equilibrium, dynamic games and rational and adaptive expectations.

During the last two decades a gap has begun to emerge between economists and practitioners (embracing both the policymakers within the public sector and the decision-makers within the private sector). It appeared to the non-economists that the economists had a world of their own, and it seemed as if the field was advanced for its own sake regardless of its relevance or application. As a result, economics as a discipline suffered to some extent. Perhaps this has been due to the way in which the thinking and findings of many economists have been made available to readers. The outcome and policy recommendations emerging out of many research projects have not been communicated in an effective manner – i.e. in a language clear and comprehensible, particularly to those who do not possess technical expertise.

Hopefully the 1990s will be a period of consolidation, bringing to the fore the work of those economists who continued their work in the difficult atmosphere of the last two decades with the dedication and the talent necessary to advance the field.

It is one of the aims of this series to bring the work and contributions of economists closer to those of practitioners and to portray the new directions in the field.

New volumes are invited by authors whose work falls in line with the aims and objectives of the series. Contributions should be sent to the Editor at the European Economics and Financial Centre, PO Box 2498, London W2 4LE.

Homa Scobie
European Economics and Financial Centre

# Preface

> Three beliefs pervade most modern accounts of scientific principles and are the principal source of confusion. The first is that in some sense scientific laws are statements made with certainty. The second is that physical measures can be exact. The third is that there is a clearly marked boundary between science and ordinary thought.
>
> (Sir Harold Jeffreys, *Scientific Inference*, p. 183)

This book largely owes its origin to my experiences trading fixed-income securities for the Investment Department of the World Bank during the late 1980s and an editorial feature that I wrote for the *Wall Street Journal* in 1989. I have long been fascinated by the behavior of speculative prices in general and how new information enters speculative prices in particular. At the same time, I find certain aspects of macroeconomic theory intriguing. These two issues are joined in the reaction of speculative prices to the release of economic reports. The often substantial reaction of bond prices to the release of selected economic data attracted my attention both as a trader and as an academician.

As a trader, I was drawn to the large price changes the release of these reports sometimes engender and the potential for large trading profits from better forecasts. As an academician, I was intrigued by the questions which the often puzzling behavior of changes in speculative prices in response to the arrival of new macroeconomic information raises for both financial and macroeconomic theory.

Of all the various areas of economics, macroeconomics receives the most attention in both the financial and the popular press. Yet, paradoxically, it is also the area which the economics profession knows the least about.

Several questions immediately arise. For instance, what, if anything, can one conclude about the validity of various alternative macroeconomic theories from watching the reaction of bond prices to the release of economic data? Put simply, is the market's reaction to economic reports more supportive of Keynesian or monetarist theory? Any discussion with traders quickly reveals that their macroeconomic or monetary views are often at variance with the predictions of the macroeconomic or monetary theories that the same traders profess to believe in. For instance, many traders believe that the predictions of monetary theory concerning a change in the rate of growth of the money supply on interest rates apply also to a change in the money supply. That is, there is a confusion between changes in the stock of an economic variable and changes in its rate of flow. Similar misperceptions exist with respect to other economic theories. The question naturally arises as to whether changes in speculative prices reflect those misperceptions, or react to new information as macroeconomic or monetary theory suggests.

The notion of an informationally efficient capital market is central to modern finance theory. At first glance, the quick reaction of bond prices to the release of economic reports is exactly what one would expect in an informationally efficient capital market. Upon closer inspection, however, seeming anomalies appear and a number of questions arise. For instance, why should speculative prices react to high frequency preliminary economic data? Are weekly money supply numbers really that important? Why are the more accurate revised numbers of past reports often seemingly ignored by market participants even when there are substantial changes from the previously reported preliminary estimate? Why are some economic reports periodically extremely important and at other times virtually ignored by market participants even though large forecast errors exist in either case? The once market-moving money supply numbers are virtually ignored today. Why? Why does the interpretation traders assign to a given piece of information sometimes change radically over time? Why is the conventional wisdom on the influence of an unexpected change in the merchandise trade balance 180 degrees different from what it was several years ago? To what extent is the reaction of bond prices to the release of new macroeconomic information indicative of trading noise?

This book attempts to answer these and other questions. It presents a blend of theory and practical applications. As such, it reflects my experience as a trader on the floor of the Chicago Mercantile Exchange and at the World Bank, as well as my training in finance and economics at the University of Chicago. The book attempts to make economic theory more intelligible to traders and trading more intelligible to economists. I have tried to make it readable by either traders or economists.

In this regard, theories are viewed simply as convenient ways of describing reality. Our interests are empirical rather than theoretical. That is, we are not interested in whether the the assumptions which underlie a theory are realistic but, rather (as Milton Friedman has argued in his *Essays on Positive Economics*), whether the predictions of the theory are supported by empirical evidence. Nor are discussions limited to the academic literature. Citations from articles in the financial press are also included.

Particular attention is directed to the role of the Federal Reserve. This does not reflect a bias toward monetarism on my part. Rather, the reason is that traders often couch their beliefs on the impact of an economic report on interest rates in terms of how the information from an economic report will influence Fed monetary policy.

The book presents several macroeconomic theories some of which are most assuredly wrong. The paucity of good econometric research in macroeconomics has led to a proliferation of macroeconomic theories many of whose propositions have never been adequately tested despite being strongly held. Some economists would, no doubt, disagree with that assessment.

Similarly, the book discusses information theory and the concept of informationally efficient capital markets at length. The notion of informational efficiency is currently under attack in many quarters and considerable attention is directed to a discussion of trading noise.

The book mentions a number of apparent anomalies in financial or macroeconomic theories. This should not be viewed as a disheartening development but rather the natural progress of science. Those of us in academia often do a great disservice to our students and the public alike by portraying the world as black and white when it is not. Readers who are looking for a black and white view of the relationship between macroeconomic information and financial market reactions will be sorely disappointed. Anomalies play an important role in scientific progress. As Thomas Kuhn has pointed out in his book *The Structure of Scientific Revolutions*, scientific advances typically occur when an accepted paradigm does not explain repeated observation of anomalies.

The book is written for individuals who have either an applied or a theoretical interest in the behavior of speculative prices in response to the arrival of new macroeconomic information. Those whose interest is largely applied will probably find chapters 1, 3, 6, 7, and 8 more appealing, while those whose interest in the behavior of speculative prices is largely theoretical will probably find chapters 2, 3, 4, 5, and 6 more appealing. As is readily apparent, chapters 3 and 6 will probably appeal to both groups.

I would like to take this opportunity to acknowledge the assistance of others without which this book may not have been written. The book has benefited greatly from the many insightful conversations I have had with Gary R. Schirr over the years on the reaction of speculative prices to the arrival of macroeconomic information. It has also benefited from the valuable comments Richard H. Leonard provided on monetary theory. I am indebted to my colleague and frequent co-author, David G. Smith, and Lauren Winer Marrus, publisher of the *Journal of Fixed Income*, for allowing me to use material drawn from our article in the *Journal of Fixed Income* in this book. I am grateful to Dr Homa Scobie, the Series Editor, for encouraging me to write the book. In addition, I would like to thank Richard Markson and the Alex Walker Foundation for providing generous financial assistance for the project. Finally, I want to thank my wife, Mary Beth, and my children, Alexander and Elizabeth, for their patience while I wrote the book and their encouragement to write it.

Robert I. Webb

# 1 Introduction

> Having the right information at the right time is nine-tenths of [winning] any battle.
>
> Napoleon Bonaparte

Large changes in speculative prices and momentary bursts in volatility frequently follow the release of macroeconomic information. Consider, for instance, the following example. On Tuesday, April 13, 1993, the Japanese government announced a 13.2 trillion yen government spending program designed to stimulate the Japanese economy. This announcement precipitated a substantial rally in Japanese stock prices with the Nikkei Average rising 4.3 percent that same day.[1]

This behavior is not unique to Japanese financial markets. Nor is it limited to announcements of unusually large, and hence infrequent, fiscal policy actions. Rather, it is a common response of speculative markets to many macroeconomic news reports. Responses occur in markets for agricultural commodities as well as in markets for securities. (Of course, the magnitude of the response in speculative prices varies greatly depending upon the nature of the perceived information.) It is especially apparent in the US bond market (the principal focus of this book) where traders follow certain periodic economic reports very closely. Indeed, there are times when most of the change in price of the on-the-run long bond during a week is due to the market's reaction to one or more economic reports.[2]

Large changes in speculative prices and momentary bursts of volatility create both risk and profit opportunities for market participants. Not surprisingly, a significant amount of trading activity occurs around the release of economic reports. At times, exceptionally quiet markets will precede the release of an economic report as many market participants anxiously await the report's release in the hope that the information in the report will give the market direction.

The attention directed to economic reports by market participants is facilitated by the fact that most of the closely watched economic reports are released according to a preannounced schedule and at a set time during the trading day. For instance, many important government economic reports in the United States are released at 8:30 a.m. (New York time). Major interest rate futures markets in the United States open 10 minutes earlier in order to accommodate market participants' desires to trade around the release of the economic reports.

Essentially, traders try to anticipate the information that will be released and also ascertain what the market, as a whole, expects. The release of periodic economic reports means that information on perceived consensus expectations can be collected and disseminated to market participants and the "forecast error" can be determined after a report's release.[3] The reaction of speculative prices to new macroeconomic information, however, depends not only on the size of the forecast error but also on the beliefs (about macroeconomic relationships) that traders use to interpret the data.

In this regard, the market's reaction to the release of economic data provides a fascinating glimpse of the macroeconomic relationships perceived by traders. The macroeconomic beliefs of traders are interesting because, as explained below, they often represent caricatures of received macroeconomic theory. Moreover, the consensus beliefs appear to change unpredictably over time. In the terminology of DeLong et al. (1990a, b) traders have *erroneous stochastic beliefs* about macroeconomic relationships. The erroneous macroeconomic beliefs of traders are not just a theoretical curiosity. Unlike economists, traders take security positions in accordance with their beliefs on how speculative prices will change. This means that vast sums of money are often wagered based on traders' mistaken views of macroeconomic relationships.

It should be noted that economic reports are followed closely not only by market participants but by macroeconomic (especially monetary) policymakers as well. Indeed, one might argue that the interest of market participants in economic reports is a reflection of the perceived interest of policymakers in the same reports as an input into the decision-making process of whether to change monetary policy.[4] Consequently, inconsistency in the market's response to a given piece of information over time may simply reflect inconsistency in the conduct of monetary or fiscal policy. Complicating matters further, policymakers may react to the market's response to macroeconomic information rather than the macroeconomic information itself. For example, an economic-report-induced inflation scare in the bond market may cause interest rates to rise and prompt the monetary authority to respond accordingly even though the macroeconomic information contained in the economic report would not have induced the central bank to act. These relationships are illustrated in figure 1.1.

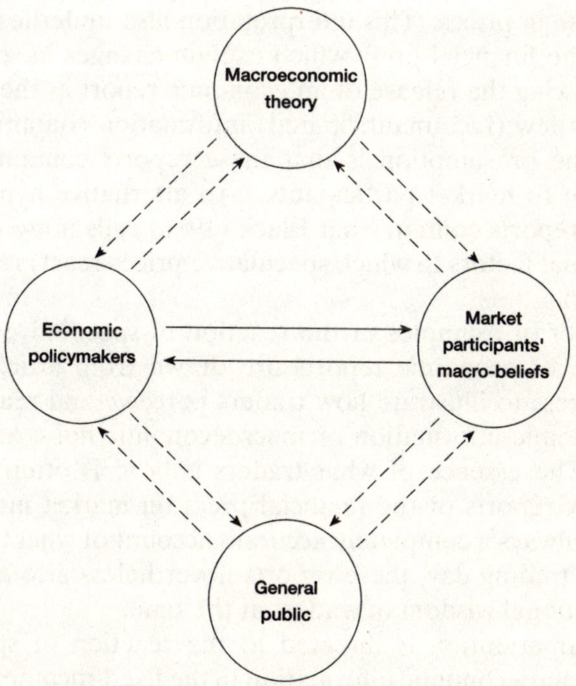


**Figure 1.1** The interrelationships of macroeconomic beliefs, theory and economic policy

As noted above, the turbulent periods that follow the release of government economic reports are often preceded by relatively tranquil periods as trading activity declines in advance of the release of an economic report. This means that recurrent patterns in the volatility of speculative prices should be observable around the release time of economic reports.[5] Engle, Ito, and Lin (1990) argue that observed clusters in the volatility of speculative prices "must lie either in the arrival process of news or in market dynamics in response to the news." On the surface, the market's reaction to various economic reports would seem to verify the above statement by Engle, Ito, and Lin, as well as illustrate the perceived information content of periodic economic reports. That is, the periodic economic reports contain new information and speculative prices change accordingly, resulting in recurrent volatility clusters. Presumably, the larger the consensus forecast error the more information conveyed by the report and hence the greater the response in prices. This interpretation also underlies most accounts in the financial press which explain changes in speculative prices following the release of an economic report as the market's reaction to new (i.e. unanticipated) information contained in the report. The presumption is that these reports contain relevant information to market participants. An alternative hypothesis is that these reports contain what Black (1986) calls noise (i.e. non-informational factors to which speculative prices react) rather than information.

A number of examples of the reaction of speculative prices to the release of economic reports are drawn from articles in the financial press to illustrate how traders perceive and react to new macroeconomic information or macroeconomic noise as the case may be. The essence of what traders believe is often captured in the daily reports of the financial press on market movements. While not always a completely accurate account of what transpired during the trading day, these reports nevertheless give a flavor of the conventional wisdom of traders at the time.

Particular attention is directed to the reaction of speculative prices to macroeconomic information in the fixed-income securities markets (both cash and derivative) to regularly scheduled economic reports.[6] The regularly scheduled release of information of interest to fixed-income market participants coupled with survey data on consensus expectations provides an opportunity to examine the influence of new information (i.e. forecast errors) on interest rates. It also provides an opportunity to examine the macroeconomic relationships perceived by traders. In addition, the reactions of speculative prices to other sources of macroeconomic information, such as monetary policy and fiscal policy actions, are discussed. This book considers these and other issues related to macroeconomic information and financial trading. Although the book focuses on the US financial market and the forces which affect it there is a presumption that financial markets are linked across national boundaries.

## 1 Sources of Macroeconomic Information

There are a number of sources of macroeconomic information of potential interest to participants in fixed-income security markets. These include periodic economic reports on employment, the merchandise trade balance, producer and consumer price indices, durable goods, and other reports released by the government. In addition, there are some privately produced economic reports which are closely followed by market participants. These include the National Association of Purchasing Managers surveys and the Johnson Redbook survey.

Many of the more important government economic reports are released to the public at 8:30 a.m. (New York time). Journalists are given the information approximately one-half hour in advance of the release to the public so that they have time to write their stories and file them immediately after the economic report is made public.[7] The news is immediately transmitted by electronic news vendors around the world. Given that some of the reports are quite lengthy, traders typically focus attention on one or, at most, a few numbers in the report. These numbers are compared with consensus expectations to determine the new information released in the report and the market's initial reaction. The released data are often preliminary and subject to revision. At the same time as new preliminary economic data are released revised data from previous reports are released. This complicates the task of identifying the new information which accompanies the release of the economic report. As noted above, the market's reaction to the release of economic reports depends not only upon the new information gleaned from the report but also upon traders' perceptions of macroeconomic relationships.

Besides regularly scheduled economic reports (produced by the government or private organizations) there are other sources of macroeconomic information which influences financial trading. These include rumors or announcements of changes in the discount rate or reserve requirements by the Federal Reserve, Treasury debt management policy, various fiscal policy actions (e.g. tax rate hikes or cuts, deficit reduction plans, economic stimulus packages), and government intervention in the currency markets. In contrast with the regularly scheduled economic reports, there are not good data on consensus expectations associated with most of the above sources of macroeconomic information. Speeches or comments on monetary or fiscal policy by policymakers occasionally influence changes in speculative prices as well. In addition, the (unofficial) reports of Federal Reserve open market operations or changes in the target Fed funds rate (for which better data on consensus expectations exist) may influence changes in interest rates as well.

Another important source of macroeconomic information which often affects bond prices is changes in the prices of other securities or commodities. There was a period during the late 1980s when bond prices were seemingly being driven by changes in the value of crude oil, the yen, the Dow Jones Industrial Average, soybeans, and the Commodity Research Bureau (CRB) index. Changes in the value of crude oil, soybeans, and the CRB were viewed as harbingers of inflation. After the stock market crash of October 1987, for instance, declining stock prices often precipitated a rally in bonds under the view that the Fed would ease monetary policy to prevent another stock market crash. Similarly, there was a widespread belief among traders that foreign (principally Japanese) investors bought a significant portion of new Treasury securities at auctions and held a substantial amount of Treasury securities in their portfolios. An increase in the value of the yen relative to the dollar was viewed as requiring higher US interest rates in order to offset foreign exchange losses and entice Japanese investors to hold Treasury debt.[8] The stated economic rationale for some of these perceived "linkages" or relationships leaves something to be desired. Not surprisingly, most of these perceived relationships between interest rates and changes in the prices of the above variables tended to be episodic and short-lived.

For instance, during the crisis in Kuwait during 1990 bond prices tended to trade off of changes in oil prices under the belief that higher oil prices cause higher inflation. Yet, only a few months earlier, the bond market virtually ignored what was at that time one of the largest one day moves in the price of oil. The question naturally arises why, if higher (lower) oil prices are a harbinger of higher (lower) future inflation, bond prices did not react earlier that year.

## 2 The Market's Reaction to Economic Reports

The impact of government economic reports on market prices is not limited to the fixed-income securities market.[9] Similarly, there is often a fairly pronounced effect of the release of weather reports and supply conditions on commodity futures prices.[10] Indeed, accurate knowledge of weather conditions in commodity-producing areas is considered so vital that many participants in commodity futures markets subscribe to the services of, or employ, private weather forecasters.[11] One consequence of the intense interest of bond market participants in economic data is increased employment opportunities for macroeconomists on Wall Street to explain what the economic reports mean and to forecast the probable content of future economic reports for traders.

To an individual schooled in economics or finance, the attention directed by market participants to the release of economic data is initially appealing. It suggests the importance of fundamental economic factors in determining changes in interest rates as economic theory would predict. This must seem reassuring to those market observers who are dismayed by the keen interest many traders have for technical analysis. The immediate, often sharp, reaction of bond market prices to the release of the report seems to confirm both the importance of the information contained in the report and the apparent informational efficiency of the bond market. Indeed, the focus by traders on the release of economic data would be exactly what one would expect in a nearly informationally efficient financial market as traders quickly assess the impact of unexpected information on financial market prices. To monetary or fiscal policymakers, the market's reaction to the release of certain economic reports provides a source of guidance about whether a given policy is correct.

Moreover, the reaction of bond prices to the release of economic reports would seem to offer the promise to resolve some disputes in macroeconomics concerning the validity of various alternative macroeconomic theories, i.e. whether the "market" is Keynesian or monetarist, for example.

Unfortunately, first appearances may be deceiving as Webb (1989) points out. Upon closer inspection, the reaction of speculative prices to macroeconomic information is often puzzling and a number of questions naturally arise. This becomes apparent when one examines the anecdotal evidence.

First, why does the interpretation traders assign to a given piece of information sometimes change radically over time? For instance, it used to be thought that a larger (in absolute value terms) than expected trade deficit number was good for the bond market since that meant that the economy was slowing down because exports were growing less rapidly than imports. Here exports served as a proxy for the strength of the economy. Exports represented production while imports represented consumption. A weaker economy, in turn, meant lower interest rates, or equivalently, higher bond prices. This past conventional wisdom of bond traders is reflected in the following excerpts from articles which appeared in the *Wall Street Journal* on September 2, 1986:

> July's record merchandise trade deficit indicates the slump is worsening for the manufacturers and farmers, and it casts doubt on prospects for an economic rebound soon. The deficit widened to \$18.04 billion from a revised June gap of \$13.25 billion....
>
> (p. 2)

> Several recent government reports, including the [above] trade figures released Friday, indicate that the economy is in the doldrums.... In the credit markets Friday, the Treasury's 7 1/4 % [long bond] due 2016 rose to 100 19/32 from 99 7/8....[12]

Simply put, a substantial rally in bond prices followed the release of this information because investors interpreted the larger than expected trade deficit as portending an economic slowdown. And this sparked a bond market rally because market participants believed (rightly or wrongly) that interest rates fall during economic slowdowns.

Contrast this interpretation and market reaction to a larger (in absolute value terms) than expected merchandise trade deficit with the conventional wisdom as explained in the following article which appeared in the *Wall Street Journal* several months later:

> Inflation fears gripped the bond market yesterday as the government reported an unexpectedly large trade deficit, oil prices spurted and the dollar fell sharply.
>
> Actively traded Treasury bonds slumped about 1 1/8 points, or around $11.25 for each $1,000 face amount, in brisk trading....
>
> The move began early in the morning after the Commerce Department said the nation's merchandise trade deficit widened to $14.4 billion in May from $13.32 billion in April. Many analysts had expected the May figure to be about the same or slightly higher than April, and there even had been rumors Tuesday of an $11 billion gap....[13]

The article goes on to report the comments of Wall Street economists who argued that the trade deficit was the major cause of the selloff in the bond market that day. In this case, there is a presumed relationship between the merchandise trade deficit and expected future rates of inflation.

Although the monthly merchandise trade balance is still closely followed by traders, the interpretation of the presumed macroeconomic relationship is entirely different. Current conventional wisdom holds that a larger (in absolute value terms) trade deficit causes bond prices to fall. The chain of reasoning is that a trade deficit implies an excess supply of dollars which causes the price of the dollar to fall and inflation to increase (because the price of imported goods rises). Higher inflation means higher interest rates and lower bond prices. In addition, a decline in the foreign exchange value of the dollar causes a decline in the demand for dollar-denominated bonds by foreigners which may, in turn, trigger a further fall in bond prices.

Notice that the interpretations of the perceived influence of unexpected changes in the merchandise trade deficit on interest rates are 180 degrees different from each other. Did macroeconomic theory change in the interim? Which view, if either, is correct?[14]

Second, why are some economic reports periodically extremely important and at other times virtually ignored by market participants even though large forecast errors exist in both cases? Consider the following. During the early 1980s, the weekly release of the US money supply announcements was closely followed by traders. Divergences of reported values from consensus expectations were often associated with substantial swings in bond prices. And then the attention stopped. The once market-moving money supply numbers are virtually ignored today. This is illustrated in the following excerpt from an article which appeared in *Barron's*:

> Like an old crooner who finds a fresh audience in a new generation, the money supply ignored for so many years is back in vogue. Its renewed importance was apparent late Thursday afternoon, when the Fed reported a surprising decline of $9.7 billion in $M_2$, the most closely watched money measure. That drop, which compared with the consensus estimate of a $3 billion gain, prompted a half-point surge in the prices of 30 year Treasury bonds and a big decline of one-fifth of a percentage point in short-term rates, as traders bet – wrongly it turned out – that the Fed would ease Friday. This post-money supply move in bonds [is], the largest in nearly a decade....[15]

This raises some troubling questions. If money supply announcements were once important why are they usually ignored today? Is it due to increased forecasting ability of Wall Street economists; a changed monetary policy regime; or an indication that money does not matter? If money supply announcements are not important in influencing changes in interest rates why were they once viewed as very important? If the response of interest rates to money supply announcements in years past was due to the pursuit of a different monetary policy regime what explains the above reaction?[16]

Similarly, some economic reports, such as durable goods orders, will receive close attention at times and then are ignored even when there are large differences between expected and reported values. Simply stated, forecast errors are large. This holds even when one standardizes for the dispersion in forecasts across forecasters.

Third, the market's focus is constantly shifting. The market's perception of what constitutes an important number changes over time. The shift in focus of traders is also apparent in the changing list of commodity and security prices that bonds sometimes seemingly "track" or trade off of. While bonds trade on their own much of the time and respond to market-specific information, during some periods bonds have traded off of changes in the price of crude oil, stocks, the yen, soybeans, and the CRB index futures contract, among others. This behavior is not unique to bonds. Changes in stock prices and foreign exchange rates are often linked to price changes in the bond market for example.

Invariably, some economic story rationalizes the linkage. For instance, there is a presumption that changes in the price of some commodity, say oil (or soybeans if there is a drought), is a proxy for inflation. Higher oil prices supposedly mean a higher rate of inflation. Never mind that the conventional wisdom in the bond market confuses changes in *relative* prices, which are not inflationary, with changes in absolute prices, which are. Inflation is largely (although not entirely) a monetary and not a real phenomenon.[17]

Fourth, the perceived economic relationship may be incorrect. Many of the macroeconomic beliefs of bond traders are discredited notions. For instance, many traders confuse changes in the stock of an economic variable, say money, with changes in its rate of flow, as illustrated in the quote from *Barron's* above.

To be sure, one would not necessarily expect individuals schooled in the finer points of macroeconomic or monetary theories to be trading on speculative markets. However, one might expect the market, as a whole, to focus on the relevant economic variables even if individual traders did not. Thus, for instance, one might expect the market, as a whole, to understand the difference between changes in money stocks or flows. Yet, as will be shown later, this does not appear to be the case.

Of all the economic reports released one can perhaps make the strongest case for the bond market's reaction to past reports of inflation (assuming, of course, that the past is prologue). Yet, the question arises as to which measure the market deems as the most important indicator of past (and presumably future) inflation. Consider, for instance, the reaction of bond prices to the release of the March 1993 producer price index (PPI) report in April 1993.

According to the *Wall Street Journal* long bond prices rose over $1\frac{1}{4}$ points largely in reaction to the report. The apparent rationale is illuminating. The article reports:

> Producer prices rose 0.4% in March, the Labor Department said, the same as in February. But the so-called core rate of inflation, considered more accurate because it excludes the volatile food and energy sectors, increased a tiny 0.1% in March. The core rate rose a more worrisome 0.3% the month before.[18]

Is the "core" rate of inflation really a meaningful measure of overall inflation? If so, why not replace the PPI with measures of the "core" rate of inflation instead? If not, why is it used? Should changes in food and energy prices be ignored by investors?

Similar misperceptions exist with respect to the predictions of other economic theories. For instance, the idea that employment beyond some "full" employment level is inflationary is widely accepted among bond traders despite the lack of any real evidence for this proposition. In fact, this idea is simply another example of the confusion between changes in relative and absolute prices discussed above. The question naturally arises as to whether changes in speculative prices reflect those misperceptions or react to new information as macroeconomic or monetary theory suggests.

Fifth, the economic data released in most economic reports cover short periods of time, are preliminary, and often subject to substantial revision. Do economic reports contain relevant information for traders in speculative markets? Simply put, why should speculative prices react to *high frequency preliminary* economic data? Are weekly money supply numbers or monthly trade balance figures really that informative? If economic reports do contain relevant information for market participants does it differ across the yield curve? For example, are weekly money supply figures as important for 13 week Treasury bills as 30 year bonds? If so, what does that suggest about the frequency of perceived *permanent* changes in the rate of growth of the money supply by market participants? Similarly, why are seemingly significant revised data sometimes ignored by market participants and at other times precipitate substantial changes in bond prices?

A number of other questions naturally arise. First, to the extent that there is a predictable relationship between forecast errors of a given economic series and changes in bond prices, can one make a superior return through bond trading by making superior forecasts of economic data? If not, is it because of informationally efficient capital markets and intense competition among forecasters or does it reflect other factors, such as changing interpretations of the value of given forecast errors? Second, are the measured consensus expectations rational? Many studies of the interest rate effects of money supply announcements used the median of survey data collected by MMS International as a proxy for consensus expectations. In a review of this literature, Clark, Joines, and Phillips (1988) demonstrate that the consensus expectations from the MMS survey data were not rational because many MMS survey participants failed to recognize a monthly seasonal pattern in the money supply induced by social security payments.

Common sense and economic theory alike suggest that timely and more accurate information is preferred to less timely and less accurate information. Nevertheless, actual market usage of information does not always conform to what one might expect. Consider the folowing story about a "new" source of macroeconomic information which appeared in *Barron's*:

> The hottest new economic indicator in the bond market isn't any government statistic, but a privately generated weekly report on retail sales called the Johnson Redbook.
>
> Why has the Redbook, which has actually been around for 32 years, recently developed a following beyond the equity analysts and industry types who have long been subscribers? Because bond traders are hungry for any good data on consumer spending and the Redbook is available way before the government's monthly retail sales report, which is widely distrusted because of frequent revisions....[19]

The article goes on to assert that the Redbook data are not only available earlier than data on retail sales released by the Commerce Department but are also more accurate. To the extent that data on retail sales are of interest to bond market participants it is not surprising that traders would react to the release of the Johnson

Redbook data. What is surprising is that bond traders ignored the Redbook numbers during the preceding 32 years. Was the reaction a fluke?

The anecdotal evidence cited above is suggestive rather than conclusive. It is possible that other factors such as incorrectly measured forecast errors, the simultaneous arrival of other information, etc. may explain the apparent anomalies. It is also possible that the contemporary news accounts reported in the financial press are inaccurate.[20] In any event, the sample size of the anecdotal evidence is too small to be used to draw valid statistical inferences.

At the very least, however, the casual empirical evidence cited above challenges the presumption that relevant information for speculative prices is necessarily contained in economic reports. Indeed, instead of containing new information such reports may contain only noise. Anyone who has ever traded fixed-income securities has observed the sometimes anomalous behavior of bond prices. Rather than being isolated examples the above examples are illustrative of a pattern in the behavior of speculative prices.

Of course, the observation of apparent anomalies in speculative prices does not necessarily suggest that market participants are necessarily irrational; unexploited profit opportunities exist; or that anything goes. Merton (1987) remarks:

> In summary, financial markets dominated by rational agents may nevertheless produce anomalous behavior relative to the perfect market model. Institutional complexities and information costs may cause considerable variation in the time scales over which different types of anomalies are expected to be eliminated in the marketplace. (p. 508)

## 3 Trading versus Investing

In order to understand why the bond market's reaction to economic reports may result in price anomalies it is important to understand the nature of trading.[21] In particular, it is important to distinguish between speculation and investment.[22] Active financial markets are driven by trading activity. This has probably always been true.[23] Most observers would probably agree that trading is a form of speculation. Both speculation and investment share many common attributes. Both are profit oriented. Both usually entail the assumption of risk. Although trading positions are typically held for short periods of time, so are some investment positions. Consequently, one cannot necessarily distinguish between the two in terms of the length of time a position is held.

What then is trading and how does it differ from investing?[24] In this book, trading is distinguished from investing in that trading decisions are assumed to be driven by expectations of future price changes of a given security or commodity irrespective of underlying or intrinsic value. In contrast, investment decisions are assumed to be driven by comparison of the current price of a security or commodity with its intrinsic value in the implicit belief that the market price will eventually converge to its intrinsic value. One implication of this approach is that prices in markets dominated by traders may deviate from intrinsic values for long periods of time.

Trading is best understood as a game requiring skill and intelligence. While the objective of the game remains constant – to make money by correctly predicting near-term price changes – the rules of the game, so to speak (i.e. the influences on short-term price changes), keep changing. As with most games, trading entails an element of strategy which is not invariant to the likely behavior of other traders.[25] In contrast to investors, who make decisions based on the perceived underlying value of a security or asset in the belief that price will eventually converge to true value, traders are primarily interested in anticipating short-term changes in price independent of the underlying value.

Keynes (1935) put it best when he said:

> Thus the professional investor is forced to concern himself with the anticipation of impending changes, in the news or in the atmosphere, of the kind by which experience shows that the mass psychology of the market is most influenced. ... The social object of skilled investment should be to defeat the dark forces of time and ignorance which envelop our future. The actual, private object of the most skilled investment to-day is "to beat the gun", as the Americans so well express it, to outwit the crowd, and to pass the bad, or depreciating, half-crown to the other fellow.

> This battle of wits to anticipate the basis of conventional valuation a few months hence, rather than the prospective yield of an investment over a long term of years does not even require gulls amongst the public to feed the maws of the professional; – it can be played by professionals amongst themselves. Nor is it necessary that anyone should keep his simple faith in the conventional basis of valuation having any genuine long-term validity. For it is, so to speak, a game of Snap, of Old Maid, of Musical Chairs – a pasttime in which he is victor who says *Snap* neither too soon nor too late, who passes the Old Maid to his neighbour before the game is over, who secures a chair for himself when the music stops. These games can be played with zest and excitement, though all the players know that it is the Old Maid which is circulating, or that when the music stops some of the players will find themselves unseated.
>
> (pp. 155–6)

Traders value economic data as providing insights into the course of the economy and as an indication of possible fiscal and monetary policy actions, as well as other traders' actions. If enough other market participants react to the release of unexpected economic data in a certain way, then traders must incorporate such behavior into their decision-making process independently of whether they believe such responses are warranted or even rational.[26] Again, Keynes (who was also a successful trader) stated:

> Or, to change the metaphor slightly, professional investment may be likened to those newspaper competitions in which the competitors have to pick out the six prettiest faces from a hundred photographs, the prize being awarded to the competitor whose choice most nearly corresponds to the average preferences of the competitiors as a whole; so that each competitor has to pick, not those faces which he himself finds prettiest, but those which he thinks likeliest to catch the fancy of other competitors, all of whom are looking at the problem from the same point of view. It is not a case of choosing those which to the best of one's judgment, are really the prettiest, nor even those which average opinion genuinely thinks the prettiest. We have reached the third degree where we devote our intelligences to anticipating what average opinion expects the average opinion to be.
>
> And there are some, I believe, who practice the fourth, fifth and higher degrees.
>
> (pp. 155–6)

Traders see changes in speculative prices up close while financial economists usually see changes in speculative prices from a distance. Put differently, traders are accustomed to viewing very high frequency data on speculative prices while financial economists are more accustomed to looking at lower frequency transaction data. This results in some misconceptions about financial markets by financial economists. For instance, it is not commonly recognized how trading activity and liquidity fall considerably around holiday periods. Similarly, traders may see thousands of price changes and spot a few price anomalies and conclude that the market is inefficient where financial economists might conclude that the low percentage of errors is evidence that financial markets are reasonably efficient. Financial economists and traders may view volatility differently.

To be sure, financial economists and practioneers alike generally measure volatility as simply the standard deviation of changes in the log of speculative prices over some time interval. Assuming that the second moment exists (as it does in a normal distribution) volatility can be readily calculated as the variance or its transform the standard deviation.[27] The choice of time interval varies across practioneers with short time intervals, such as 14 to 20 trading days, generally preferred for changes in futures prices.[28]

Focus on the standard measure of volatility, however, fails to capture the fact that traders also perceive different types of volatility. The world of trading has its own argot with colorful and descriptive terms. For example, traders use the term "choppy" to describe markets with violent price swings, where prices oscillate wildly without seeming to stop at intervening prices.[29] Moreover, the volatility (as measured by the variance) may remain *unchanged* during a choppy market. This results from the fact that *effective* transaction prices may differ sharply even though *measured* transaction prices do not. Most traders fear choppy markets because of the increased danger of uncontrollable losses due to sudden price swings.

A closely related phenomenon which frequently precedes and may precipitate a "choppy" market is a "vacuum." As the name implies, vacuums cause traders to get "sucked up" into believing that a price move will continue and it then suddenly reverses, thus "blowing out" the trader with a position on the wrong side.

A vacuum represents a market condition that arises when all or most of the outside or public orders on the books (i.e. non-market orders) are executed in some price range due to prior price action in that range. This may result, for example, from "gunning for stops" when futures prices are momentarily pushed up or down during periods of light trading and "stop-loss" orders are triggered in the process. In the absence of a heavy inflow of market orders, the intervening prices in that range are determined solely by demand on the floor. However, the floor population, known as "locals," largely consists of "scalpers" or marketmakers who usually desire to be "flat" (i.e. without a long or short futures position) most of the time. As a result, price action tends to be dominated by individuals who desire to hold a zero inventory of futures contracts at any point in time. This tends to exacerbate price moves as locals attempt to exit or enter the market. In this sense, a vacuum may help create the conditions for a choppy market by creating uneven order flows. Whether vacuums precipitate choppy markets is not known for certain, however.

The intelligent trader must keep in mind how other traders may react to market events. A price move which precipitates a rash of short covering may be the trader's cue to go long *first* or to go short just prior to the move losing its "steam" when prices break again. Similarly, a price move which precipitates a rash of long covering may be the cue for the trader to go short *first*, or long prior to the bottom of the break. This strategy is expressed in the market adage "sell rallies and buy breaks." Implicitly it assumes that changes in speculative prices are characterized by mean reversion. Of course, this strategy makes sense only if the trader believes that the market has, indeed, overreacted. A strategy of "selling rallies" and "buying breaks" could be potentially disastrous if the market is adjusting to a new level of prices.

It should be noted that economic analysis has certain limitations when applied to trading. Economic theory indicates the influence of economic factors on speculative prices in market equilibrium. That is, it indicates what should happen in the *long term*. It is of less value in predicting what will happen to prices during the next second, minute, hour, or day. Nor does relevant economic information enter speculative markets continuously. Consequently, it is not surprising that traders are interested in the "information" content of macroeconomic reports as guides to market direction.

Options allow one to trade expected volatility. The simple rule "buy low and sell high" applies to volatility as well as price. One would buy options if one expected the volatility of the underlying security to increase by more than the market expects. One would sell or write options if one expected the volatility of the underlying security to decrease by more than the market expects it to.

Finally, traders approach the market differently from investors. Personality characteristics, such as stick-to-itiveness, may be admirable in many areas of life. Such characteristics are potentially disastrous to a trader who must have the flexibility to change his views on a dime.[30] The objective of traders is always the same – to make money. What differs across traders are the means of doing so (i.e. the trading strategy). It is in the execution of his trading plan that the trader must apply discipline.

## 4 Conclusion

Ultimately, the behavior of security prices will determine the validity of a particular economic theory. However, the relevant relationship may not be apparent in the immediate reaction of market prices to macroeconomic information. The shifting foci of traders, the changing interpretations traders assign to the same event over time, the perceived economic relationship itself, and the preliminary and high frequency character of much of the economic data released illustrates the danger of attributing too much significance to the initial market reaction to the release of economic reports.

The inconsistency of the market's response to economic data means that traders with more accurate forecasts of the information contained in economic reports do not necessarily have a comparative advantage over less well-informed traders. One must be aware of the changing (perhaps stochastic) interpretations that traders assign to these numbers. Being a good forecaster of the economy or even of specific components is not enough to make a good trader on the information contained in economic reports.

The question of whether participants in financial markets should respond to the periodic release of macroeconomic reports is logically distinct from the question of whether they do. The fact is that the presumed information content of periodic macroeconomic reports often drives financial markets. Although the effects are sometimes felt in the foreign exchange and equity markets, probably the biggest impact is in the fixed-income security markets. Indeed, the sharp response of fixed-income prices to the release of economic data suggests that there is significant information in these reports. It also suggests that the *consensus* forecasts of bond market participants are relatively poor, for otherwise the response would be more muted on average. As we shall see in this book, the reasons motivating a response are often spurious. And economic reports may contain more noise than information.

## Appendix 1.1: Derivative Securities and Markets

> In a modern market contracts are not confined to sales for immediate delivery. People will endeavor to forecast the future and make agreements according to their prophecy. Speculation of this kind is the self adjustment of society to the probable. Its value is well known as a means of avoiding or mitigating catastrophes, equalizing prices, and providing for periods of want. It is true that the success of the strong induces imitation by the weak, and that incompetent persons bring themselves to ruin by undertaking to speculate in their turn. But legislatures and courts have recognized that the natural evolutions of a complex society are to be treated with a very cautious hand,and that such coarse attempts at a remedy for the waste incident to every social function as a simple prohibition, and laws to stop its being, are harmful and vain.
>
> (Oliver Wendell Holmes, *Annual Report of the Chicago Board of Trade*)

Derivative securities are based on or derived from (hence the name) other securities. The markets for these securities are sometimes called *shadow* markets to indicate their linkage to underlying securities. This analogy, while descriptive, does an injustice to derivative securities in the sense that these markets often drive the underlying cash markets. Treasury bond prices are determined not by the primary government securities dealers on and off Wall Street but on (Chicago's) La Salle Street in the Treasury bond futures pit on the floor of the Chicago Board of Trade. Similarly, the yield on many money market securities in the United States is largely determined in the Eurodollar futures pit on the floor of the Chicago Mercantile Exchange.

The securities market can be dichotomized into the cash and forward markets. The cash market is the market for immediate delivery and payment. The forward market entails setting a price today for future delivery and payment. Forward markets have long existed and represent a means of transferring price risks among market participants.[31] Forward contracts require the purchaser to take delivery and the seller to make delivery of the commodity or security in question. Parties to forward market transactions face counterparty risk – the risk that the counterparty may default.

Futures are simply standardized forward contracts. Contracts are standardized with respect to size, delivery location, type of commodity or security, etc. Because futures contracts are exchange traded (and the clearinghouse interposes itself in every transaction) offsetting a futures position is relatively easy. Although futures trading on agricultural commodities has long existed, financial futures trading began in the United States with the introduction of futures contracts on foreign currencies at the International Monetary Market of the Chicago Mercantile Exchange in 1972. Today financial futures include currency, interest rate and stock index futures contracts. Financial futures markets are well developed in many nations around the world.

Option contracts impose asymmetric obligations on buyers and sellers. Option buyers have the *right* but not the obligation to buy (in the case of a call option) or sell (in the case of a put option) a specific commodity or security at a specified price within a specified period of time. Option sellers, in contrast, are obligated to sell (in the case of a call) or buy (in the case of a put) a specified commodity or security at a specified price within a specified period of time *if* the buyer exercises his right to buy or sell as the case may be.

Option markets have long existed. However, option trading really took off with the advent of exchange traded options and the development of the Black and Scholes (1973) option pricing model. Exchange traded equity option contracts began trading on the Chicago Board Options Exchange in 1973. Today, options are traded on a variety of securities including futures contracts.

Volatile financial markets have increased the need of market participants to manage exposure to financial risks and simultaneously created new trading and investment opportunities. Not surprisingly, there has been a substantial increase in the volume of derivative securities in recent years. The growth has been most pronounced in the over-the-counter markets. This has meant increased profits for banks and other firms making a market in these securities.

Derivative securities allow one to manage exposure to financial risk more effectively and economically than many cash market alternatives. The development of derivative securities and other financial innovations is driven by a number of factors including the desire to lower transaction costs; increase return; facilitate risk transference; facilitate shorting; facilitate circumvention of regulation; facilitate speculation; avoid, reduce, or defer taxes; and achieve certain accounting objectives.

## Notes

1 *Wall Street Journal*, Wednesday, April 14, 1993, p. C1.
2 The on-the-run long bond is the most recently issued 30 year Treasury bond. It is the benchmark security for the US bond market.
3 The determination of consensus expectations is simplified because most market participants use the predictions of economists in the employ of firms on and off Wall Street for forecasts of the likely content of economic reports. This means that surveys of economists are a good proxy for the consensus expectations of market participants.
4 The current chairman of the Federal Reserve System, Alan Greenspan, has been described in the financial press as someone with an intense interest in the minutiae of economic data.
5 In an analysis of Chicago Mercantile Exchange Eurodollar futures prices Webb and Smith (1994) report recurrent patterns in the behavior of volatility during the trading day. In particular, they report greater volatility at the open and close of trading and during the *information period* (i.e. 7:30 a.m., Chicago time) when government economic reports are often released.
6 Trading in fixed-income securities dwarfs trading in equity securities and, in turn, is dwarfed by trading in foreign currencies if one considers any single type of fixed income security. For a discussion of derivative markets see appendix 1.1.

7 To avoid creating differential information opportunities, journalists are confined to the room and not allowed to communicate information on the economic report to others until the scheduled release time.

8 For instance, the *Wall Street Journal* reported the following story on May 5, 1987:

> A falling dollar and increasing nervousness about how much Japanese investors will buy in this week's Treasury refunding pushed bond prices lower in light trading.
>
> Prices of some actively traded 30 year Treasury bonds fell almost 1 1/4 points, or nearly $12.50 for each $1,000 face amount, after falling about 1 1/2 points Friday. The two day loss erased all the gains made last Thursday when Federal Reserve Board Chairman Paul Volcker confirmed that the Fed was pushing up short term interest rates to help stabilize the dollar....
>
> (p. 3)

9 Barnhart (1988) examines the response of selected commodity futures prices to the release of certain economic reports as well as Federal Reserve announcements of discount rate changes in order to test the policy anticipations and inflationary expectations hypotheses.

10 Colling and Irwin (1990) report that hog futures prices respond quickly to the unanticipated (but not the anticipated) information contained in US Department of Agriculture *Hogs and Pigs Reports*. This is consistent with what one would expect in an informationally efficient capital market.

11 Babcock (1990) shows that more accurate weather information may hurt, rather than help, producers who face an inelastic demand for their commodities.

12 *Wall Street Journal*, September 2, 1986, p. 28.

13 *Wall Street Journal*, July 16, 1987.

14 To make matters more confusing there is evidence that the perceived macroeconomic relationship between unexpected changes in the merchandise trade deficit and bond prices may have changed 180 degrees again. On August 19, 1993, bond prices rose substantially on the news of a larger than expected merchandise trade deficit. The bond rally was largely attributed in the financial press to market participants interpreting the greater than expected trade deficit as evidence of a slowing economy. For instance, the *Wall Street Journal* for August 20, 1993, reported:

> Long-term bond prices responded strongly to further evidence of a sluggish economy. The Commerce Department reported

> that the merchandise trade deficit widened in June far more than expected to the largest level in more than five years....
>
> (p. C1)

15 *Barron's*, May 11, 1992, p. 42.

16 The money supply report did not remain "in vogue" very long, however. Subsequent weeks did not indicate renewed interest in the weekly money supply announcements by market participants.

17 Inflation is largely although not entirely a monetary phenomenon. It is often described as "too much money chasing too few goods." When the supply of goods is held constant but money is allowed to vary it is clear that inflation is a monetary phenomenon. However, it is also possible to imagine inflation in an economy where the money supply is held constant if real output declines at some rate. Such a situation might arise in a war torn economy, for example. It is also possible to imagine that real growth rates in excess of the growth rate of the money supply (holding money demand constant) may reduce inflationary pressures by increasing the supply of goods relative to the supply of money.

18 *Wall Street Journal*, April 1993.

19 *Barron's*, April 6, 1992, p. 56.

20 The often substantial reaction of speculative prices to questionable economic data has not escaped the attention of the financial press. Consider the following excerpt from an article by Gene Epstein which appeared in the May 24, 1993, issue of *Barron's*:

> It would be funny if it weren't scary. Fears about inflation were fanned two weeks ago when the U.S. Bureau of Labor Statistics released worrisome data about rising consumer and producer prices. In response, hundreds of billions of dollars worth of stocks and bonds declined in value, and then, last Tuesday, the US central bank duly deliberated whether to respond by hiking short term interest rates. All this because of inflation estimates that were fuzzy, at best....
>
> (p. 47)

21 To an outside observer trading behavior may seem completely irrational. For instance, in a discussion of whether some commonly regarded speculative bubbles have fundamental explanations, Garber (1990) states:

> Though several authors have proposed market fundamental explanations for the well documented Mississippi and South Sea Bubbles, these episodes are still treated in the modern literature

as outbursts of irrationality. This may be attributable to the influence of Mackay's (1852) graphic description of the frenzied speculative crowds which materialized in Paris and London in 1719 and 1720; from our current perspective, though such "irrational" speculation probably looked a lot like a normal day in a pit of the Board of Trade.

(p. 36)

22 Keynes (1935) uses the terms speculation and enterprise instead. He states:

> If I may be allowed to appropriate the term speculation for the activity of forecasting the psychology of the market, and the term enterprise for the activity of forecasting the prospective yield of assets over the whole life, it is no means always the case that speculation predominates over enterprise. As the organization of investment markets improves, the risk of the predominance of speculation does, however, increase. In one of the greatest investment markets in the world, namely, New York, the influence of speculation (in the above sense) is enormous.
>
> (pp. 158–9)

23 Keynes (1935) points out that over half of the trading volume on a busy day on the New York Stock Exchange is attributable to day traders.

24 There is an element of truth in the old adage that an investment is simply a trade gone sour.

25 There is a dichotomy in the economics literature concerning the relevance of trading strategies. While there is an extensive literature on optimal trading strategies for various auctions, much of the financial economics literature seems to ignore the possibility that trading may involve an element of strategy. One exception is an article by Ho, Schwartz, and Whitcomb (1985) who argue:

> In much of the economics literature, the price information process is assumed to be a Walrasian *tâtonnement* in which market participants trade at equilibrium prices. But when friction (information, decision and order handling costs) impedes the trading process, such prices are generally not attained in a single round of trading, and the very act of trading becomes a process that requires analysis.
>
> (p. 40)

26 Another illustration of the importance of understanding how other traders make their decisions is contained in the following excerpt from

an article which appeared in the May 6, 1993, issue of the *Wall Street Journal*:

> Panic about London chart points, or index levels sent the market diving, and the FT 100 sank as much as 26 points [approximately 1 percent] in intraday trading. So-called chartists who believe that the market's path can be tracked by looking at recurring patterns, predicted that once the key index fell through the 2800 level, it couldn't be stopped from hitting 2730, and once there would drop again and find support only at 2700. But late in the session investors decided the panic was overdone, and buyers emerged to push prices back up a bit....
>
> (p. C12)

27 There is a significant amount of empirical evidence which suggests that the distribution of changes in speculative prices is non-normal but nevertheless stable paretian.

28 The variance is simply defined as the expectation of the squared deviation from the mean. The expected deviation from the mean cannot be used since it must by definition be equal to zero for any probability distribution. Squaring each deviation before an expectation is taken allows one to calculate a measure of dispersion which has the desirable property that it minimizes the deviation from the mean. Since population parameters are not known, the sample variance is calculated as the average of the squared deviations from the sample mean. As Marsh and Rosenfeld (1986) note, the measured volatility of changes in speculative prices may be distorted by "market-making noise."

29 It is important to note that small quantities may be traded at intervening prices during a choppy market. Transaction price data on many financial markets are widely and instantly disseminated by electronic news vendors. Data on the associated volume traded at each price are not always readily available especially on US financial futures markets. Thus, an outside observer looking only at transaction prices generated over some time interval (and not the associated volumes traded at each price) may not recognize a market as "choppy." For a discussion of the effects of choppy markets on the pricing of futures options see Webb (1987).

30 In this regard, the following passage in Lefèvre's classic book on trading, *Reminiscences of a Stock Operator* (1923), is illustrative:

> The successful trader has to fight these two deep-seated instincts [of hope and fear]. He has to reverse what you might call his natural impulses. Instead of hoping he must fear; instead of fearing he must hope. He must fear that his loss may develop

into a much bigger loss, and hope that his profit may become a big profit. It is absolutely wrong to gamble in stocks the way the average man does.

(p. 131)

31 In his classic book, *Value and Capital*, Hicks (1939) remarks:

> It is often supposed that capitalism is entirely devoid of any organization of plans; but that is not altogether the case. A way does exist, within the orbit of private enterprise, whereby expectations and plans can be (at least partially) coordinated. This is the device of forward trading (including not only dealing in forward markets, commonly so called, but also all orders given in advance, and all longterm contracts). It is very instructive, even at this stage, to pay some attention to the working of this sort of coordination, and to examine why it is not more efficient, and its range more extensive, than it is in fact.
>
> (p. 135)

## References

Babcock, B. A. 1990: "The Value of Weather Information in Market Equilibrium," *American Journal of Agricultural Economics*, 86, February, 63–72.

Barnhart, S. W. 1988: "Commodity Futures Prices and Economic News: An Examination Under Alternative Monetary Regimes," *Journal of Futures Markets*, 8 (4), 483–510.

*Barron's*, selected issues.

Black, F. 1986: "Noise," *Journal of Finance*, 41 (3), July, 529–43.

Black, F. and M. Scholes 1973: "The Pricing of Options and Other Corporate Liabilities," *Journal of Political Economy*, 81, May–June, 637–59.

Clark, T., D. H. Joines, and G. M. Phillips 1988: "Social Security Payments, Money Supply Announcements, and Interest Rates," *Journal of Monetary Economics*, 22, 257–78.

Colling, P. L., and S. H. Irwin 1990: "The Reaction of Live Hog Futures Prices to USDA *Hogs and Pigs Reports*," *American Journal of Agricultural Economics*, 86, February, 84–94.

DeLong, B., A. Shleifer, L. Summers, and R. Waldman 1990a: "Noise Trader Risk in Financial Markets," *Journal of Political Economy*, 98 (4), August, 703–38.

DeLong, B., A. Shleifer, L. Summers, and R. Waldman 1990b: "Positive Feedback Investment Investment Strategies and Destabilizing Rational

Speculation," *Journal of Finance*, 45 (2), June, 379–96.

Engle, R. F., T. Ito, and W. Lin 1990: "Meteor Showers or Heat Waves? Heteroskedastic Intra-Daily Volatility in the Foreign Exchange Market," *Econometrica*, 58 (3), May, 525–42.

Garber, P. M. 1990: "Famous First Bubbles," *Journal of Economic Perspectives*, 4 (2), Spring, 35–54.

Hicks, J. R. 1939: *Value and Capital*, Oxford: Oxford University Press.

Ho, T. S. Y., R. A. Schwartz, and D. K. Whitcomb 1985: "The Trading Decision and Market Clearing under Transaction Price Uncertainty," *Journal of Finance*, 40 (1), March, 21–42.

Keynes, J. M. 1935: *The General Theory of Employment, Interest, and Money*, New York: Harcourt, Brace & World.

Lefèvre, E. 1923: *Reminiscences of a Stock Operator*, New York: George H. Doran.

Marsh, T., and E. Rosenfeld 1986: "Non-Trading, Market-Making and Estimates of Stock Price Volatility," *Journal of Financial Economics*, 15, 359–72.

Merton, R. C. 1987: "A Simple Model of Capital Market Equilibrium with Incomplete Information," *Journal of Finance*, 42 (3), July, 483–510.

*Wall Street Journal*, various issues.

Webb, R. I. 1987: "A Note on Volatility and the Pricing of Futures Options During 'Choppy' Markets," *Journal of Futures Markets*, 7 (3), June, 333–7.

Webb, R. I. 1989: "To Understand the Economy, Ignore Traders," *Wall Street Journal*, Thursday, August 24.

Webb, R. I., and D. G. Smith 1994: "The Effect of Market Opening and Closing on the Volatility of CME Eurodollar Futures Prices," *Journal of Futures Markets*, February (forthcoming).

# 2

# Information and the Behavior of Speculative Prices

The immaturity of our science is illustrated by the conspicuous lack of predictive content about some of its most intensely interesting phenomena, particularly *changes* in asset prices. General stock prices are notoriously unpredictable and financial economists have even developed a coherent theory (the theory of efficient markets) to explain why they *should* be unpredictable.

(Richard Roll "$R^2$," p. 541)

## 1 Introduction

The behavior of speculative prices and information are inextricably intertwined. Changes in speculative prices not only reflect information, they also convey it to the uninformed. As Nobel laureate economist Friedrich von Hayek once argued, prices are signals for resource allocation. Changes in speculative prices are no exception in this regard.[1]

Similarly, uncertainty and information are also intimately related. Uncertainty reflects a lack of information. Future changes in speculative prices are uncertain because there is incomplete information. The uncertainty surrounding changes in speculative prices can be characterized by a probability distribution. This allows the uncertainty to be quantified. Uncertainty can be thought of as the absence of complete information. Much of the variation in speculative prices is attributable to the flow of new information. However, because changes in speculative prices can still occur even in a world of certainty the volatility of changes in speculative prices is not entirely a reflection of uncertainty alone.[2]

Participants in financial markets are confronted by an incredible amount of data to choose from. It is impossible for any one individual to digest all of it. This task is made somewhat easier because speculative prices aggregate information across market participants. In this sense, speculative prices represent the consensus values placed on shared information.

Available information frequently differs across individuals. Black (1986) argues that a necessary condition for trading to occur is the existence of differences in information across market participants. An alternative view is that trading may occur even when individuals share the same information if market participants interpret the same information differently (or need to transact for portfolio rebalancing purposes), in which case the choice of a particular trading strategy depends not only on the information one possesses but also on the information one believes others possess and the interpretation they will probably assign to it. Put simply, differences in opinion not only make horse races possible but also account for much of the activity on financial markets.

The manner by which new information enters the marketplace and how it is incorporated into security prices is not well understood at present. Existing information theoretic models have yet to influence the design of alternative models of asset pricing or add much to our knowledge of how markets work. Indeed, the comments Ross (1978) made in his review of the current status of the capital asset pricing model (CAPM) still apply:

> The work on information is highly provocative, but definitive positive conclusions have yet to emerge. In particular, we are still groping for an adequate understanding of exactly how competitive prices are determined in such markets with asymmetric information and at present there are several competing conceptions of what constitutes an equilibrium. A resolution of these issues is going to turn on a closer examination of the microtheory of price formation in these markets, and that is a task that is just beginning.
>
> (p. 891)

In this chapter, the implications of informationally efficient capital markets and equilibrium models of asset pricing for the behavior of speculative prices are considered. Some of the extensive empirical literature in this area is reviewed. In addition, the role that costly information production, uncertain information dissemination, discontinuous trading, and the existence of asymmetric information play in the determination of speculative prices and the informational efficiency of speculative markets is examined.

## 2 The Behavior of Speculative Prices

The early empirical literature on the behavior of speculative prices suggested that changes in speculative prices follow simple time series processes or "fair game" models. For instance, the early empirical literature reported that changes in grain futures prices (Working, 1934) and stock prices (Kendall, 1953; Roberts, 1959) followed random or quasi-random walks. Kendall also reported that changes in spot cotton and wheat prices appeared to follow a random walk.[3] (Measured serial correlation was approximately zero and independence of successive price changes was assumed.)

These results initially puzzled researchers as they seemed at variance with economic theory, yet these apparent anomalies ignited a scientific revolution. As with other scientific revolutions, the discovery of apparent anomalies through empirical research preceded the development of a theory to explain the anomalies.[4] The theory which eventually resulted is the efficient capital markets hypothesis. The first general equilibrium explanation for the observed random behavior of changes in speculative prices was offered by Samuelson (1965) who demonstrated that changes in futures prices will follow martingale or submartingale processes under some very general assumptions about the behavior of the spot price.[5]

It should be pointed out that seasonal patterns in certain speculative price series have been reported in the financial economics literature. Black (1976) argues that seasonality in commodity futures prices is not necessarily inconsistent with market efficiency if knowledge of such patterns is known by all market participants. For instance, there is strong evidence of seasonality in short-term interest rates in the United States during the late ninteenth and early twentieth centuries. The desire to eliminate this seasonality was one factor which led to the establishment of the Federal Reserve System. Clark (1986) suggests that the disappearance of seasonality in short-term interest rates following the First World War was a worldwide phenomenon and not necessarily the result of Federal Reserve policy actions. In any event, the existence of seasonal patterns in US interest rates is not, in itself, indicative of unexploited profit opportunities.

## 3 Informationally Efficient Capital Markets

Properly considered, finance is really a branch of economics that deals with certain resource allocation problems which usually involve both time and uncertainty. Not surprisingly, some concepts encountered in the context of the simple timeless certain world of elementary economic analysis have a counterpart in financial economics where both time and uncertainty are important. One example is the concept of an informationally efficient capital market or, more simply, market efficiency.

Jensen (1978) has defined an informationally efficient capital market as a market in which it is not possible to earn a "pure" or "economic" profit based on a given and presumably shared information set. This concept should not be too surprising since pricetaking firms in competitive markets are expected to earn only enough to cover their costs (including a normal profit) and consequently earn zero "pure" profits. This "zero pure profit" condition imposed on firms in competitive markets in a certain timeless world has its parallel in the concept of market efficiency in a world with both time and uncertainty. Alternatively stated, an informationally efficient capital market is simply a market in which speculative prices do not systematically deviate from the prices the securities would be expected to command given available information commonly shared by rational investors.

Other definitions of market efficiency also exist. Fama (1970) has defined an informationally efficient capital market as one in which speculative prices fully (and correctly) reflect available information. In this case, speculative prices are a "sufficient statistic" (i.e. all one needs to know). Speculative prices then reflect the aggregate of individual pieces of information and perhaps more than any one individual knows. In which case, speculative prices both reflect the aggregate of available information in the marketplace and convey that information to the uninformed.

Latham (1986) has advanced an alternative definition of informational market efficiency. Namely, he contends that a market is efficient with respect to some information set $\theta$ if prices would not change if all traders were revealed information set $\theta$. Similarly, one may view an informationally efficient market as one in which speculative prices do not *systematically* deviate from the prices which the securities should command given available information.

It should be noted that, in an efficient market, changes in speculative prices occur only in response to new information or reassessments of existing information. As a result, a sequence of speculative prices for a given security reflects a sequence of market equilibria. That is, prices adjust to new information immediately and without any intervening price disequilibria. In essence, the sequence of price changes mirrors the underlying economic events in the economy. Fama (1963) notes that:

> New information, in turn, should ultimately reflect changes in the underlying economic conditions that determine equilibrium prices in speculative markets. Thus, following this line of reasoning, the underlying economic conditions must themselves have an asymptotically paretian character and are therefore subject to a larger number of abrupt changes than would be the case if the distribution of price changes in speculative markets conformed to the Gaussian hypothesis.
>
> (pp. 426–7)

This suggests that the new information arrives in the same process that changes in speculative prices follow,[6] and that changes in the economy itself follow a similar process. The empirical literature suggests that the variance of speculative prices is nonstationary. Nonstationarity in the variance of new information may explain otherwise inexplicable successive large price changes.

The sufficient conditions for market efficiency are (1) zero taxes and transactions costs; (2) zero information production and dissemination costs; and (3) complete agreement among investors regarding the future distribution of security returns. Not surprisingly, these conditions parallel those underlying the assumptions of perfect competition in elementary economics. Obviously, the conditions are not encountered in actual market environments where conducting transactions and acquiring information costs money and unanimity of beliefs across investors is rare. Indeed, if investors shared the same information and attached the same interpretations to it trading would only occur for portfolio rebalancing purposes and not for speculative purposes.

Informational market efficiency may still exist, however, even in a world often characterized by the above imperfections. That is, the above conditions are sufficient but not necessary for market efficiency. The reason why transaction costs may not impede market efficiency is that prices may adjust without transactions. Alternatively stated, information may be conveyed through a variety of channels including transactions. The closure of one channel may not close others. If information is conveyed through channels other than transactions the need for transactions to eliminate price anomalies is reduced. Similarly, all investors need not have access to all available information if "enough" investors do. Finally, heterogeneous expectations across investors may not cause a problem for market efficiency unless there are individuals who have superior forecasting talents. In any event, whether the frictions introduced by these imperfections impede market efficiency is an empirical issue.

Roberts (1959) divides informational market efficiency into three types: weak form; strong form; semistrong form. The three forms of market efficiency differ only in the amount of information that security prices are assumed to be conditioned on.

Weak-form market efficiency posits that the sequence of previous price changes does not contain any information about future price changes. That is, one cannot predict future price changes on the basis of knowledge of the past sequence of price changes. Under such a regime, attempts to exploit such information (e.g. through technical analysis) are fruitless.[7] This is not to say that the past history of price changes does not contain useful information. Rather, it merely says that the past sequence of price changes does not contain useful information which is not already incorporated into market prices. The reasoning underlying the concept of weak-form market efficiency is that the sequence of security prices is information which is readily available at minimum cost to all investors. As a result, strategies based on exploiting such information should not be very valuable.

In contrast, strong-form market efficiency posits that the market is efficient with respect to all available information. Unfortunately, tests of strong-form market efficiency are possible only in a negative sense. That is, one can only test whether the market is efficient with respect to a certain piece of information.

Finally, semistrong-form market efficiency assumes that the market is efficient only with respect to all publicly available information. Inside information possessed by investors could be profitably exploited in a capital market that is only semistrong-form efficient.

The concept of market efficiency, as stated above, does not have any testable propositions. In order to derive testable propositions concerning market efficiency certain restrictions are necessarily imposed on the price formation process. Namely, it is assumed that one can state market equilibrium in terms of expected returns and that expected returns are conditioned upon the set of available information. (There is also an implicit assumption of linearity in the process generating security returns.[8])

## 4 Equilibrium Models of Asset Pricing

The concept of an informationally efficient capital market is inextricably linked with the process assumed to generate asset returns in market equilibrium. In turn, the process by which new information is produced, disseminated, and ultimately incorporated into market prices influences whether the capital market is informationally efficient and the equilibrium model of asset pricing is appropriate. As a result, tests of market efficiency are always joint tests of market efficiency and the model of market equilibrium chosen.

The simple one-period CAPM of Sharpe (1964), Lintner (1965), and Mossin (1966) remains the basic model for equilibrium asset pricing in the financial economic literature. Essentially, the CAPM posits that expected one-period returns may be decomposed into a return for the time value of money and a return for bearing risk. In conformity with the portfolio theory of Markowitz (1959) risk is defined as the covariance of the return of an asset with the return on the market portfolio or the set of all assets including human capital. Of course, in empirical tests a subset of all assets is used as a proxy for the market portfolio.[9] The CAPM may be written as follows:

$$R_{i,t} = R_{\mathrm{f}} + B_{i,\mathrm{m}}(R_{\mathrm{m},t} - R_{\mathrm{f}}) + u_{i,t} \tag{2.1}$$

where $R_{i,t}$ is the uncertain return on security $i$ at time $t$, $R_{\mathrm{f}}$ is the risk-free (zero variance) or riskless (zero covariance with the market) interest rate at time $t$, $B_{i,\mathrm{m}}$ is the measure of the risk of security $i$ relative to the risk of the market portfolio m (i.e. the covariance of return on security $i$ with the return on the market portfolio), and $u_{i,t}$ is the error term which has a mean equal to zero. If the expectations operator $E$ is passed through equation (2.1) there is a simple interpretation for the equation

$$E(R_{i,t}) = R_{\mathrm{f}} + B_{i,\mathrm{m}}[E(R_{\mathrm{m},t}) - R_{\mathrm{f}}] \tag{2.2}$$

that results. Namely, $R_{\mathrm{f}}$ is the return for the time value of money (note that the expectation of a constant is a constant) and $B_{i,\mathrm{m}} \times [E(R_{\mathrm{m},t}) - R_{\mathrm{f}}]$ is the expected premium for bearing risk. Note that there is only one source of systematic risk in the CAPM.

There are several assumptions underlying the CAPM: (1) security returns are multinormally distributed (this means that security returns are completely described by the first two moments of the distribution); (2) investors' expectations are homogeneous with respect to means and variances (agreement with respect to the first two moments among investors represents agreement about the future); (3) markets are complete with zero transaction costs; (4) investors are risk-averse wealth maximizers (this simply means that more expected wealth is always preferred to less); and (5) there is a single time period. The assumptions of zero transaction costs and homogeneous expectations are the same as two of the three sufficient conditions for market efficiency. The assumptions underlying the CAPM differ from assumptions underlying general expected return models of market equilibrium in that security returns are assumed to be multinormally distributed and certain constraints are placed on investors' utility functions. Models of asset pricing which assume that investors make decisions on the basis of knowing only the first two moments or parameters of the probability distribution of security returns or assume that the probability distribution of security returns can be completely described by the first two moments are called two-parameter models. The CAPM is a member of the family of two-parameter models. It differs from other members of the family such as the market model principally in its specification of the risk-free rate as the constant term.

Although the CAPM is still widely accepted in the financial economic literature its use remains controversial. The validity of tests of the CAPM has been challenged from a methodological viewpoint by Roll (1977). Moreover, much empirical evidence has been produced which suggests that either the CAPM is inappropriate or the capital market is informationally inefficient.[10] More recently, Fama and French (1992) have presented evidence that suggests that beta is not a good measure of risk. This and similar studies are frequently misinterpreted by the financial press as academic admission of market inefficiency rather than simply that the model of asset pricing is incorrect.[11] Given the widespread acceptance of informational market efficiency by financial economists attention has largely concentrated on alternative theories of asset pricing. One such theory is the arbitrage pricing theory (APT) of Ross (1976).

The basic premise underlying the APT is that, in market equilibrium, securities must be priced such that no arbitrage opportunities exist. In particular, the APT precludes portfolios with common return covariances (expected returns) from having different expected returns (return variances). The APT posits that in equilibrium the return generating process may be characterized by a linear relationship between the return on any asset, its expected return and the compensation for various risk factors. Moreover, it is argued that the APT is appropriate in a multiperiod setting and the model may be derived with only minor restrictions on investors' utility functions. That is, it is assumed only that investors are risk averse, and prefer more return for a given level of risk to less. That is,

$$E(R_{i,t}) = R_f + b_{i1}L_1 + b_{i2}L_2 + b_{i3}L_3 + b_{i,k}L_k \cdot \qquad (2.3)$$

Equation (2.3) states that the expected return on security $i$ is a linear function of the risk-free interest rate $R_f$ and its sensitivities

$b_i$ to each of the $k$ risk factors $L$. There is a further restriction that $k < n$ (the number of securities). This equation is presumed to hold for every security and hence every possible portfolio as well. The APT does not specify *a priori* anything about the size or sign of the risk factors.

The primary point of contention between the two alternative models of asset pricing centers on the number and nature of the risk indices (although the APT also requires fewer restrictive assumptions than the CAPM). Various empirical studies suggest that there are at least three or four unique risk factors rather than only one as the CAPM posits.[12] Unfortunately, the methodology employed in these tests does not allow one either to identify the individual risk factors located nor to be certain that they are the same general risk factors across samples.

In evaluating the two asset pricing theories attention should be focused not on the differences in assumptions but rather on the predictive power of the theories. This is in keeping with positive economics as expressed by Friedman (1953). That is, one accepts or rejects a theory not on its "theoretical merits" but rather on whether the predictions of the theory conform most closely with the evidence in the data. The impressions given in many discussions of models of asset pricing is that models such as the CAPM or the APT explain most of the variation in speculative prices. Unfortunately, it must be pointed out that neither theory explains most of the variation in individual security return variances. In fact, in an early study, which also considers the possibility of multiple risk factors, King (1966) reports that the market factor explains only about 50 percent of individual security return variation on average. The existence of significance-explained security return variation using the existing models of asset pricing is an indication of their inadequacy.

## 5 The Empirical Evidence on Market Efficiency

The concept of informationally efficient capital markets is central to modern financial economic theory.[13] Whether speculative markets behave in such a fashion, however, is largely an empirical rather than a theoretical issue. Most financial economists would view strong-form market efficiency more as a theoretical construct than a plausible description of actual markets. Consequently, attention has centered on whether the market is weak-form or semistrong-form efficient.

Early tests of informational market efficiency focused on whether or "how quickly" speculative prices respond to new information. The slower the response the more opportunities there exist to profit from the information. The slower the response the more serial correlation present in successive price changes. The quick response of changes in speculative prices to the arrival of new information has been interpreted as evidence that the market is at least semistrong-form informationally efficient.

For instance, Fama (1965) reports that stock returns for the 30 companies which comprise the Dow Jones Industrial Average appear to follow a fair game process. Similarly, Fama (1975) reports that the interest rate implicit in the prices of US Treasury bills with one month to maturity is autocorrelated and appears to follow a first-order autoregressive process. The exact moving average representation of the above equation is an infinite-order moving average process. However, because the size of the first coefficient casts doubt on whether even the second moving average parameter would be significant it may be modeled as a first-order moving average process.

In assessing market efficiency it is always important to keep in mind that efficiency is defined with respect to transaction costs. That is, price may deviate from full information prices if the amount of deviation is such that one cannot take advantage of perceived profit opportunities or only floor traders can take advantage of such opportunities. Alternatively stated, the value of exploiting the information is exceeded by its costs. It is also important to determine whether observed or reported prices are actual transaction prices. Often potential profit opportunities turn out to be more apparent than real. Attempts to exploit such profit opportunities would not be successful precisely because the prices are not true transaction prices. This often occurs in the cash bond market. Moreover, one may only be able to execute trades for a limited amount of the security in question without affecting the price.

Similarly, it is always important to consider whether the reported transaction prices are identical with respect to time. Prices which are different with respect to time may simply reflect different information sets and not potential arbitrage profit opportunities.

## 6 Information, Volume, and the Volatility of Changes in Speculative Prices

There is a widely held belief that volume causes price changes in speculative markets. If financial markets are informationally efficient one would not expect to observe a causal relationship between changes in volume (absent the simultaneous arrival of new information) and changes in speculative prices at all. Perhaps the landmark study in this area was Myron Scholes' dissertation at the University of Chicago and the article adapted from it which was subsequently published in the *Journal of Business*.

In it, Scholes (1972) examines three competing hypotheses (the price pressure, substitution, and information hypotheses). He states:

> Few people will quarrel with the idea that buyers and sellers on an organized exchange such as the New York Stock Exchange can buy and sell small quantities of stock at approximately the prevailing market price. But when the size of the trade is large relative to these small trades there is a belief that the price of a stock must fall to induce investors to purchase these additional shares. This inducement, or "sweetener" as it is called, results from an increase in the quantity of shares that must be held by market participants. If the excess demand curve is downward sloping, the additional shares will only be held at lower prices.... An alternative hypothesis to the price pressure hypothesis [described above] can be called the substitution hypothesis.... To obtain a desired consumption investment program, investors can buy various combinations of assets. Each security is a potential candidate for inclusion in investors' portfolios.... A risky asset is a small percentage of all assets that investors may hold in their portfolios. As a result, the demand curve facing individual investors is essentially horizontal.... The information hypothesis states that when a large block of stock is sold in the market, we should see a downward price adjustment in the price of the stock. This fall is the expected value of information contained in large block trades. It is a permanent adjustment in the stock price and not an inducement followed by abnormal returns in the future as the price pressure

> hypothesis suggests. Whether or not the value of information is an increasing function of the size of the trade, or is relatively constant once a trade is made is an empirical question.... The efficient markets model would imply that the value of information in trades is much smaller than the implied effects suggested by the price pressure adherents....
>
> (pp. 180–3)

Scholes reports evidence in favor of the substitution–information hypotheses.

Several studies (Wood, McInish, and Ord, 1985; Amihud and Mendleson, 1987; Stoll and Whaley, 1990) report the presence of U-shaped patterns in the volatility of stock returns during the trading day.[14] Webb and Smith (1994) report similar findings for Eurodollar futures prices on the Chicago Mercantile Exchange (CME) even though a financial market trading virtually identical Eurodollar futures contracts is already open when the CME opens for trading. The question naturally arises as to whether these results reflect (and are induced by) a curvilinear pattern in volume as well.

Webb and Smith contend that the various volatility measures they employ are *information* dependent rather than *volume* or *time* dependent. Simply stated, the arrival of new information is the driving force behind the influence of trading volume on price changes and *not* volume *per se.* Similar arguments can be found in the financial economic literature that reports a relationship between volume and changes in speculative prices.

For instance, Clark (1973) states in his classic *Econometrica* article:

> The different evolution of price series on different days is due to the fact that information is available to traders at a varying rate. On days when no new information is available, trading is slow, and the price process evolves slowly. On days when new information violates old expectations, trading is brisk, and the price process evolves much faster.
>
> (p. 137)

Clark reports a curvilinear relationship between daily trading volume and daily changes in cotton futures prices. He explains that relationship as follows:

> To see how this curvilinear dependence of price change variance on volume might occur, consider how the futures market actually works.... When new information (in the form of data that the traders consider relevant) flows to the market, both prices and traders' price expectations will change. If the information is uncertain (i.e., some traders shift expectations up and others down on the basis of the information), or if only "inside" traders get the information first, then large price changes will be coincident with high volumes. On the other hand, very large price moves will probably be due to information that is perceived by all traders to move the price in one direction. News of widespread insect problems might be an example of this sort of information in the cotton futures market. In this case, all traders would revise their expectations in the same direction, and the price change would have relatively low volume.
>
> (pp. 144–5)

The puzzling element of the Webb and Smith study is that the mere opening of a market is *not* an informational event when another financial market trading virtually the same commodity is already open elsewhere. That is, one would not expect new information to cluster around the opening when another financial market trading the same security is already open elsewhere. Consequently, there are unlikely to be *information*-induced changes in trading volume which would result in changes in prices around the opening of such markets.

## 7 Market Anomalies

Although the concept of market efficiency is widely accepted in the financial economic literature there is growing evidence which suggests that the hypothesis may not be valid. Not surprisingly, much of the attention has focused on the behavior of stock returns in the cash market. Nevertheless, the results are interesting for what they may indicate about the validity of accepted models of asset pricing.

For example, an apparent "firm size" effect, first reported by Banz (1981) and Reinganum (1981), suggests that the returns on equity securities of firms with small capitalizations exceed those of firms with larger capitalizations even after adjustments for differences in perceived risk (as measured by the CAPM beta) are made.[15] Keim's (1983) subsequent discovery that most of the size effect occurred during the first part of January only spawned another anomaly which has been aptly dubbed the "January effect." The observation of "weekend" and "day of the week," and in particular "Monday," effects was made by Gibbons and Hess (1981), French (1980), and Keim and Stambaugh (1984) among others. Essentially, the "Monday effect" was the observation that the average return on Standard and Poor (S&P) 500 equities and the 30 stocks in the Dow Jones Industrial Average was consistently negative on Mondays (open to close) or some would argue only over the weekend (i.e. from Friday's close to Monday's open).[16]

The results are more puzzling when the behavior of stock index futures prices are considered since Cornell (1985) indicates an absence of any consistent "Monday effect." Indeed, if anything, it appears that the return is higher on Monday than on any other trading day of the week. Another anomaly has been observed by Harris (1986) who reports evidence which suggests that stock returns exhibit a tendency to rise during the first 45 minutes of trading for all trading days except Monday.

In fairness, it should be pointed out that the financial economics literature is replete with papers which attempt to explain apparent market anomalies within the context of an informationally efficient capital market.[17] Early attempts to explain one or more of the above effects focused on whether trading in the stocks of small firms was less frequent than or asynchronous with the trading in the stocks of large capitalization firms (Oldfield and Rogalski, 1980; Roll, 1981); implicit or hidden transaction costs were ignored (Stoll and Whaley, 1983); security returns were nonstationary (Brown, Kleidon, and Marsh, 1983). These arguments met with varying degrees of success as Reinganum (1982) demonstrates.[18] Additional market anomalies will be considered in the next chapter.

There is some evidence that the response of speculative prices to the arrival of new information may differ across related financial markets. For instance, Stephan and Whaley (1990) conclude that changes in stock and related stock option prices differ in the speed of response to new information. Moreover, contrary to what one might expect given the apparent transaction cost advantage of stock options, Stephan and Whaley report that stock prices react before the related stock options.

It would also be misleading to present the reader with the view that the only anomalies observed in the financial literature are those mentioned above. While the above anomalies have received and continue to receive considerable attention in the financial economics literature other apparent anomalies exist. Indeed, a special issue of the *Journal of Financial Economics* was devoted, a number of years ago, to articles reporting anomalies. Examples include the potential for abnormal security returns for investments in closed-end funds based on a simple trading rule (Thompson, 1978); the existence of arbitrage profit opportunities for members in traded call options on the Chicago Board Options Exchange (Galai, 1978); and Chiras and Manaster (1978) report that a simple trading rule based on the variances implicit in option prices meant that excess profits could be earned by Chicago Board Options Exchange members and nonmembers alike.

## 8 Information Theoretic Models

Considerable attention has been directed in the economic literature to issues concerning the effects on market prices and market efficiency of differences in information across individuals (Grossman, 1976; Green, 1978; Shefrin, 1978; Laffont, 1980), uncertain information dissemination (Beja and Hakansson, 1977; Goldman and Sosin, 1979), and costly information production (Grossman and Stiglitz, 1976, 1980). Obviously, information theoretic models have implications for asset pricing as well as market efficiency. Conversely, the stochastic behavior of changes in speculative prices also has implications for the validity of alternative information theoretic models.

It is important to emphasize that prices may perform one or more roles with respect to the information production or dissemination process. First, prices may be a source of information. That is, information may be conveyed to the uninformed through price or price changes as Grossman (1975) has shown. Alternatively, prices are sometimes considered merely to aggregate information across investors. In such a case, no information is conveyed through price changes *per se*. Indeed, prices are merely reflecting existing information which is obtainable elsewhere.

Many of the articles in the information theory literature consider information issues in the context of Arrow–Debreu complete markets. As noted above, Grossman and Stiglitz (1980) consider the implications of costly information production for the informational efficiency of security markets. Essentially, they contend that it is not possible for security markets to be informationally efficient if positive information production costs exist. Their reasoning is that the presence of information production costs deters the incorporation of costly information into market prices. Individual investors have no economic incentive to expend resources to produce information if market prices already reflect that information. However, if no one produces such information then the market cannot reflect all available information and therefore cannot be efficient.

The way around this problem is obvious. Individual investors who invest in information production activities must earn a normal return from such investments. If investors earned more than a normal return competitive forces in the information production market would force down the return as others entered the business or existing individuals produced more information. Conversely, if the return from information production was below normal then firms would leave this unprofitable business activity until profitability returned. Whenever the latter situation arises Grossman (1975) considers that market prices reveal too much information and the market is "over informationally efficient."

In his study of futures markets, Grossman (1975) considers the effects of differential information upon market efficiency and market prices. In his model, each investor has a distinct piece of information. Essentially, Grossman argues that in such a market the market price becomes a sufficient statistic. That is, the market price aggregates existing information in a "perfect" way such that the information reflected in market prices is superior to that possessed by any one individual investor. In order to avoid the aforementioned problem of eliminating the incentive to the production of information Grossman introduces noise into the system. As a consequence, it is then possible to earn a normal return on the information production due to the presence of noise but this also means that security prices can no longer be sufficient statistics. The consequence of the latter result is that the "allocative efficiency" of the price system is questioned. That is, the presence of noise in the pricing process means that (security) prices are no longer (good) signals for resource allocation. In another paper, Grossman (1976) considers the deleterious effect upon the market when too much information is produced.

Grossman notes, however:

> On the other hand, when there is noise [in the price system] so that the price system does not aggregate information perfectly, the allocative efficiency properties of a competitive equilibrium may break down .... Individuals need not know why the price has risen, the fact that there is a higher price induces them to counteract the scarcity in an efficient way. This argument breaks down when the price system is noisy.
>
> (p. 574)

Grossman (1976) has shown that it does not matter whether we consider information to be conveyed through prices or whether one considers prices merely to aggregate information. In either case, the aforementioned problem of costly information arises. As a result, the existence of capital market efficiency is tied to what happens in another market, namely the market for information.

Beja and Hakansson (1977) take an entirely different tack. Essentially, they note that because the auction process is itself time-consuming – unlike the Walrasian *tâtonnement* used to describe the process by which competitive markets reach equilibrium – intervening price disequilibria will exist. The price disequilibria are the result of the fact that the information cannot be incorporated quickly enough to achieve a sequence of competitive equilibria.

Goldman and Sosin (1979) consider a disequilibrium model in which there is uncertainty surrounding the dissemination of information across investors. They examine the consequences for market prices of such uncertainty under various market structure scenarios. They state:

> Specifically, we are concerned with how the *process of information dissemination* interacts with specific *market structures* to produce prices. That is, whereas Fama et al. were concerned simply with

> whether prices adjust quickly to information once it is publicly available, we are concerned with *how quickly* and *how much* prices adjust *as* information becomes publicly available and how the adjustment process is altered by alternative market structures.
>
> (p. 30, emphasis in original)

Goldman and Sosin contend that uncertainty with respect to the speed of information dissemination and uncertainty with respect to the sequence or order in which traders are informed results in "undershooting" and "overshooting" the equilibrium price (i.e. investors will not fully or correctly impound all information). Simply stated, serial correlation in prices results in a world where information dissemination is uncertain and information production is costly. Goldman and Sosin argue: "The intuition behind this result is that with continuous trading although investors may learn at any future instant and adjust prices accordingly, on average they will not learn instantaneously." Thus, when information dissemination is time consuming temporary price disequilibria result.

The effects of differential information across market participants may affect market efficiency and market prices. To the extent that the market price becomes a sufficient statistic when information differs across investors market efficiency is not affected. That occurs if the market price aggregates existing information in a manner such that the information reflected in market prices is superior to that possessed by any one individual investor. Of course, difficulties arise if information is also costly to produce. Unfortunately, disincentives to the production of information can be eliminated only if speculative prices are not sufficient statistics. It is then possible to earn a normal return on information production but this also means that speculative prices are no longer good signals for resource allocation.

It has been argued that when the auction process is itself time consuming (unlike the Walrasian *tâtonnement* used to describe the process by which competitive markets achieve equilibrium in elementary economics) intervening price disequilibria will exist. The price disequilibria are the result of the fact that information cannot be incorporated quickly enough to achieve a sequence of competitive equilibria. Put differently, trading at "false" prices will occur.

## 9 The Market for Information

Information is a commodity, and as with any commodity, there is a market for it. Information must be produced before it is consumed and disseminated to others before its full impact on speculative prices occurs. As discussed above, there are usually costs to information production and uncertainty surrounding information dissemination.

Gonedes (1976) has considered the implications of the market for accounting information. In particular, Gonedes assesses the role that the dissemination of "accounting numbers" plays in the information production process with respect to the determination of security prices for individual firms. Gonedes makes the important point that in analyzing the capital market it is imperative to also consider the market for information. Evidence which appears inconsistent with capital market equilibrium may be indicative of problems with the market for information instead.

## 10 Information and Market Regulation

Regulation permeates the US financial system much as it does in other countries. Derivative security markets are no exception. Much of the regulation of derivative security markets, for example, originates with, and is largely administered by, market participants themselves or their self-regulatory organizations. The implicit or explicit acceptance of these private-sector-based, or market-initiated, regulations is often a necessary precondition to trade on organized futures and option markets. Other regulations originate with the public sector and are imposed on derivative security markets by federal and state governments, their agencies, or the courts. In a world where competing international financial futures and options markets are located in regulatory environments with widely varying degrees of both private and public regulation, the regulatory environment itself becomes a matter of choice to market participants. It is instructive to consider some of the effects of regulations on the flow of information in exchange-traded derivative security markets.

Regulation may take many forms. For instance, it may limit the size of security positions one may take. Or it may specify the auction system. For instance, the open outcry auction system which is mandated by the rules of most US futures exchanges, in particular the requirement that only the "best" (highest) bid or "best" (lowest) offer prevail in the market at any one time, also helps to ensure that information is impounded into market prices. Thus, more valuable information is not impeded in being incorporated into market prices.

Certain regulations, such as restricting the release of new information until after US markets are closed, are inconsistent with, and ineffective in, an open global economy where securities are traded continuously. In such an environment, regulators effectively must compete with one another. This may, in turn, limit their ability to impose and enforce regulations. Consequently, the effects of regulation on derivative security markets are not always immediately apparent.

Even within the United States there are differing degrees of both private- and public-sector-imposed regulation on derivative security contracts and markets. For instance, interest rate and currency swaps are largely outside the purview of government regulation. Certain over-the-counter options also escape close government or private-sector-based regulatory scrutiny. Exchange-traded futures, options, and futures options are extensively regulated in the United States and deserve attention.

There is a surprising dichotomy in the regulatory treatment of information across countries and financial markets. In some countries trading on inside information is perfectly legal while in others, such as the United States, it is not legal. Even within the United States there is a disparity in the regulatory view of information in the cash and financial futures markets. For instance, the Commodity Futures Trading Commission (CFTC) which regulates US financial futures markets regards the information on large futures positions (which certain traders must report to the CFTC) as private property which is not released to the general public in a timely fashion. In contrast, the Securities and Exchange Commission requires investors who acquire more than 5 percent of the stock of a company whose stock is publicly traded in the United States to indicate whether they intend to acquire additional shares before doing so. This information is released to the public.

Similarly, the rules of the various futures and options exchanges also provide a perspective on the importance market participants attach to the value of certain types of information or the effects on speculative prices of its dissemination. For instance, Rule 432 of the Chicago Mercantile Exchange states:

> It shall be a major offense: ... to make or report a false or fictitious trade; to knowingly disseminate false, misleading or inaccurate reports concerning crop or market information or conditions that affect or tend to affect the price of any commodity upon the Exchange; ... to make use of or reveal any confidential information obtained by reason of participating in any investigation proceeding or hearing; ....

Violation of this rule may be punishable by suspension of, or expulsion from, membership in the Exchange, or payment of a fine up to $100,000.

This rule is also a testament to the influence of rumors on market prices. There is a probability distribution associated with the veracity of any piece of information. That is, there is always some possibility that the information received is incorrect. For rumors, these probability distributions are considerably wider, on average, than with other types of information. What makes rumors special is the power that they exert in the financial marketplace. Frequently, prices react out of all proportion to the likely veracity of the content of the rumor. The low transaction costs in futures and options markets make these markets especially susceptible to even minor rumors.[19]

The issue of whether the public sector should impose regulations on financial markets is a matter of much controversy. Many individuals have some strongly held views concerning regulation of financial markets. It is not uncommon to find individuals who believe that government regulation of otherwise free markets is entirely detrimental and society is better off without it. Alternatively, there are individuals who believe that government regulation of financial markets is absolutely vital and markets with it are inherently superior to markets without it. Both views ignore important elements of economic reality.

It is important to recognize that one cannot draw any inferences about social optimality or welfare from the existence of market equilibrium alone. There is a danger in believing, like the character Pangloss in Voltaire's novel *Candide*, that market equilibrium means it is the best of all possible worlds. Market equilibrium is simply the equation of quantity demanded and quantity supplied. The market clears during periods when competition is absent or price manipulation is present, as well as during normal periods with market competition. The voluntary nature of the exchange of goods in the marketplace does not imbue such transactions with any social desirability or necessity. One need only consider the trade in illicit drugs to reject that point of view.

Similarly, one must be careful not to presume that a regulated environment is inherently superior to a *laissez-faire* or unregulated one. The existence of regulation requires only a political, as opposed to economic, rationale to justify it. In a democratic society, regulation reflects an attempt to satisfy the perceived needs of a variety of political constituencies whose economic interests often conflict with one another. In addition, the regulatory agency itself has a vested interest in the regulation it imposes, and its self-interest may differ from that of society as a whole. Not surprisingly, the end result is frequently regulation which is inconsistent with the economic interest of society as a whole.

Regulations may also have unintended results such as reducing competition and innovation by creating barriers to entry in the industry or regulatory delays in the introduction of new products. Moreover, the existence of deficiencies in the market process does not necessarily justify the regulation imposed. There is a cost associated with market regulation and, quite simply, the cost may exceed the benefit. In this sense, government-imposed regulation may be viewed as merely another form of taxation with its own set of disincentive effects.

Nevertheless, government regulation of many speculative markets is a fact of life and is likely to remain so. As a result, the relevant issue is not so much whether government regulation of speculative markets should exist, but rather what effects such regulation has on speculative markets.

The imposition of effective regulations is not always an easy task for either private- or public-sector regulatory organizations. Regulations may be misdirected, unenforced, or easily circumvented.

It is even more difficult when alternative markets in competing political jurisdictions exist.[20]

## 11 Information and "Fast" Futures Markets

The release of new information in futures markets is often followed by a short period of rapidly changing futures prices, a significant increase in trading activity, and perceived "choppiness" in futures prices.[21] Such markets are often officially designated as "fast" by traders on the floor. The designation of a fast market serves as a signal to traders off the floor that there is greater uncertainty about the price at which market orders may be executed at. It also provides an alternative (albeit arbitrary) measure of the length of time it takes the market to fully digest and impound a piece of new information into futures prices.

To most participants, fast markets represent periods of increased volatility in future prices. As noted earlier, Engle, Ito, and Lin (1990) have argued that the observed patterns in the clusters of volatility in speculative prices reflect either "the arrival process of news or market dynamics in response to the news."

Fast markets represent a *market-participant*-described period of perceived increased volatility and heavy trading activity. The designation that a market is fast is simultaneously released with futures prices.[22] Most fast markets arise in response to the arrival of new information. Not surprisingly, large changes in futures prices often occur in fast markets. The rapid (and often large) price changes associated with fast markets may, in turn, trigger buy or sell orders which further exacerbate price volatility. Some observers contend that the trading volume during this time period can be several times the trading volume during normal futures markets for a comparable time period.

The rules for determining whether a market should be designated as "fast" are set by the individual exchanges. Generally, fast markets are determined at the discretion of the relevant pit committee.[23] As one might imagine, in a busy futures pit, the process for designating a fast market is informal. While the number of members of the pit committee differs across markets, it takes two or more members to instruct exchange clerks to designate a market as fast or to remove that designation. Because of the arbitrary way in which fast markets are set it is possible that not all market participants will agree that a market designated as fast is indeed fast.[24] For certain key government reports and other information announcements with scheduled release times (previously known to market participants), the pit committee may agree in advance that the market should be designated as fast immediately after the announcement. Conversely, the impetus to remove a "fast" market designation may first arise from the exchange staff on the floor asking whether the designation should be lifted.

Contrary to popular belief, the designation of a market as fast does not relieve brokers of any legal liabilities associated with executing trades on behalf of customers. It may, however, allow brokers to better explain their actions (or lack thereof) in exchange hearings.

The length of most fast markets extends beyond what would be needed for price adjustment in an informationally efficient capital market. This may suggest that the market is informationally inefficient; that information dissemination uncertainty is more important than commonly thought; or that *reported* fast markets exaggerate the length of *actual* fast markets, that is, the factors inducing fast markets may not last the full length of a reported fast market. Consequently, it is possible (consistent with an informationally efficient market) that speculative prices adjust quickly yet the other factors which determine a fast market – price choppiness and increased trading activity – remain. Indeed, it would seem that one could decompose a fast market into three principal components: the adjustment of speculative prices to reflect the new information; price choppiness; and increased trading activity. Nevertheless, the notion that "fast" markets last for more than a moment means that there is an adjustment period when new information enters the market.

Although fast futures markets are characterized by rapid and often large changes in futures prices, increased trading activity and perceived choppiness in speculative prices, each of these factors may not last the entire length of a fast market. Indeed, financial economic theory would suggest that futures prices would react quickly to new information. Thus, the large price adjustment to new information should come very quickly. If futures prices overreact to new information than one would expect the period of perceived price choppiness also to be relatively short-lived as well. Rapid changes in futures prices following the news item may largely be a reflection of increased market-making. One can contend that the response of changes in speculative prices to new information during a fast market is a form of information dissemination uncertainty.

The existence of fast markets increases the need to distinguish between calendar time and transaction time when measuring the volatility of changes in speculative prices. For instance, Clark (1973) argues that transaction time is more appropriate than calendar time to measure volatility.

## 12 Conclusions

The chapter began with a discussion of the behavior of speculative prices. The observed simple time series behavior of speculative prices was the impetus behind the development of the efficient capital markets hypothesis. Ultimately, macroeconomic or financial economic models must explain the observed behavior of speculative prices over time. In an informationally efficient capital market the process by which new information enters the market is mirrored by changes in speculative prices themselves. Consequently, as Fama (1963) has pointed out, the observed "fair game" processes that most changes in speculative prices follow simply reflects the flow of new information into financial prices and the "abrupt nature" of changes in the real economy. From an econometric perspective, changes in speculative prices may be regarded as the output variables of some financial "black box."

Put differently, the hypothesis of market efficiency is not directly observable. Speculative prices, however, are the observable output variables drawn from an unobservable "black box" representing the model of asset pricing within either an efficient or an inefficient capital market. As a result, judgments concerning market efficiency are based on the behavior of changes in speculative prices. The behavior of changes in speculative prices over time also has implications for the structure of the econometric model presumed to be generating the output variables. Using the methodology pioneered by Zellner (1979) and Zellner and Palm (1974) one can integrate the development of a simultaneous equations model with time series analysis (SEMTSA). Alternatively, one can employ SEMTSA methodology to delimit the class of acceptable linear models consistent with the observed (and correctly measured) time series behavior of the output variables.

It should be pointed out that interest rates are the output variables of various financial economic models of asset pricing but also various macroeconomic and monetary models. The observed time series behavior of changes in speculative prices imposes some restrictions on possible *linear* models of asset pricing as well as macroeconomic/monetary models in which interest rates or other speculative prices are the output variables. The observed simple time series behavior of changes in speculative prices also imposes strict limits on the potential joint time series process of the input variable(s) (i.e. new information about the real economy) and hence models of information production. Moreover, these restrictions apply whether the market is informationally efficient or not. Thus, the class of possible disequilibrium models of asset pricing within an informationally inefficient captial market is restricted as much as possible equilibrium models of asset pricing are within an informationally efficient capital market.

Simply stated, there is information contained in the time series behavior of speculative prices. This information can be exploited in determining possible models of asset pricing as Webb (1985) has shown.[25]

## Notes

1 In his review of the literature on efficient capital markets, Eugene Fama (1970) takes a similar tack when he states:

> The primary role of the capital market is allocation of ownership of the economy's capital stock. In general terms, the ideal is a market in which prices provide accurate signals for resource allocation: that is, a market in which firms can make production–investment decisions, and investors can choose among the secu-

> rities that represent ownership of firms' activities under the assumption that security prices at anytime "fully reflect" all available information. A market in which prices always "fully reflect" available information is called "efficient".
>
> (p. 109)

2 The reason for this is that changes in speculative prices may occur even in a world of certainty. For instance, the price of a default-free zero coupon will change as interest rates change and with the passage of time alone. This is because the price of a default-free zero coupon bond will approach par as it approaches maturity.

3 As Fama (1970) notes, the assumption that changes in speculative prices follow a random walk is unnecessarily restrictive in that it requires that changes in speculative prices are *both* independent and identically distributed.

4 In his classic book *The Structure of Scientific Revolution*, Kuhn (1970) argues that scientific revolutions occur when one paradigm replaces a previously widely held paradigm. Specifically, Kuhn states:

> Discovery commences with the awareness of anomaly, i.e., with the recognition that nature has somehow violated the paradigm induced expectations that govern normal science. It then continues with a more or less extended exploration of the area of the anomaly. And it closes only when the paradigm theory has been adjusted so that the anomalous has become the expected.
>
> (pp. 52–3)

5 Samuelson's classic paper provided the theoretical foundation for the efficient capital markets hypothesis.

6 Ross (1989) shows that for a simple martingale model in an arbitrage-free economy the "variance of security prices equals the rate of information flow" (p. 8).

7 Technical analysis is an attempt to exploit the perceived information in the past sequence of speculative prices in order to ascertain the *direction* of future price changes or identify *turning points*. The usefulness of technical analysis remains a matter of controversy in the academic literature. A recent article by Brock, Lakonishok, and LeBaron (1992) suggests that the use of certain technical analysis tools in the past would have produced greater returns than a simple buy and hold strategy even after transaction costs have been taken into account. Other studies (e.g. Cutler, Poterba, and Summers, 1990) note the use of technical trading systems by many market practitioners to exploit observed serial correlation in speculative prices.

8 As Fama (1970) points out, such an assumption

> elevates the purely mathematical concept of expected value to a status not necessarily implied by the general notion of market efficiency. The expected value is just one of many possible summary measures of a distribution of returns, and market efficiency *per se* (i.e. the general notion that prices "fully reflect" available information) does not imbue it with any special importance. Thus, the results of tests based on this assumption depend to some extent on its validity as well as on the efficiency of the market. But some such assumption is necessary to give the theory of efficient markets empirical content.
>
> (p. 385)

9 It should be pointed out that in empirical tests of the CAPM it is necessary to use a proxy for the market portfolio. In the early empirical literature, a portfolio of US exchange traded stocks was used to represent the market portfolio. The effect of omitted assets on estimates of the return on the market portfolio has been considered by Fama and Schwert (1977). Indeed, Fama and Schwert contend that some observed pricing anomalies may be attributable to the use of the incorrect market portfolio (see for example Black and Scholes dividend effects).

10 Breeden (1979) suggests the use of aggregate consumption as a proxy for the market portfolio. Essentially, Breeden contends that aggregate consumption may be used as an instrumental variable since the true market portfolio is difficult to measure. Breeden's analysis has the virtue of recognizing that consumption is the ultimate objective of all wealth creation activities. Thus, if one cannot measure the value of the asset directly but can measure aggregate consumption then one can conclude that it represents the return on all capital.

Employing this approach to analyzing futures markets Breeden (1980) reports that several commodities and hence the futures contracts they represent are quite risky *vis-à-vis* the market portfolio (i.e. aggregate consumption). In particular, he reports beta coefficients significantly different from zero for a number of commodities. These results are in sharp contrast to those obtained by Dusak (1973) who used the more standard measure of the market portfolio. Dusak reports beta coefficients close to zero for the commodities she examined with one exception, corn, which enjoyed a small but statistically significant positive beta coefficient.

11 The interested reader is referred to an article by Nichols (1993).

12 Indeed, with respect to the identification of the APT systematic risk factors, Roll and Ross (1980) argue:

> This question is equivalent to asking what causes the particular values of the covariance term in the CAPM. If there are only a few systematic components of risk, one would expect these to be related to fundamental economic aggregates, such as GNP, or to interest rates or weather (although no causality is implied by such relations). The factor model formalism suggests that a whole theoretical and empirical structure must be explored to better understand what economic forces actually affect returns systematically. But in testing the APT, it is no more appropriate for us to examine this issue than it would be for tests of the CAPM to examine what, if anything, causes returns to be multivariate normal. In both instances, the return generating process is taken as one of the primitive assumptions of the theory. We do consider the basic underlying causes of the generating process of returns to be a potentially important area of research, but we think it can be investigated separately from testing asset pricing theories.
>
> (p. 1077)

13 Jensen (1978) states: "Indeed, the Efficient Market Hypothesis progressed from the state of a curiosity taken seriously by only a few scientists in economics and finance communities, to that of a dominant paradigm in finance and the basis for an emerging revolution in macroeconomics (where the principle is still generally referred to as rational expectations)."

14 Ekman (1992) reports a similar finding with respect to Standard and Poor 500 stock index futures prices.

15 It should be noted that size is a relative concept. Many of the small capitalization stocks examined in the early stocks were traded on the New York Stock Exchange or American Stock Exchange and were small only in relation to the market capitalizations of the other stocks listed on the exchange.

16 French (1980) asserts:

> If one concludes that the expected return for Monday is negative, it is tempting to also conclude that the market is inefficient. However, any test of the efficient market hypothesis is simultaneously a test of efficiency and of assumptions about the nature of market equilibrium. Because of this, one can never unambiguously reject market efficiency. Nevertheless, it is difficult to imagine any reasonable model of equilibrium consistent with both market efficiency and negative expected returns to a portfolio as large as the Standard and Poor's Composite.

17 Not surprisingly, this is exactly what one would expect to observe if Kuhn's theory of scientific change is correct. Kuhn (1970) states:

> Let us then assume that crises are a necessary precondition for the emergence of novel theories and ask next how scientists respond to their existence. Part of the answer, as obvious as it is important, can be discovered by noting first what scientists never do when confronted by even severe and prolonged anomalies. Though they may begin to lose faith and then to consider alternatives, they do not renounce the paradigm that has led them into crisis. They do not, that is, treat anomalies as counterinstances, though in the vocabulary of the philosophy of science that is what they are.
>
> (p. 77)

18 Not surprisingly, a significant counter literature on this topic has also developed. The interested reader is referred to Keim (1986) and Jensen (1978) for a review of the literature on market anomalies (excluding excessive volatility of speculative prices). Many of the early studies in the empirical financial economics literature did not specify a specific equilibrium model of price formation (other than that the model of market equilibria is a member of the class of linear expected return models) and are not subject to as much criticism as those that used the CAPM.

19 To the extent that a rumored event is *possible* although *improbable*, speculative prices should react to the *expected* value of the information. Any reaction in excess of this may reflect market psychology.

20 These points are illustrated in the following account of Mehl (1934) of futures option trading on the Chicago Board of Trade in the late nineteenth and early twentieth centuries:

> Trading in privileges [futures options] on the Chicago Board of Trade had been carried on at intermittent periods since the early [eighteen] sixties. From time to time the exchange tried to prohibit its members from trading in privileges, but such efforts did not meet with success as the members resorted to the Open Board of Trade, another market in Chicago, and to an exchange in Milwaukee, where trading in privileges was permitted. The disciplining of members who persisted in the practice was not feasible, as there were so many engaged in the privilege trading that to have disciplined all who violated the rules would have meant the disruption of the board. The Illinois law of 1874 which prohibited trading in privileges was not strictly enforced, and in 1913 it was amended, apparently to exempt privilege

> transactions not settled by the payment of "differences" [i.e. in cash]. It was the payment of differences that was considered a gambling feature of privilege trading....
>
> (p. 77)

21 As noted in the previous chapter, traders use the term "choppy" to characterize markets with violent swings in *effective* transaction prices. Such price swings increase the danger of uncontrollable losses (i.e. getting "chopped" up).

22 Although fast markets may arise from noninformational factors such as a sudden increase in trading volume (due perhaps to triggering a number of large stop-loss orders) or as the result of a "spillover" of sharp changes in other futures prices, say due to a crash, most fast markets arise from the release of new information. Noninformational factors are rarely the proximate cause of a fast market.

23 The "pit" committee is an exchange committee composed of several members who customarily trade in a given futures pit. It represents the first layer of regulation by the exchange. Each financial or commodity futures pit has its own pit committee.

24 Fast markets need not commence with the release of the information. Indeed, with unscheduled information releases one would imagine that the designation of a fast market occurs shortly after the news becomes available to market participants. Consequently, one must be cognizant of the lag time between the time the news is released and the time that a fast market is designated. Similarly, it is unlikely that fast markets end before they have returned to normal. Consequently, one must be cognizant of the lag between the actual end of a fast market and the reported end of a fast market.

25 Essentially, this result follows from the observed simplicity of the time series process that changes in speculative prices follow and the application of some simple consistency constraints from econometrics. If changes in future prices, stock returns, interest rates and inflation follow simple fair game processess such as an IMA(I) as the empirical evidence suggests then the asset pricing model is subject to certain constraints. This becomes apparent where time series analysis is integrated with structural econometric model building as Zellner and Palm (1974) have proposed. In essence, financial economic structural econometric models are subject to various consistency constraints as are other structural econometric models. The simple time series processes which speculative prices follow severely constrains the complexity of the appropriate model of asset pricing and the time series processes for the explanatory or input variables.

## References

Amihud, Y., and H. Mendleson 1987: "Trading Mechanisms and Stock Returns: An Empirical Investigation," *Journal of Finance*, 42 (3), July, 533–55.

Banz, R. W. 1981: "The Relationship Between Return and Market Value of Common Stocks," *Journal of Financial Economics*, 9, March, 3–18.

Beja, A., and H. Hakansson 1977: "Dynamic Market Processes and the Rewards to Up-to-Date Information," *Journal of Finance*, 32, June, 291–304.

Black, F. 1976: "The Pricing of Commodity Contracts," *Journal of Financial Economics*, 3, January–March, 167–79.

Black, F. 1986: "Noise," *Journal of Finance*, 42 (3), July, 529–43.

Breeden, D. T. 1979: "An Intertemporal Asset Pricing Model with Stochastic Consumption and Investment Opportunities," *Journal of Financial Economics*, 7 (3), 265–96.

Breeden, D. T. 1980: "Consumption Risks in Futures Markets," *Journal of Finance*, 35 (2), May, 503–20.

Brock, W., J. Lakonishok, and B. LeBaron 1992: "Simple Technical Trading Rates and the Stochastic Properties of Stock Returns," *Journal of Finance*, 47 (5), December, 1731–64.

Brown, P., A. W. Kleidon, and T. A. Marsh 1983: "New Evidence on the Nature of Size Related Anomalies in Stock Prices," *Journal of Financial Economics*, 12, June, 33–56.

Chiras, D. P., and S. Manaster 1978: "The Information Content of Option Prices and a Test of Market Efficiency," *Journal of Financial Economics*, 6, June–September, 213–33.

Clark, P. K. 1973: "A Subordinated Stochastic Process Model with Finite Variance for Speculative Prices," *Econometrica*, 41 (1), January, 135–59.

Clark, T. 1986: "Interest Rate Seasonals and the Federal Reserve," *Journal of Political Economy*, 94 (1), February, 76–125.

Cornell, B. 1985: "The Weekly Pattern in Stock Returns: Cash vs. Futures: A Note," *Journal of Finance*, 40, June, 583–8.

Cutler, D. M., J. M. Poterba, and L. Summers 1990: "Speculative Dynamics and the Role of Feedback Traders," *American Economic Review*, 80 (2), May, 63–8.

Dusak, K. 1973: "Futures Trading and Investor Returns: An Investigation of Commodity Market Risk Premiums," *Journal of Political Economy*, 81 (6), November–December, 1387–406.

Ekman, Peter D. 1992: "Intraday Patterns in the S&P 500 Index Futures Market," *Journal of Futures Markets*, 12 (4), December, 365–81.

Engle, R. F., T. Ito, and W. Lin 1990: "Meteor Showers or Heat Waves? Heteroskedastic Intra-Daily Volatility in the Foreign Exchange Market," *Econometrica*, 58 (3), May, 525–42.

Fama, E. F. 1963: "Mandlebrot and the Stable Paretian Hypothesis," *Journal of Business*, 36 (4), October, 420–9.

Fama, E. F. 1965: "The Behavior of Stock Market Prices," *Journal of Business*, 38, 34–105.

Fama, E. F. 1970: "Efficient Capital Markets: A Review of Theory and Empirical Work," *Journal of Finance*, 25 (2), May, 383–417.

Fama, E. F. 1975: "Short-Term Interest Rates as Predictors of Inflation," *American Economic Review*, 65, June, 269–82.

Fama, E. F. 1991: "Efficient Capital Markets: II," *Journal of Finance*, 46 (5), December, 1575–617.

Fama, E. F., and K. R. French 1992: "The Cross-Section of Expected Stock Returns," *Journal of Finance*, 47 (2), June, 427–66.

Fama, E. F., and G. W. Schwert 1977: "Asset Prices and Inflation," *Journal of Financial Economics*, 5, November, 113–45.

French, K. 1980: "Stock Returns and the Weekend Effect," *Journal of Financial Economics*, 8, March, 55–69.

Friedman, M. 1953: *Essays in Positive Economics*, Chicago, IL: University of Chicago Press.

Galai, D. 1978: "Empirical Tests of Boundary Conditions for CBOE Options," *Journal of Financial Economics*, 6, June–September, 187–211.

Gibbons, M., and P. Hess 1981: "Day of the Week Effects and Asset Returns," *Journal of Business*, 54 (4), October, 579–96.

Goldman, B., and H. Sosin 1979: "Information Dissemination and Market Efficiency," *Journal of Financial Economics*, 7, March, 29–61.

Gonedes, N. J. 1976: "The Capital Market, the Market for Information, and External Accounting," *Journal of Finance*, 31 (2), May, 611–30.

Green, J. 1978: "Sequential Structure of Futures Markets and the Value of Improving Information," *Economics Letters*, 1 (1), 29–32.

Grossman, S. 1975: "The Existence of Futures Markets, Noisy Rational Expectations and Informational Externalities," Ph.D. Dissertation, University of Chicago.

Grossman, S. 1976: "On the Efficiency of Competitive Stock Markets Where Traders Have Diverse Information," *Journal of Finance*, 31, 573–85.

Grossman, S., and J. Stiglitz 1976: "Information and Competitive Price Systems," *American Economic Review*, 66, May, 246–53.

Grossman, S., and J. Stiglitz 1980: "The Impossibility of Informationally Efficient Markets," *American Economic Review*, 70, June, 393–408.

Harris, L. 1986: "A Transaction Data Study of Weekly and Intradaily Patterns in Stock Returns," *Journal of Financial Economics*, 16, May, 99–117.

Jackson, M. 1991: "Equilibrium, Price Formation, and the Value of Private Information," *Review of Financial Studies*, 4 (1), 1–16.

Jensen, M. C. 1978: "Some Anomalous Evidence Regarding Market Efficiency," *Journal of Financial Economics*, 6, June–September, 95–101.

Keim, D. B. 1983: "Size Related Anomalies and Stock Market Seasonality: Further Empirical Evidence," *Journal of Financial Economics*, 12, June, 13–32.

Keim, D. B. 1986: "The CAPM and Equity Return Regularities," *Financial Analysts Journal*, 42 (3), May–June, 19–39.

Keim, D. B., and R. F. Stambaugh 1984: "A Further Investigation of the Weekend Effect in Stock Returns," *Journal of Finance*, 39, July, 819–37.

Kendall, M. G. 1953: "The Analysis of Economic Time Series Part I: Prices," *Journal of the Royal Statistical Society*, 96, Part I, 11–35.

King, B. F. 1966: "Market and Industry Factors in Stock Price Behavior," *Journal of Business*, 39 (1), Part II, 139–90.

Kuhn, T. S. 1970: *The Structure of Scientific Revolutions*, Chicago, IL: University of Chicago Press.

Laffont, J. 1980: *Essays in the Economics of Uncertainty*, Cambridge, MA: Harvard University Press.

Latham, M. 1986: "Informational Efficiency and Information Subsets," *Journal of Finance*, 41 (1), March, 39–52.

Lintner, J. 1965: "Security Prices, Risk and Maximal Gains from Diversification," *Journal of Finance*, 20, December, 587–615.

Markowitz, H. M. 1959: *Portfolio Selection: Efficient Diversification of Investments*, New Haven, CT: Yale University Press.

Marsh, T. A., and E. Rosenfeld 1986: "Information Dissemination and Market Efficiency," *Journal of Financial Economics*, 15, 359–72.

Mehl, P. 1934: "Trading in Privileges on the Chicago Board of Trade," US Department of Agriculture Circular 323, Washington, DC, December.

Mossin, J. 1966: "Equilibrium in a Capital Asset Market," *Econometrica*, 34, October, 768–83.

Nichols, N. A. 1993: "Efficient? Chaotic? What's the New Finance?," *Harvard Business Review*, 71, March–April, 50–60.

Oldfield, G., and R. Rogalski 1980: "A Theory of Common Stock Returns Over Trading and Nontrading Periods," *Journal of Finance*, 35, June, 729–51.

Reinganum, M. R. 1981: "Misspecification of Capital Asset Pricing: Empirical Anomalies Based on Earnings' Yields and Market Values," *Journal of Financial Economics*, 9, 19–46.

Reinganum, M. R. 1982: "A Direct Test of Roll's Conjecture on the Firm Size Effect," *Journal of Finance*, 37, March, 27–35.

Roberts, H. V. 1959: "Stock Market Patterns and Financial Analysis: Methodological Suggestions," *Journal of Finance*, 14, March, 1–10.

Roll, R. 1977: "A Critique of the Asset Pricing Theory's Test: Part 1," *Journal of Financial Economics*, 4, May, 129–76.

Roll, R. 1981: "A Possible Explanation of the Small Firm Effect," *Journal of Finance*, 36, 879–87.

Roll, R. 1988: "$R^2$," *Journal of Finance*, 43 (2), July, 541–66.

Roll, R., and S. A. Ross 1980: "An Empirical Investigation of the Arbitrage Pricing Theory," *Journal of Finance*, 35, December, 1073–1104

Ross, S. A. 1976: "The Arbitrage Theory of Capital Asset Pricing," *Journal of Economic Theory*, 13, December, 341–60.

Ross, S. A. 1978: "The Current Status of the Capital Asset Pricing Model," *Journal of Finance*, 33 (3), May, 885–901.

Ross, S. A. 1989: "Information and Volatility: The No-Arbitrage Martingale Approach to Timing and the Resolution Irrelevance," *Journal of Finance*, 43, 1–16.

Samuelson, P. A. 1965: "Proof that Properly Anticipated Prices Fluctuate Randomly," *Industrial Management Review*, Spring, 341–60.

Scholes, M. 1972: "The Market for Securities: Substitution Versus Price Pressure and the Effects of Information on Share Prices," *Journal of Business*, 45 (2), April, 179–211.

Sharpe, W. F. 1964: "Capital Asset Prices: A Theory of Market Equilibrium Under Conditions of Risk," *Journal of Finance*, 19, September, 425–42.

Shefrin, H. M. 1978: "Differential Information and Informational Equilibrium," *Economics Letters*, 1 (1), 33–7.

Stephan, J., and R. E. Whaley 1990: "Intraday Price Change and Trading Volume in the Stock and Stock Option Markets," *Journal of Finance*, 45 (1), March, 191–220.

Stoll, H. R., and R. E. Whaley 1983: "Transaction Costs and the Small Firm Effect," *Journal of Finance*, 12, June, 57–79.

Stoll, H. R., and R. E. Whaley 1990: "Stock Market Structure and Volatility," *Review of Financial Studies*, 3 (1), 37–71.

Thompson, R. 1978: "The Information Content of Discounts and Premiums on Closed-End Fund Shares," *Journal of Financial Economics*, 6, June–September, 157–85.

Webb, R. I. 1985: "The Behavior of Speculative Prices and the Consistency of Economic Models." *Journal of Econometrics*, 27, January, 123–30.

Webb, R. I., and D. G. Smith 1994: "The Effect of Market Opening and Closing on the Volatility of Eurodollar Futures Prices," *Journal of Futures Markets*, 14 (1), February, forthcoming.

Wood, R. A., T. H. McInish, and J. K. Ord 1985: "An Investigation of Transactions Data for NYSE Stocks," *Journal of Finance*, 40 (3), July, 723–41.

Working, H. 1934: "A Random Difference Series for Use in the Analysis of Time Series," *Journal of the American Statistical Association*, 29, March, 11–24.

Zellner, A. 1979: "Statistical Analysis of Econometric Models," *Journal of the American Statistical Association*, 74, September, 628–43.

Zellner, A., and F. Palm 1974: "Time Series Analysis and Simultaneous Equation Econometric Models," *Journal of Econometrics*, 2 (1), 17–54.

# 3
# Noise and the Behavior of Speculative Prices

> The science of political economy, to be of practical utility, should not teach, *what necessarily* must take place, if even deduced by legitimate reasoning, and from undoubted premises; it must show, in what manner that which in reality does take place is the consequence of other facts equally certain. It must discover the chain which binds them together, and always, from observation, establish the existence of the two links at their point of connection.
>
> (Jean Baptiste Say,
> *Elements of Pure Economics or the Theory of Social Wealth*)

## 1 Introduction

As was noted in the previous chapter, the influence of information on changes in speculative prices has long received much attention in the financial economics literature. This is reflected in the substantial empirical literature on informationally efficient capital markets as surveyed by Fama (1970, 1991).[1] Indeed, the idea that speculative prices fully and correctly reflect available information is central to modern financial economic theory. However, there is growing evidence that the capital market may not be informationally efficient and that speculative prices change in response to both the arrival of new information and traders' reactions to "noise" (i.e. noninformational factors).

Observations of apparent market inefficiencies have, in turn, sparked the development of a theoretical literature that seeks to explain the observed behavior of changes in speculative prices in terms of the reaction to noise (or the overreaction to new information), or allow for speculative bubbles to occur in the context of models where individuals form expectations rationally. Fischer Black's (1986) provocative article on the influence of "noise" on the behavior of speculative prices is an example in this regard.

The evidence against market efficiency remains controversial and the implications of some alternative models of the behavior of speculative prices have yet to be adequately tested. Nevertheless, the initial results are interesting enough to warrant further investigation. This chapter examines some of the theoretical and empirical literature in this area and assesses whether market inefficiency represents a plausible explanation for how speculative prices sometimes react to the arrival of macroeconomic information.

## 2 Review of the Literature

The idea that speculative prices might change in response to both informational and noninformational factors is not new. For instance, Keynes (1935) explicitly rejects (what is now called) informational market efficiency when he argues that noninformational factors influence changes in speculative prices.[2] Although not new, the idea that noninformational factors influence changes in speculative prices has only recently received serious attention in financial economics as the empirical evidence against market efficiency has increased.

Roll (1984) examines the influence of weather on frozen concentrated orange juice (FCOJ) futures prices. He notes that almost 98 percent of total US frozen concentrated orange juice production is centered in central Florida and yet changes in central Florida weather conditions explain only a small fraction of the total variation in FCOJ futures prices while other seemingly important factors (such as changes in demand or production costs) explain even less. Roll concludes that much of the variation in FCOJ futures prices is unrelated to the arrival of new information. Similarly, Roll (1988) argues that much of the variation in individual stock prices cannot be explained by the reaction to fundamental news.[3]

French and Roll (1986) report significantly greater volatility in stock returns during the trading day than overnight. This is a surprising result if one believes that new information arrives evenly throughout the full day. French and Roll attribute the differential volatility primarily to traders acting on private information and, to a lesser extent, to mispricings by traders or traders acting on public information. It should be noted that their results, as well as the results of Roll (1984, 1988) are consistent with several explanations including the effects of noise trading.

The above three articles provide only a glimpse of the puzzling results many researchers have reported. Much of the theoretical and empirical financial economics literature on apparent market inefficiencies can be summarized around various topical areas. This approach is taken below.

## 2.1 Excessive Volatility in Speculative Prices

It was noted in the previous chapter, that an informationally efficient capital market suggests that speculative prices change only in response to the arrival of new information. Consequently, changes in speculative prices reflect the flow of new information in the market.

There is a significant strand of research in the financial economics literature which suggests that changes in speculative prices are too volatile to be accounted for by changes in information on economic fundamentals alone.[4] In particular, Shiller (1981a, b) and LeRoy and Porter (1981) make this argument for stock prices. Financial economic theory suggests that the price of a common stock is simply the present value of the stream of expected future dividends. Thus, the volatility of stock prices should approximate the volatility of expected future dividends holding the discount rate constant.[5] Consequently, Shiller's findings suggest that the market is informationally inefficient.

These articles sparked a substantial counter literature. Not surprisingly, much of the initial criticism of the findings of excessive volatility focused on methodological issues. For instance, Flavin (1983) and Kleidon (1986) criticize, among other things, the validity of the variance bounds test methodology as a means for determining whether changes in speculative prices are excessively volatile.[6]

Marsh and Merton (1986) suggest that managers may set dividends out of permanent income which may explain the appearance of excessive volatility of stock prices. The thrust of this literature is to demonstrate that the behavior of changes in speculative prices is still potentially consistent with an informationally efficient capital market.

This, in turn, has led to responses by Shiller (1986, 1990). Shiller (1990) argues that the Marsh and Merton hypothesis that managers set dividends out of permanent income implies that past changes in real dividends should help forecast future changes in real income. Using Granger causality tests, Shiller does not find any empirical support for this implication of the Marsh and Merton hypothesis.

Hodrick (1990) points out that before one can regard changes in speculative prices as excessive the volatility implied by market fundamentals must be known. This entails a more complete specification of market fundamentals, including the effects of taxes, the evolution of required return over time, and how market participants learn, than is contained in the simple present value model of real stock prices. Hodrick also points out the central importance of the assumption of risk neutrality in these models. He states:

> Without risk neutrality, there is no presumption that asset returns are expected to be the same either across assets or over time. Time-varying risk premiums complicate studies of excess asset price volatility because things that change risk premiums on assets are legitimate market fundamentals.
>
> (p. 187)

## 2.2 Varying Risk Premia

Even if stock market efficiency can be reconciled with seemingly excessively volatile stock prices, the question naturally arises as to what might explain the apparently volatile nature of stock prices. Malkiel (1979) and Pindyck (1984), for example, contend that the apparent excess volatility in stock prices might be explained by varying risk premia. Consequently, periods of increased volatility would be associated with greater risk premia.[7]

However, Poterba and Summers (1986) contend that long-term changes in stock prices cannot be adequately explained by changes in volatility. The reason for this is that changes in volatility do not last long enough to affect returns (and hence prices) for other than short time periods. Moreover, this is true for both historical volatility and expected volatility (as proxied from the implied volatility in the Chicago Board Options Exchange index of the prices of standardized stock options).

## 2.3 Fads versus Fundamentals

The notion that changes in speculative prices are excessively volatile suggests that they may be influenced by nonfundamental factors. Shiller (1986) argues that fads in investor behavior are reflected in the behavior of speculative prices. Shiller proposes integrating "modern financial theory with behavioral alternatives." Any model of asset pricing, however, must explain the observed time series behavior of changes in speculative prices. Webb (1990) contends that the simple time series models that changes in speculative prices follow impose sharp limits on the class of possible *linear* disequilibrium models of asset pricing. Webb (1990) concludes:

> Financial models of asset pricing are subject to the same rules of econometrics as other structural econometric models. Although there is considerable disagreement over whether capital markets are informationally efficient, there is general agreement that observed changes in speculative prices follow simple time series processes. While the ultimate goal of any model of asset pricing is to explain the behaviour of changes in speculative prices over time, the observed time series behaviour of changes in speculative prices likewise imposes restrictions on possible models of asset pricing. An application of the Zellner–Palm SEMSAT methodology shows that the simplicity of the observed time series behaviour of changes in speculative prices imposes severe constraints on the class of possible linear disequilibrium models of asset pricing in an inefficient capital market. In particular, disequilibrium models which possess long lags are not consistent with the observed behaviour of speculative prices. Moreover, the results suggest that the *joint* time series process of the input variables must be quite simple. All of which illustrates the practical

> importance of using the information contained in the time series behaviour of changes in speculative prices in developing a model of asset pricing.
>
> (p. 398)

Shiller (1990) considers the possibility that high correlation between real stock prices and real dividends may make it more likely that stock prices change in response to fundamentals and not fads. Shiller argues that the relationship between real stock prices and real dividends is highest at low frequencies (i.e. over long periods of time) and lowest at high frequencies (i.e. over short periods of time).[8] Moreover, Shiller argues that the dividends set by management are themselves potentially subject to fads.[9] Shiller (1990) also argues that the observed absence of short-term serial correlation in changes in speculative prices may simply mean that any feedback effects associated with speculative bubbles may occur over a longer time period.

## 2.4 Mean Reversion in Speculative Prices

There is considerable evidence that changes in speculative prices exhibit mean reversion.[10] Using data covering the period 1926–85, Fama and French (1988) report significant negative autocorrelation of stock returns over certain holding periods exceeding one year in length. They contend that this is consistent with mean reversion and indicate that over 35 percent of the variation of three to five year nominal stock returns is predictable (more for portfolios of small capitalization firms; less for portfolios of large capitalization firms). These findings are potentially consistent with two alternative models as Fama and French point out:

> Such price behavior is consistent with common models of an irrational market in which stock prices take long temporary swings away from fundamental values. But the predictability of long-horizon returns can also result from time-varying equilibrium expected returns generated by rational pricing in an efficient market.... More informed choices between the competing explanations of return predictability will require models which restrict the relations between

> the behavior of macroeconomic driving variables and equilibrium returns.
>
> (pp. 247–8)

Fama and French also contend that the observed negative autocorrelation in long-period stock returns is attributable to a common macroeconomic factor rather than factors unique to individual firms. They conjecture that the significant negative autocorrelation observed may primarily reflect the first 15 years of the sample (1926–40). Poterba and Summers (1988) present similar evidence indicating the presence of mean reversion in real stock returns.

DeBondt and Thaler (1985) take a behavioral approach to explain the apparent overreaction of stock prices to new information. Specifically, they test whether there is any evidence of mean reversion and, if so, whether it is related to the size of the initial move. Examining the behavior of cumulative average residuals they report evidence consistent with mean reversion.

The studies indicating mean reversion have been criticized by Nelson (1990). He notes that almost all of the evidence for mean reversion is in the pre-Second World War part of the sample.[11] This suggests that financial economists may be premature in suggesting that mean reversion is indicative of irrational behavior by individuals.

## 2.5 More Market Anomalies

Mehra and Prescott (1985) present evidence of a large difference between the realized real return on equities and short-term real interest rates in the United States during the period 1889–1978. The result is puzzling because the high realized return on equities (6.18 percent) during this period would lead one to expect a higher realized real return on short-term risk-free investments in a perfect market than that observed (0.80 percent).[12] They note that their results are not sensitive to whether the economic growth rate persists or the degree of leverage of corporations. Mehra and Prescott conclude that the relevant question "may not be why was the average equity return so high but rather why was the risk-free rate so low" (p. 158).

Siegel (1992) pursues that suggestion in his article on the behavior of realized real interest rates in the UK and the United States, during the period 1800–1990. Siegel reports evidence that the realized real return was substantially greater than what Mehra and Prescott report (0.80 percent) for the periods preceding and following their sample even though the realized real return on equity was essentially the same as what Mehra and Prescott reported. (Moreover, Siegel reports this result was true for both short-term and long-term interest rates.) That is, Siegel reports an average annual real short-term interest rate of 5.19 percent outside the Mehra and Prescott sample period versus a real interest rate of 0.87 percent within the Mehra and Prescott sample period using US data. Siegel obtains similar results using UK data. He concludes that his evidence indicates "that the period since 1925, which is so often studied by finance economists, may be uncharacteristic of returns on fixed income securities" (p. 248).

Much financial economic research has been conducted on US stock market price data. Cutler, Poterba, and Summers (1990) consider whether similar patterns observed in the US equity markets are also apparent in other speculative markets in the United States and outside. They report evidence of statistically significant positive autocorrelation in one month returns for equities, bonds, foreign exchange, gold, houses, and collectibles during the period 1960–88 or some subperiod of it. Cutler, Poterba, and Summers point out that certain types of technical analysis may work well in an environment where changes in speculative prices exhibit positive autocorrelation followed later by negative autocorrelation. They contend that multi-year returns can be readily predicted by comparing market prices with intrinsic value (one possible interpretation of this result would be that "value" investing works).

Other researchers have noted the widespread use of technical analysis by many market participants as a possible reason that speculative markets do not always reflect fundamental factors. In this regard, Frankel and Froot (1990) investigate the possibility that the rapid appreciation (and subsequent rapid collapse) of the US dollar in 1984–5 might be an example of a speculative bubble. Frankel and Froot argue that one interpretation of the observed large volume of trading in the foreign exchange markets is that "much trading is based on noise rather than news, and leads to excessive volatility" (p. 183). Further, they point out that many foreign exchange traders use technical analysis or other models which extrapolate recent price trends to forecast future changes in foreign exchange rates. They suggest that a pronounced shift away from forecasting services using fundamental analysis toward technical analysis might explain how a speculative bubble could arise. Frankel and Froot state:

> It is now widely accepted that standard observable macroeconomic variables are not capable of explaining, much less predicting *ex ante*, the majority of short-term changes in the exchange rate.
>
> (p. 181)

The question naturally arises as to whether anomalies can persist especially in an environment where market participants learn from past errors or where significant sums are involved. Research by Camerer (1987) using experimental data suggests not. This means that there are limits to the persistence of anomalies.

Sometimes market anomalies are more apparent than real. An excellent case in point is the observation of negative nominal yields on certain Treasury securities as they approached maturity during the Great Depression of the 1930s. Given that cash has a zero nominal return, purchases of Treasury securities with negative nominal returns seem irrational. This seeming anomaly is readily explained, however. Cecchetti (1988) points out that during the Great Depression the US Treasury issued securities at par even though the securities had a market value greater than par (because the coupon rate exceeded the market interest rate). New securities could be purchased by paying cash or exchanging eligible existing securities. The implicit option or exchange privilege contained in existing securities was not taken into account by previous economics studies (although its existence was widely known on the Street). Cecchetti contends that the size of the spread was tantamount to an underwriting spread which fully reflected the risks that the purchasers of the debt undertook.[13]

Another example in this regard is Gibson's paradox. It is a puzzle that baffled economists for several generations. Essentially, Gibson's paradox is the observation made by Keynes and others of a close correlation between nominal interest rates and the level of prices and a virtual absence of relationship between nominal interest rates and the rate of change in prices even though economic theory would suggest otherwise. That is, as is explained in more detail in the next chapter, economic theory suggests that the nominal interest rates should be highly correlated with the rate of change in prices.

Barsky and Summers (1988) provide a convincing (albeit partial) explanation for Gibson's paradox. First, they start with an observation attributed to Friedman and Schwartz (1982) that the period when Gibson's paradox is operative coincides with the period that countries in which it was observed, such as the UK, were on the gold standard. Second, the opportunity cost of holding gold is the real interest forgone. As a result, the relative price of gold varies inversely with changes in the real rate of interest. Third, because the monetary authorities fixed the nominal price of gold, changes in the relative price of gold translate directly into changes in the price level.[14] Barsky and Summers provide some evidence in support of their explanation.

## 2.6 Tests of Market Efficiency and Linearity

There is a substantial amount of empirical evidence in support of the concept of informationally efficient capital markets, yet a number of studies provide often persuasive evidence of gross persistent market inefficiencies (e.g. Modigliani and Cohn, 1979).[15] How does one explain these conflicting results? One approach is to challenge the validity of the tests that purport to show evidence of market efficiency. Essentially, this is the approach that Summers (1986) takes when he argues that many of the tests of market efficiency have little power. This has an extremely important implication; namely, that the tests commonly used in these studies may not be able to detect certain departures from market efficiency. In particular, Summers (1986) argues:

> [C]ertain types of inefficiency in market valuations are not likely to be detected using standard methods. This means the evidence found in many studies that the hypothesis of efficiency cannot be rejected should not lead us to conclude that market prices represent

> rational assessments of fundamentals valuations.... In particular, the hypothesis that market valuations include large persistent errors is as consistent with the available evidence as is the hypothesis of market efficiency. These are exactly the sort of errors in valuation one would expect to see if market valuations involved inflation illusion or were moved by fads as some have suggested.
>
> (p. 598)

Another approach to reconciling the substantial evidence of market efficiency with the more recent evidence of market inefficiency is to question whether changes in speculative prices are well described by linear models. That is, nonlinear models of changes in speculative prices (where market participants form expectations rationally) might be more appropriate.

Meese and Rose (1990) observe that existing linear models of exchange rates do not show a strong relationship to economic fundamentals.[16] Meese and Rose (1990) use a nonparametric technique (known as locally weighted regression) to investigate whether nonlinearities in exchange rate relationships exist. However, with the notable exception of the franc–US dollar exchange rate, they report little evidence of significant nonlinearities in exchange rates.

## 2.7 Rationality of Expectations Data

The empirical evidence indicating that changes in financial market prices exhibit speculative bubbles, mean reversion, or excessive volatility calls into question the underlying assumption of rationality in the expectations formation process.

Increased understanding of how individuals form expectations may help to explain the observed behavior of changes in speculative prices. Ito (1990) uses Japanese survey data on expectations of the yen–dollar exchange rate over a two year period to examine the expectations formation process. Ito's findings suggests that the assumption that individuals form rational expectations of the yen–dollar exchange rate may not be valid given the heterogeneous expectations he observes across individuals. Moreover, Ito contends that information disparities across investors are unlikely to explain heterogeneous expectations across market participants. Another interesting finding that Ito reports is the tendency for forecasted changes in the exchange rate to be in the direction which would benefit the forecaster's likely exposure to exchange rate risk. Thus, importers (exporters) would be more likely to forecast a fall (rise) in the foreign exchange value of the dollar, which (if they were not fully hedged) would have the effect of increasing profits. Finally, Ito shows that short-term and long-term forecasts are not internally consistent. He states:

> One might think that people use different economic variables for forecasting the future spot rate with different horizons. For example, chart (technical) analysis ... is used for the short-term horizon, but other factors come into consideration for the long-term horizon ... [i.e. economic fundamentals]. ... However, if these factors are relevant in the long-run, they should be relevant in the short-run, although the effect may be small in the short-run.
>
> (p. 447)

## 2.8 Speculative Prices and the Aggregation of Information

It was stated earlier that speculative prices are sufficient statistics in an informationally efficient capital market. That is, speculative prices aggregate information across individual traders/investors – each of whom may possess only a little piece of knowledge.

There are theoretical reasons why one might expect the hypothesis of informationally efficient capital markets not to hold under some circumstances, especially given that traders differ in size (and perhaps influence).[17] Laffont and Maskin (1990) demonstrate that when imperfect competition is introduced into financial markets (i.e. an individual can affect the price of a security) security prices do not aggregate information effectively, thereby causing potentially inefficient prices. This result follows from the fact that it is in the self-interest of traders who can affect market prices to behave strategically.

Auction bidding strategies are not invariant to perceived informational differences among auction participants. Put simply, the greater the expected uncertainty of what other participants know the less one is willing to bid. Cammack (1991) examines the Treasury bill auction market. She presents evidence which indicates that the prices for Treasury bills are downwardly biased relative to the secondary market and increase directly with the expected dispersion of bids (i.e. when there is more uncertainty about what others know).

Cammack also examines whether Treasury auctions convey information to the secondary market. She reports that when actual dispersion in Treasury auctions exceeds expected dispersion the prices of Treasurys in the secondary market fall. However, with information that the number of competitive bidders at an auction exceeds what was expected the prices of Treasurys increase in the secondary market. Cammack interprets these relationships as suggesting that market structure influences how information is aggregated into speculative prices.[18]

## 2.9 The Influence of Psychological Factors on Economic Decisions

The behavior of speculative prices is often viewed from the perspective of classical economics, i.e. a world where individual economic agents make rational decisions which they perceive to be in their best interests and the forces of supply and demand combine to produce equilibrium prices. An alternative approach to explaining seemingly irrational prices is to consider the influence of psychological factors on economic decisions as suggested by Arrow (1982). There is a growing literature in economics and finance (e.g. Tversky, Slovic, and Kahneman, 1990; Patel, Zeckhauser, and Hendricks, 1991) which challenges the assumption of rational decision-making.

In this regard, DeBondt and Thaler (1990) examine whether the forecasts of professional security analysts share some of the systematic biases that have been observed for other groups in the behavioral literature. In particular, they test whether forecasted changes in earnings per share (or revisions) and forecast errors are correlated with each other and, if so, whether any observed bias increases directly with uncertainty. They conclude:

> The same pattern of overreaction found in the predictions of naive undergraduates is replicated in the predictions of stock market professionals. Forecasted changes [in earnings per share] are simply too extreme to be considered rational. The fact that the same pattern is observed in economists' forecasts of changes in exchange rates and macroeconomic variables adds force to the conclusion that generalized overreaction can pervade even the most professional of predictions.
>
> (p. 57)

## 2.10 Is Rational Speculation Destabilizing?

There is a longstanding debate in the economics literature on whether speculation is price stabilizing or price destabilizing. It has been argued that *rational* speculation must necessarily be price stabilizing otherwise speculators would expect to lose money. This view essentially assumes that prices converge toward their equilibrium level. This means that departures from equilibrium cannot last for long periods of time and casts doubt on the existence of speculative bubbles. Consequently, understanding how speculation may destabilize prices is potentially important to understanding how speculative bubbles may arise.

Hart and Kreps (1986) advance a model in which rational speculation can be destabilizing even if speculators compete with one another. Stein (1987) takes a different approach to examining the question of whether speculation is potentially price destabilizing. His concern is not with whether some speculation is preferred to none, as Hart and Kreps contend, but rather whether "more speculation is better than less" as Stein puts it. In practical terms, Stein believes that additional speculation might arise from the opening of a new futures or options market where one did not exist before.

In Stein's model individual economic agents are rational and risk averse, have simple utility functions, and are profit maximizers. He finds that there are two conflicting effects from increased speculation. First, increased speculation facilitates risk transference (Stein calls it risk sharing) which, in turn, enables those individual economic agents who have transferred price risk to speculators to respond more fully to the signals for resource allocation implicit in changes in commodity prices. A positive externality is created by transferring price risk from hedgers to speculators. Not surprisingly, this leads to a better allocation of economic resources and thus increases social welfare.

The second effect of increased speculation concerns the impact on the amount of information that speculative prices convey. Stein finds that under some circumstances additional speculation decreases the informational content of speculative prices which may (if it exceeds the first effect) destabilize prices and reduce social welfare. The circumstances which drive this result are imperfections in information across speculators.

## 2.11 Rational Speculative Bubbles

Some of the theoretical economic literature on speculative bubbles advance models where speculative bubbles are possible but are inherently unstable. Moreover, these models do not explain the factors which cause speculative bubbles to develop or to end. In contrast, Leach (1991) advances a theoretical model in which speculative bubbles may arise in an environment where expectations are formed rationally and equilibria are stationary.[19] The model is a variant of a model proposed by Blanchard and Watson (1982).

Flood and Garber (1980) both explain how a speculative bubble can occur in markets where individuals form expectations rationally and define it. They state:

> A bubble can arise when the actual market price depends positively on its own expected rate of change, as normally occurs in asset markets. Since agents forming rational expectations do not make systematic prediction errors, the positive relationship between price and its expected rate of change implies a similar relationship between price and its actual rate of change. In such conditions, the arbitrary self-fulfilling expectation of price changes may drive actual price changes independently of *market fundamentals*; we refer to such a situation as a *price bubble*.
>
> (p. 746)

Diba and Grossman (1988a) advance a model where stock prices have two components, one due to a rational positive (i.e. price increasing) bubble and the other due to economic fundamentals. The bubble begins at inception of trading and cannot restart once it has burst. Diba and Grossman (1988b) use such a model to test for the existence of a rational speculative bubble in US stock prices. They report no evidence of significant explosive bubbles in stock prices.

Froot and Obstfeld (1991) advance a simple rational speculative bubble in order to explain observed variation in US stock prices. Unlike other models of rational speculative bubbles which rely upon noise or other noninformational factors to explain variation in stock prices Froot and Obstfeld consider a rational speculative bubble in which all of the volatility in stock prices is a (nonlinear) function of fundamental economic factors. Because "intrinsic" bubbles depend solely on economic fundamentals, stable economic fundamentals may cause over- or under-valuation of stock prices to persist for long periods of time. New information on economic fundamentals, however, may cause stock prices to change too much. Moreover, Froot and Obstfeld contend that (otherwise unexplained) long-term changes in stock prices may be explained by an intrinsic bubble which depends on dividends. Using data on US stock prices Froot and Obstfeld reject the no speculative bubble hypothesis because of an observed nonlinear relationship between stock prices and dividends.

## 2.12 Empirical Evidence on the Existence of Speculative Bubbles

Although there is a strong belief, among many individuals, in the existence of speculative bubbles, rigorous empirical studies to ascertain whether bubbles exist within an environment in which individual economic agents are assumed to form expectations rationally are relatively recent. Whether or not speculative bubbles exist depends, in part, on how they are defined as well as how the model of market fundamentals is defined. The danger in testing for the existence of speculative bubbles is that the model of market fundamentals may not be defined correctly.

Two interesting tests of the existence of speculative bubbles were conducted by Flood and Garber (1980) and by Meese (1986). The studies reach conflicting conclusions on the existence of speculative bubbles.

Flood and Garber (1980) examine the German hyperinflation of the 1920s. Hyperinflations represent interesting periods to test for the existence of speculative bubbles because, as they note, theory would suggest that expectations exert a significant influence on price changes during periods of hyperinflation and hyperinflations are characterized by accelerating prices. These conditions are necessary for speculative bubbles to exist.[20] They reject evidence of a price-level bubble during the German hyperinflation.

Meese (1986) tests whether the existence of speculative bubbles could explain the behavior of selected foreign exchange rates using *monthly* data during the period 1973–82. The basic objective is to determine whether speculative bubbles might explain some of the perceived departures of exchange rates from what fundamental factors would suggest. Meese rejects the null joint hypothesis of no bubbles and stability for the processes that drive relative money supplies and real incomes between the countries he examines.

Meese (1986) recognizes the potential influence of noise on changes in speculative prices when he concludes:

> While many economists believe that asset prices reflect the values of the underlying market fundamentals, asset market participants often express the view that fundamentals are just part of the story. Characterizations of asset price movements from the latter group often include discussions of "extraneous events"....
>
> (p. 369)

There are a number of other articles in the literature which test whether speculative bubbles characterized a number of historical episodes. Flood and Hodrick (1990) review many of these articles in their survey of the empirical economics literature on tests for the existence of speculative bubbles or, to use their terminology, "rational dynamic indeterminacies." They contend that none of the empirical studies provide convincing evidence of the existence of speculative bubbles. Rather, those studies that purport to find speculative bubbles may simply reflect misspecified models or have ignored some relevant market fundamental factor(s).

## 2.13 Were the Classic Speculative Bubbles Really Bubbles?

Given the above results, the question naturally arises whether commonly perceived speculative bubbles in the more distant past ever actually existed. That is, can one advance fundamental explanations for these bubble episodes? Put differently, were the speculative markets during various well-known "bubbles" informationally inefficient? After all, an extreme example of an informationally inefficient capital market would be a speculative bubble.

Perhaps the classic example of a speculative bubble is the Dutch tulip bulb mania of 1634–7. Other commonly cited examples of speculative bubbles are the South Sea Company in England and John Law's Mississippi Company in France (both of which enjoyed a spectacular rise and suffered an equally spectacular collapse in the price of their stock).[21]

A closer examination of the period of speculation in tulip bulbs is provided by Garber (1989). Garber (1989) notes that, contrary to widespread belief, the period of tulip mania was relatively short-lived, being largely confined to common bulbs during the last month of futures trading. However, the implications of Garber's findings extend beyond whether this particular episode should be properly classified as a speculative bubble as Garber notes in his conclusion:

> Ironically, theories of rational asset pricing do not generally preclude bubbles. A precondition for the existence of a rational bubble is the belief that a bubble can exist. The ancient examples usually cited may not themselves have been bubbles. Yet if market participants now believe that these historical events prove the existence of bubbles, rational bubbles can emerge in asset markets.
>
> (p. 558)

Similarly, Garber (1990) advances highly plausible market fundamentals explanations for the Missisippi and South Sea bubbles. As Garber essentially points out, many economists have incorrectly concluded that these episodes were speculative bubbles, in part, because their ultimate failure was apparently not foreseen by investors. In contrast, White (1990) argues that there is much qualitative evidence to suggest that the stock market crash of October 1929 was indeed a speculative bubble.

## 2.14 Incomplete Markets

The concept of rational expectations has come to dominate much of the economic literature. Indeed, the assumption that individuals form expectations rationally lies at the heart of many modern macroeconomic and financial economic models. As noted earlier, the efficient markets hypothesis is in essence nothing more than the application of rational expectations to financial markets. Implicit in many models, however, is the notion that markets are complete.

Hahn (1988) argues that insufficient attention has been paid to the effects of incomplete markets in macroeconomics and asset pricing. Hahn notes:

> With incomplete asset markets the claim that asset prices reflect "fundamentals" is not to be taken at face value. Some of the states in question may be "sunspots." The money supply for instance is a notorious sunspot. Similarly, the claim that asset markets are "efficient" could in the model be applied to all markets if what is meant is that prices reflect all the information which agents have. But we must remember that it is supposed to be common knowledge that this is the case. In any event rational expectations do not buy "fundamentals" as the term is usually understood. This of course does not mean that agents are systematically disappointed.
>
> (p. 967)

Similarly, Benassy (1991) uses a simple two-good overlapping generations model where individuals cannot trade wealth between time periods to examine whether rational expectations are optimal in an incomplete market environment. In such an environment, Benassy concludes that rational expectations may be dominated by irrational expectations.

## 2.15 "False" Prices in Walrasian Auctions

Price disequilibria may arise from the structure or way financial markets are organized. Classical economic theory assumes that prices (including speculative prices) are determined by a Walrasian *tâtonnement*.

As Webb (1991) notes, there is no assurance that transaction prices on US futures markets are true equilibrium prices. The reason for this is that excess demand or supply may exist at any given transaction price, thus resulting in trading at "false" prices. In contrast, Japanese commodity futures markets which employ the single fixed-price auction (and are not open continuously) do not have this problem.

Actual auction markets, even those modelled on Walrasian *tâtonnements*, may sometimes produce price disequilibria or "false" prices. Walras (1977) recognizes this possibility when he considers auction markets that are open continuously. He states:

> Finally, in order to come still more closely to reality, we must drop the hypothesis of an annual market period and adopt in its place the hypothesis of a continuous market. Thus, we pass from the static to the dynamic state. For this purpose, we shall now suppose that the annual production and consumption which we had hitherto represented as a constant magnitude for every moment of the year under consideration change from instant to instant along with the basic data of the problem.... Such is the continuous market, which is perpetually tending toward equilibrium without ever actually attaining it because the market has no other way of approaching equilibrium except by groping, and, before the goal is reached, it has to renew its efforts and start over again, all the basic data of the problem, .... Viewed in this way, the market is like a lake agitated by the wind, where the water is incessantly seeking its level without ever reaching it. But whereas there are days when the surface of a lake is almost smooth, there never is a day when the effective demand for products and services equals their effective supply and when the selling price of products equals the cost of the productive services in making them. The diversion of productive services from enterprises that are losing money to profitable enterprises takes place in various ways, ..., but at best these ways are slow. It can happen and frequently does happen in the real world, that under some circumstances a selling price will remain for long periods of time above cost of production and continue to rise in spite of increases in output, while under other circumstances, a fall in price, following upon this rise, will suddenly bring the selling price below cost of production and force entrepreneurs to reverse their production policies. For, just as a lake is, at times, stirred to its very depths by a storm, so also the market is sometimes thrown into violent confusion by *crises*, which are sudden and general dis-

> turbances of equilibrium. The more we know of the ideal conditions of equilibrium, the better we shall be able to control or prevent these crises.
>
> (pp. 380–1)

Thus, Walras recognizes that price disequilibria may result if new information arrives in a market that is always open. Moreover, Walras recognizes that such price disequilibria may last "for long periods of time"; the difference between (selling) price and (intrinsic) value (in this case the cost of production) may continue to widen ("in spite of increases in output"); and the eventual convergence to market equilibrium may be sudden (i.e. a crisis). Note also that Walras admits the possibility of periodic chaotic markets (i.e. "violent confusion [induced] by *crises* which are sudden and general disturbances of equilibrium").

## 2.16 Noise

Black (1986) contends that a necessary condition for active, liquid financial markets is the existence of noise trading. Black advances a model of financial markets where speculative prices change in response to noise or noninformational factors. In Black's model there are noise traders (who only trade off of noninformational factors and, on average, lose money) and information traders (who trade off of information and, on average, make money). Further, noise traders may incorrectly believe that they are information traders. That is, they do not recognize that they are trading off of extraneous factors. The trading activity of noise traders creates the liquidity which market participants desire and the mispricings which information traders *partially* exploit. Risk aversion and uncertainty over how much of the information they possess is already in speculative prices keeps information traders from fully exploiting the perceived mispricings. Morover, Black contends that the noise that noise traders put into speculative prices is "cumulative."

One implication of Black's analysis is that increases in the amount of noise trading make market prices less efficient even while creating greater liquidity and profit opportunities for information traders.

Another implication of Black's analysis is that noise trading will cause excessive volatility in the short run. Put differently, noise trading causes the volatility of speculative prices to exceed the volatility of the intrinsic value of a security in the short run. The more noise trading there is, the greater is the potential departure of price from intrinsic value and the greater the (excess) volatility of speculative prices.[22]

Unlike the volatility of changes in speculative prices, the volatility of intrinsic value responds only to the arrival of new information. Black contends that the volatility of a security's price will converge to the volatility of its intrinsic value in the long run.

There is another implication of Black's analysis worth noting given the French and Roll (1986) results discussed above; namely, that one would expect to observe greater volatility of speculative prices during the trading day when noise traders may impact market prices from their actions than overnight (i.e. the close to open price change) when markets are closed and are subject only to potentially market-moving information events. Further, Black argues that this result applies only for the dominant market in a commodity or security (i.e. the market on which most noise traders trade). This implication, of Black's analysis, of course, fits the empirical results reported by French and Roll (1986).

Black's analysis produces some interesting implications that appear consistent with the puzzling observations of excessive volatility of speculative prices relative to fundamental factors and greater volatility during the trading day than overnight. However, tests of many of Black's propositions are complicated because speculative prices in continuous auction markets may be characterized as a virtually indistinguishable mixture of equilibrium and false prices.[23]

Put differently, it may not be possible to distinguish between the intrinsic value of some security and its price. Indeed, Black contends that most of the propositions he advances about noise cannot be tested.

The problem of distinguishing between value and price in auction markets which trade continuously does not arise in some periodic call auction markets.[24] This suggests some possible tests of Black's propositions. It also suggests that the amount of noise in a given market is a function, in part, of its market structure – i.e. of the way the market is organized. There is no reason to believe that the noise level is the same across market structures. Indeed, certain types of market structures are inherently less noisy than others.

DeLong et al. (1990b) consider a model where the beliefs of noise traders are stochastic and incorrect (i.e. traders have "erroneous stochastic beliefs"). Noise trader risk (which results from unpredictability in the beliefs of noise traders) introduces additional uncertainty as to future speculative prices and causes speculative prices to be more volatile. The activity of noise traders also introduces risk into what would otherwise represent potential arbitrage opportunities. The existence of impediments to arbitrage means that speculative prices can diverge from intrinsic value for significant periods of time. Noise trader risk introduces inefficiencies into speculative prices but also serves to make noise trading profitable.

DeLong et al. (1990a) take a similar tack when they advance a model where speculation *destabilizes* prices. Essentially, they posit where some market participants are not always rational and sometimes trade off of noise. Rational market participants are precluded from fully exploiting the apparent profit opportunities due to perceived risks. In such an environment, speculation can destabilize prices because the natural corrective forces in the marketplace are not fully operative.

Shleifer and Summers (1990) note that the noise trader risk model is consistent with how many individuals perceive financial markets. Moreover, they argue that the noise trader risk model may explain several anomalies that have puzzled financial economists over the years. For instance, they contend that the presence of noise trader risk may explain why closed-end funds often sell at a discount.[25] Other puzzles that they believe their model may explain include the equity premium puzzle of Mehra and Prescott (1985) and French's and Roll's (1986) puzzle of greater volatility in speculative prices during the trading day than overnight.

It should be pointed out that the term noise has several meanings in the financial economic literature. Even Black uses it in two different ways; namely, to describe the noninformational factors which affect speculative prices, and to measure the extent to which speculative prices depart from intrinsic value. In contrast, DeLong et al. use the term noise to denote erroneous stochastic beliefs or extraneous information held by market participants. Financial economists use the term noise to describe certain recurrent patterns in the behavior of changes in speculative prices or returns (e.g. day-of-the-week or January effects in stock returns) or mispricings by traders.

## 3 Auctions and the Behavior of Speculative Prices

Speculative prices are frequently determined through auctions. Both the frequency with which transaction prices are determined and the auction method employed, however, may differ sharply across financial markets.

Englebrecht-Wiggans (1980) notes that: "Auctions may be viewed as games with incomplete information." This means that there is often an element of gamesmanship or strategy in determining the bids one submits in an auction. Moreover, the strategy one employs is not invariant to the structure of the auction. It stands to reason that if the auction's structure influences the prices and amounts that participants (who behave strategically) submit as bids or offers, then it should also influence the behavior of the transaction prices which arise from the auction. The *winner's curse* is common to many auctions.

The *winner's curse* arises when an individual is successful in an auction and later finds that he bid too high or he offered the commodity at too low a price. The winner's curse is absent from some auctions. For instance, the single fixed-price auction encourages individuals to bid or offer the true value of the commodity by reducing the risk of being wrong. This suggests that prices in a single fixed-price auction or another auction without a winner's curse should reflect more information, on average, than prices in auctions where there is a winner's curse.

The design of an auction has important practical implications because the auction design can influence the incentives of auction participants to bid or offer and the amount that they are willing to bid and offer. An example in this regard is a "Dutch" auction (one type of single price auction where all transactions occur at the lowest accepted price).[26] In a Dutch auction, individuals who submitted higher bids than the lowest bid accepted are thus able to acquire the commodity at a price less than they bid. Essentially, a Dutch auction reduces the risk of the winner's curse. Because the risk of the winner's curse is lower, individuals are more willing to submit higher bids for larger quantities than they otherwise would.[27]

Another illustration of the effects of market structure on the behavior of changes in speculative prices is the development of "electronic" or screen-based exchanges. The adoption of this type of trading system eliminates the need for an exchange trading floor and with it certain types of noise.[28]

## 4 Summary

The theoretical and empirical literature on noise is rich in potential explanations for the often puzzling reaction of speculative prices to macroeconomic information. For instance, the behavioral approach to finance would explain the consistent overreaction of speculative prices to new information. The noise models of Black and DeLong, Shleifer, Summers, and Waldman offer an especially promising explanation for the the behavior of changes in speculative prices in response to the release of economic reports and other sources of macroeconomic information. The above noise models are very intellectually appealing because they explain how rational investors are unable to exploit the mispricing of noise traders fully. The concept of "erroneous stochastic beliefs" might explain such puzzling phenomena as the complete reversal of interpretation that traders assign to the merchandise trade balance; irrational expectations by market participants; the tendency of bond prices to track changes in other commodities from time to time; or why some economic reports are closely followed for a while and then virtually ignored.

The other lesson of this chapter is that seeming aberrations in speculative prices may have fundamental explanations upon closer examination. The evidence which sparked the development of the noise models remains controversial. It is premature to explain the reaction of changes in speculative prices to macroeconomic information in the context of these models without further statistical evidence.

The lessons of the influence of noise on speculative markets, however, extend beyond a potential explanation of why speculative prices change in a particular fashion in response to new macroeconomic information. After all, the primary role of a capital market is to facilitate the allocation of resources to their best use by producing prices which represent accurate signals for resource allocation. If speculative prices are informationally inefficient there is no assurance that scarce societal resources will be allocated to their best use.

## Notes

1 As previously noted, the time series behavior of changes in speculative prices in an informationally efficient capital market can be viewed as mirroring the flow of new information into the marketplace. Fama (1963) and Ross (1989) argue that changes in speculative prices are erratic only because the flow of new information into the marketplace is itself erratic.

2 Keynes (1935) argues:

> We are assuming, in effect, that the existing market valuation, however arrived at, is uniquely *correct* in relation to our existing knowledge of the facts which influence the yield of the investments, and that it will only change in proportion to changes in this knowledge; though, philosophically speaking, it cannot be uniquely correct, since our existing knowledge does not provide a sufficient basis for a calculated mathematical expectation. In point of fact, all sorts of considerations enter into the market valuation which are in no way relevant to the prospective yield. (p. 152)

3 Roll (1988) states:

> There was, however, a dramatic decline in sample kurtosis from public news events. A simple mixture of distributions model (i.e. one distribution for a non-news date and a second higher variance distribution for a news date) yielded two suggestive results: (1) the average minimum ratio of news variance to background noise variance was around 20 for all sample dates but

> only around 7 for nonnews dates, and (2) the estimated probability of news was modest but material for *both* identifiable news dates and other dates. This seems to imply either the existence of private information or else occasional frenzy unrelated to concrete information.
>
> (p. 566)

4 The findings of excessive volatility in speculative prices by Shiller (as well as the 1987 stock market crash) probably precipitated much of the academic interest in the influence of noise on changes in speculative prices.

5 Volatility in the discount rate may also explain part of the variation in stock prices.

6 Some observers have argued that the thrust of this criticism is misplaced. For instance, Summers (1985) states:

> The volatility test controversy is like a scientific debate about whether one can reject the hypothesis that the earth is flat with a microscope. Shiller's conclusion that the joint hypothesis of rationality and a constant required return on the market can be rejected is exactly the conclusion reached by most modern work in financial economics. ... Why then has work on volatility testing generated such hostility from mainstream finance researchers. In part, because users of volatility tests have interpreted their rejections of the null hypothesis in controversial ways. In part, because volatility tests raise some interesting and complex methodological issues. But a large part of the answer must be a deep distrust of research purporting to explore fundamentals valuations.
>
> (pp. 634–5)

7 Simple present value models suggest that bond and stock prices should move together. Barsky (1989) advances a model to explain the observed relationship between stock and bond prices. He contends that increased risk or decreased productivity growth may lead to either higher or lower stock prices even though the real riskless interest rate falls in both cases. Essentially, Barsky argues that whether stock prices rise or fall with respect to a change in one of the two factors depends upon the degree of aversion to intertemporal substitution (as distinct from risk aversion). Shiller and Beltratti (1992) report evidence showing that real stock prices are more sensitive to changes in interest rates than what a simple present value model would suggest.

8 It should be pointed out that, in the context of Shiller's paper (where he examines the correlation of real stock prices and real dividends

over the period 1871–1987), year-over-year changes are considered high frequency data. One can only imagine what the relationship is on an intra-daily basis.

9 Shiller states: "If managers become optimistic at the same time that the public does, they may increase dividends at the same time that fashions cause prices to increase" (p. 59).

10 For a survey of the literature in this area see DeBondt and Thaler (1989).

11 Nelson (1990) states:

> When we look at the pre and post World War II periods separately, however, dividing the sample at 1947, we see very different patterns.... The post-war data suggest some mean reversion at short horizons, but strong mean aversion for six years and longer. Evidently, the mean reversion result for the full time period was entirely due to pre-war behavior....
>
> (pp. 39–40)

12 Mehra and Prescott (1985) state the argument for expecting a higher real interest rate as follows:

> In the case of a growing economy, agents with high risk aversion effectively discount the future to a greater extent than agents with low risk aversion (relative to a nongrowing economy). Due to growth, future consumption is less than that of present consumption, real interest rates will be higher on average.
>
> (p. 146)

13 Cecchetti notes that Treasury bills also occasionally had negative nominal yields. In those cases the absolute value of the yield was quite small. Cecchetti argues that cases of negative nominal yields for Treasury bills can be explained by tax exemption (at the state and local level) and other institutional factors.

14 Barsky and Summers do not contend that their explanation accounts fully for the observed Gibson's paradox. Indeed, they contend that their explanation does not account for the impact of new discoveries of gold.

15 Essentially, Modigliani and Cohn (1979) argue that investors have money illusion with respect to the discount rates they employ. This leads to a substantial undervaluation of assets during periods of inflation. Pindyck (1984) notes that the real value of the stocks which comprise the New York Stock Exchange index declined by about 68 percent between 1965 and 1981. Pindyck (1984) attributes the decline in real stock values to a rise in capital risk during this period.

16 In particular, Meese and Rose (1990) state:

> There is little evidence that conclusively links the bilateral exchange rates of typical OECD countries to "fundamental" macroeconomic determinants of exchange rates such as money, output, relative prices, or interest rate differentials. Coeffficient estimates are notoriously unstable and frequently "missigned" (compared with theoretical predictions); exchange rate equations do not fit particularly well, and forecast no better than the simplest naive alternatives.
>
> (p. 192)

17 Rumors and occasionally confirmed news that a particular (presumably exceptionally savvy) trader has taken a particular position or completed a certain transaction often enter speculative markets. Sometimes this precipitates a significant change in speculative prices. A case in point was the news that the renowned investor George Soros acquired a large position in the gold market. The subsequent rally in gold was attributed (correctly or incorrectly) to him.

18 Cammack states: "the secondary and auction markets aggregate traders' private information differently" (p. 101).

19 Leach's definition of a bubble does not allow for continuous increases in speculative prices over an indefinite period of time.

20 In Flood and Garber (1980) the form of the bubble is sensitive to market fundamentals, in this case, whether the money supply is exogenously or endogenously determined. Evans (1978) provides evidence that the money supply was endogenously determined during the German hyperinflation.

21 More recently, the Japanese financial and popular press has referred to the mid- to late 1980s (a period which witnessed a rapid rise and subsequent sharp decline in Japanese stock and real estate prices) as the bubble economy.

22 Marshall (1961) would agree with Black that increased trading activity increases liquidity (i.e. reduces the bid–ask spread) but would disagree with Black that it increases the volatility of changes in speculative prices. For instance, Marshall (1961) argues:

> If there are two securities equally good, but one of them belongs to a large issue of bonds, and the other to a small issue by the same government, so that the first is constantly coming on the market, and the latter but seldom, then the dealers will on this account alone require a larger margin between their selling price and their buying price in the latter case than in the former. This illustrates the great law, that the larger the market for a

commodity the smaller generally are the fluctuations in its price, and the lower is the percentage on the turnover which dealers charge for doing business in it.

(p. 328)

23 Garbade and Silber (1979) argue that the frequency of market clearing is an important "structural characteristic" of financial markets.

24 Domowitz and Wang (forthcoming) suggest that periodic auction markets such as the single fixed price auction have lower price variability. The Itayose-hoh auction system employed on the Tokyo Grain Exchange is an example of one type of market structure which may minimize the effects of trading noise. The Itayose-hoh auction system closely resembles a classical single commodity Walrasian *tâtonnement* where recontracting is allowed at provisional futures prices until an equilibrium (i.e. market clearing transaction) price is determined. As a result, all *transaction* futures prices are market clearing prices on the Tokyo Grain Exchange. Marsh and Webb (1983) compare the volatility of soybean futures prices traded under a single fixed-price auction with soybean futures prices traded in an open out-cry auction. They report no significant difference between the two volatilities. An unpublished paper by Webb (1993) uses Tokyo Grain Exchange price and volume data to test some of Black's propositions on the influence of noise. He reports evidence inconsistent with them.

25 Shleifer and Summers state: "Put differently, the reason why there are discounts *on average* is that discounts fluctuate, and investors require an extra return for bearing the risk of fluctuating discounts" (p. 27).

26 The single fixed-price auction system differs from the Dutch auction in at least two important respects: the quantity offered in a Dutch auction is fixed, and recontracting is not allowed in a Dutch auction.

27 This characteristic of Dutch auctions has led Friedman (1963) to argue that substantial savings (in the form of lower borrowing costs) would result if the US Treasury adopted a "Dutch" auction system for the sale of new Treasury securities. In September 1992 the US Treasury began a one year experiment by using a Dutch auction system to sell new two and five year Treasury notes.

28 Domowitz and Wang (forthcoming) recognize that differences in auction systems essentially reflect differences in the algorithms employed.

## References

Arrow, K. J. 1982: "Risk Perception in Psychology and Economics," *Economic Inquiry*, 20, January, 3–24.

Barsky, R. B. 1989: "Why Don't the Prices of Stocks and Bonds Move Together?," *American Economic Review*, 79 (5), December, 1132–45.

Barsky, R. B. and L. H. Summers 1988: "Gibson's Paradox and the Gold Standard," *Journal of Political Economy*, 96 (3), 528–50.

Benassy, J. 1991: "Incomplete Markets and the Suboptimality of Rational Expectations," *Economics Letters*, 36, 341–6.

Black, F. 1986: "Noise," *Journal of Finance*, 41 (3), July, 529–43.

Blanchard, O. J., and M. W. Watson 1982: "Bubbles, Rational Expectations, and Financial Markets," in P. Wachtel (ed.), *Crises in the Economic and Financial Structure*, Lexington, MA: Lexington Books.

Camerer, C. 1987: "Do Biases in Probability Judgment Matter in Markets?," *American Economic Review*, 77, December, 981–97.

Cammack, E. B. 1991: "Evidence on Bidding Strategies and the Information in Treasury Bill Auctions," *Journal of Political Economy*, 99 (1), 100–30.

Cecchetti, S. C. 1988: "The Case of the Negative Nominal Interest Rates: New Estimates of the Term Structure of Interest Rates during the Great Depression," *Journal of Political Economy*, 96 (6), 1111–41.

Cutler, D. M., J. M. Poterba, and L. Summers 1990: "Speculative Dynamics and the Role of Feedback Traders," *American Economic Review*, 80 (2), May, 63–8.

DeBondt, W. F. M., and R. Thaler 1985: "Does the Stock Market Overeact?," *Journal of Finance*, 40 (3), July, 793–805.

DeBondt, W. F. M., and R. H. Thaler 1989: "A Mean-Reverting Walk Down Wall Street," *Journal of Economic Perspectives*, 3 (1), Winter, 189–202.

DeBondt, W. F. M., and R. H. Thaler 1990: "Do Security Analysts Overreact," *American Economic Review*, 80 (2), May, 52–7.

DeLong, B. J., A. Shleifer, L. Summers, and R. J. Waldman 1989: "The Size and Incidence of Losses from Noise Trading," *Journal of Finance*, 44, July, 681–96.

DeLong, B. J., and A. Shleifer, L. Summers, and R. J. Waldman 1990a: "Positive Feedback Investment Strategies and Destabilizing Rational Speculation," *Journal of Finance*, 45 (2), June, 379–96.

DeLong, B. J., and A. Shleifer, L. Summers, and R. J. Waldman 1990b: "Noise Trader Risk in Financial Markets, *Journal of Political Economy*, 98 (4), August, 703–38.

Diba, B. T., and H. I. Grossman 1988a: "Explosive Rational Bubbles in Stock Prices?," *American Economic Review*, 78, June, 520–30.

Diba, B. T., and H. I. Grossman 1988b: "The Theory of Rational Bubbles in Stock Prices," *Economic Journal*, 98, September, 746–54.

Domowitz, I., and J. Wang, forthcoming: "Auctions as Algorithms: Computerized Trade Execution and Price Discovery," *Journal of Economic Dynamics and Control.*

Englebrecht-Wiggans, R. 1980: "Auctions and Bidding Models: A Survey," *Management Science*, 26 (2), February, 119–42.

Evans, P. 1978: "Time Series Analysis of the German Hyperinflation," *International Economic Review*, 19, February, 195–209.

Fama, E. 1963: "Mandlebrot and the Stable Paretian Hypothesis," *Journal of Business*, 36 (4), 420–9.

Fama, E. 1970: "Efficient Capital Markets: A Review of the Theory and Empirical Work," *Journal of Finance*, 25, May, 343–417.

Fama, E. 1991: "Efficient Capital Markets: II," *Journal of Finance*, 46 (5), December, 1575–1617.

Fama, E. F., and K. French 1988: "Permanent and Temporary Components of Stock Prices," *Journal of Political Economy*, 96 (2), 246–73.

Flavin, M. 1983: "Excess Volatility in the Financial Markets, A Reassessment of the Empirical Evidence," *Journal of Political Economy*, 91, December, 929–56.

Flood, R. P., and P. M. Garber 1980: "Market Fundamentals versus Price Level Bubbles: The First Tests," *Journal of Political Economy*, 88, August, 745–70.

Flood, R. P., and R. J. Hodrick 1986: "Asset Price Volatility, Bubbles, and Process Switching," *Journal of Finance*, 41, September, 831–42.

Flood, R. P., and R. J. Hodrick 1990: "On Testing for Speculative Bubbles," *Journal of Economic Perspectives*, 4, Spring, 85–101.

Frankel, J. A., and K.A. Froot 1990: "Chartists, Fundamentalists, and Trading in the Foreign Exchange Market," *American Economic Review*, 80 (2), May, 186–91.

French, K., and R. Roll 1986: "Stock Return Variances: The Arrival of Information and the Reaction of Traders," *Journal of Financial Economics*, 17, 5–26.

Friedman, M. 1963: "Price Determination in the United States Treasury Bill Market, A Comment," *Review of Economic Statistics*, 45, 318–20.

Friedman, M., and A. J. Schwartz 1982: *Monetary Trends in the United States and the United Kingdom: Their Relation to Income, Prices, and Interest Rates, 1867–1975*, Chicago, IL: University of Chicago Press for the National Bureau of Economic Research.

Froot, K. A., and M. Obstfeld 1991: "Intrinsic Bubbles: The Case of Stock Prices," *American Economic Review*, 81 (5), December, 1189–1214.

Garbade, K. G. and W. L. Silber 1979: "Structural Organization of Secondary Markets: Clearing Frequency, Dealer Activity, and Liquidity Risk," *Journal of Finance*, 34, 577–93.

Garber, P. M 1989: "Tulipmania," *Journal of Political Economy*, 87 (3), 535–60.

Garber, P. M. 1990: "Famous First Bubbles," *Journal of Economic Perspectives*, 4 (2), Spring, 35–54.

Hahn, F. 1988: "On Monetary Theory," *Economic Journal*, 98, December, 957–73.

Hart, O. D., and D. Kreps 1986: "Price Destabilizing Speculation," *Journal of Political Economy*, 94 (5), 927–52.

Hodrick, R. J. 1990: "Volatility in the Foreign Exchange and Stock Markets: Is it Excessive?," *American Economic Review*, 80 (2), May, 186–91.

Ito, T. 1990: "Foreign Exchange Rate Expectations: Micro Survey Data," *American Economic Review*, 80 (3), June, 434–49.

Keynes, J. M. 1935: *The General Theory of Employment, Interest, and Money*, New York: Harcourt, Brace & World.

Kleidon, A. W. 1986: "Variance Bounds Tests and Stock Price Valuation Models," *Journal of Political Economy*, 94 (5), 953–1001.

Laffont, J., and E. S. Maskin 1990: "The Efficient Market Hypothesis and Insider Trading on the Stock Market," *Journal of Political Economy*, 98 (1), 70–93.

Leach, J. 1991: "Rational Speculation," *Journal of Political Economy*, 99 (1), 131–44.

LeRoy, S., and R. D. Porter 1981: "The Present-Value Relation: Tests Based on Implied Variance Bounds," *Econometrica*, 49, May, 555–74.

Malkiel, B. G. 1979: "The Capital Formation Problem in the United States," *Journal of Finance*, 34, May, 291–306.

Marsh, T. A., and R. C. Merton 1986: "Dividend Variability and Variance Bounds Tests for the Rationality of Stock Prices," *American Economic Review*, 76, June, 483–98.

Marsh, T. A., and R. I. Webb 1983: "Information Dissemination Uncertainty, the Continuity of Trading and the Structure of International Futures Markets," *Review of Research on Futures Markets*, 2, 36–71.

Marshall, A. 1961: *Principles of Economics*, vol. 1, 9th edn, New York: Macmillan.

Meese, R. A. 1986: "Testing for Bubbles in Exchange Markets: A Case of Sparkling Rates?," *Journal of Political Economy*, 94 (2), 345–73.

Meese, R. A., and A. K. Rose 1990: "Nonlinear, Nonparametric, Nonessential Exchange Rate Estimation," *American Economic Review*, 80 (2), May, 52–7.

Mehra, R., and E. C. Prescott 1985: "The Equity Premium: A Puzzle," *Journal of Monetary Economics*, 15, 145–61.

Milgrom, P. R. 1989: "Auctions and Bidding: A Primer," *Journal of Economics Perspectives*, 3, Summer, 679–88.

Modigliani, F., and R. Cohn 1979: "Inflation, Rational Valuation and the Market," *Financial Analysts Journal*, 35, March–April, 3–23.

Nelson, C. R. 1990: "Are Stock Returns Predictable? A Critique of the Evidence," in W. F. Sharpe and K.F. Sherrerd (eds), *Quantifying the Market Risk Premium for Investment Decision Making*, Charlottesville, VA: Association for Investment Management and Research.

Patel, J., R. Zeckhauser, and D. Hendricks 1991: "The Rationality Struggle: Illustrations from Financial Markets," *American Economic Review*, 81 (2), May, 232–6.

Poterba, J. M., and L. Summers 1986: "The Persistence and Volatility of Stock Market Fluctuations," *American Economic Review*, 76, December, 1142–51.

Poterba, J. M., and L. Summers 1988: "Mean Reversion in Stock Prices: Evidence and Implications," *Journal of Financial Economics*, 22, September, 27–60.

Pindyck, R. S. 1984: "Risk, Inflation, and the Stock Market," *American Economic Review*, 74, June, 335–51.

Roll, R. 1984: "Orange Juice and the Weather," *American Economic Review*, 74, December, 861–80.

Roll, R. 1988: "$R^2$," *Journal of Finance*, 43 (2), July, 541–66.

Ross, S. 1989: "Information and Volatility: The No-Arbitrage Martingale Approach to Timing and Resolution Irrelevance," *Journal of Finance*, 43, 1–16.

Shiller, R. J. 1981a: "Do Stock Prices Move Too Much to be Justified by Subsequent Changes in Dividends?," *American Economic Review*, 71, June, 421–36.

Shiller, R. J. 1981b: "The Use of Volatility in Assessing Market Efficiency," *Journal of Finance*, 36, May, 291–304.

Shiller, R. J. 1983: "Do Stock Prices Move Too Much to be Justified by Subsequent Changes in Dividends? Reply," *American Economic Review*, 73, March, 236–7.

Shiller, R. J. 1986: "The Marsh–Merton Model of Managers' Smoothing of Dividends," *American Economic Review*, 71, June, 499–503.

Shiller, R. J. 1990: "Market Volatility and Investor Behavior," *American Economic Review*, 80 (2), May, 58–62.

Shiller, R. J., and A. E. Beltratti 1992: "Stock Prices and Bond Yields," *Journal of Monetary Economics*, 30, 25–46.

Shleifer, A., and L. Summers 1990: "The Noise Trader Approach to Finance," *Journal of Economic Perspectives*, 4 (2), Spring, 19–33.

Siegel, J. 1992: "The Real Rate of Interest from 1800–1990," *Journal of Monetary Economics*, 28, 227–52.

Stein, J. C. 1987: "Informational Externalities and Welfare-Reducing Speculation," *Journal of Political Economy*, 95 (6), 1123–45.

Summers, L. H. 1985: "On Economics and Finance," *Journal of Finance*, 40 (3), July, 633–35.

Summers, L. H. 1986: "Does the Stock Market Rationally Reflect Fundamental Values?," *Journal of Finance*, 41, July, 591–601.

Tversky, A., P. Slovic, and D. Kahneman 1990: "The Causes of Preference Reversal," *American Economic Review*, 80 (1), March, 204–17.

Walras, L. 1977: in *Elements of Pure Economics or the Theory of Social Wealth*, trans. and ed. W. Jaffé, Fairfield, CT: Augustus M. Kelly.

Webb, R. I. 1985: "The Behavior of Speculative Prices and the Consistency of Economic Models," *Journal of Econometrics*, 27, January, 123–30.

Webb, R. I. 1990: "Asset Pricing in an Inefficient Market," *Economic Modelling*, 7 (4), October, 395–9.

Webb, R. I. 1991: "The Behavior of 'False' Futures Prices," *Journal of Futures Markets*, 11 (6), December, 651–68.

Webb, R. I. 1993: "Futures Trading in Less 'Noisy' Markets," Mimeo, University of Virginia, February.

White, E. N. 1990: "The Stock Market Boom and Crash of 1929 Revisited," *Journal of Economic Perspectives*, 4 (2), Spring, 67–83.

# 4

# A Review of Monetary Theories

> There is no denying that views on money are as difficult to describe as are the shifting clouds.
>
> (Joseph A. Schumpeter, *History of Economic Analysis*)

## 1 Introduction

Broadly speaking, the reaction of speculative prices to the forecast error in economic reports can be divided into two components: that due to a perceived change in the economic outlook, and that due to an anticipation of a change in macroeconomic policy. For instance, a worse than expected employment report might lead market participants to conclude (rightly or wrongly) that interest rates will fall because of a worsening economic outlook. It may also cause interest rates to decline because of the belief that the monetary authority will "ease." Conversely, a worse than expected inflation report (producer price index or consumer price index) may cause interest rates to rise because of fears of higher future inflation (a worsening economic outlook) or the belief that the monetary authority will "tighten" (or not loosen if that was previously expected), thus raising interest rates (under some monetary theories). As is readily apparent these two effects may reinforce one another.

Not surprisingly, the reaction of speculative prices to the forecast errors contained in periodic economic reports is intimately intertwined with economic policy in general and monetary policy in particular. In order to understand the policy anticipation effect fully one must understand the relationship between changes in speculative prices and monetary policy actions under various alternative monetary theories.

The principal objective of this chapter is to review a number of alternative monetary theories and assess their implications for changes in speculative prices in general and interest rates in particular. The task is made difficult because of the large number of competing monetary theories which have been advanced in the economics and financial economics literature and the general paucity of empirical evidence to distinguish between the competing hypotheses. This state of affairs may explain, in part, the substantial confusion that exists among many market participants over what economic theory posits about the influence of monetary policy actions on changes in speculative prices.

In addition, most models of modern monetary theory either preceded or have ignored advances in the theory of financial economics. As a result, some of the implications or underlying assumptions of many monetary models are inconsistent with the theory of efficient capital markets.[1] An ancillary objective of this chapter is to consider the influence of monetary policy on changes in speculative prices in an informationally efficient capital market. The next two chapters provide a review of the empirical evidence and an assessment of the influence of Federal Reserve monetary policy, respectively.

## 2 Active and Passive Monetary Policy

Essentially, the monetary authority may pursue either an *active* or a *passive* monetary policy. The primary objective of active monetary policy is to alter the money supply in order to affect interest rates, prices, or output. In a fractional reserve banking system this can be accomplished by changing reserves. Ignoring stochastic fluctuations, reserves can be altered through changes in (1) reserve requirements or (2) the discount (or similar) rate, or through (3) open market operations (security transactions in the open market), all of which are available as policy instruments to the US monetary authority, the Federal Reserve.[2] Open market operations are probably the most important (and most frequently used) instrument of transmission of Federal Reserve monetary policy on the economy.[3] In contrast, under a passive monetary policy the monetary authority simply accommodates the demands of the public for money. Simply put, the money supply is endogenously determined when the monetary authority pursues a passive monetary policy. Under a passive monetary regime, the monetary authority does not attempt or is unable to influence changes in the real rate of interest or real economic growth.

Briefly stated, the interest rate effects attributed to monetary policy actions by monetary theories that posit an exogenously determined money supply extend from transitory or permanent effects on the real rate of interest and an eventual impact on price expectations (hence on any price expectations component of the nominal interest rate as well) to an immediate impact on price expectations alone. Alternatively, those monetary theories that posit an endogenously determined money supply generally hypothesize an absence of real (and sometimes nominal) interest rate effects associated with monetary policy actions. It is also conceivable that monetary policy actions may be correlated with but not causally related to changes in interest rates (both real and nominal) if monetary policy is primarily passively determined.

It is important to recognize that the issue of the influence of monetary policy actions on interest rates may be viewed from two perspectives. First, from a macroeconomic perspective, attention focuses on whether open market operations or other monetary policy actions influence changes in interest rates within the context of the implications of alternative monetary theories. From a purely financial economics perspective, attention focuses on whether the government securities market is efficient with respect to central bank security transactions in the open market or other monetary policy actions. To a large extent, one perspective is merely the mirror image of the other, although in some aspects the latter perspective may be temporally narrower than the former.

One must be careful to distinguish two separate but related questions. First, do monetary policy actions affect changes in interest rates or changes in the rate of change of prices? Second, does the central bank exercise control over the short-run nominal money supply through its monetary policy actions? This chapter is chiefly concerned with the former question, although the latter question is also considered.

It should be noted at the outset that some of the monetary theories discussed below are better known than others. For instance, this chapter reviews the neo-Keynesian, Keynesian New View, neoclassical (with adaptive and rational expectations) and monetary approaches to the balance of payments, as well as the monetary theories of Fischer Black, Arthur Laffer, Neil Wallace, Eugene Fama, and James Tobin. This serves to illustrate the wide range of often conflicting implications of alternative monetary theories. It also reflects the paucity of empirical evidence on this subject.

## 3 Neo-Keynesian Monetary Theory

Neo-Keynesian monetary theory (associated with Samuelson and others) states that a change in the money supply will cause interest rates to change inversely.[4] This occurs in the first instance by the bidding up (or down) of security prices through open market operations. Since investors are presumed to be in portfolio equilibrium before the open market purchase (sale) the price of bonds must rise (fall) to induce individuals to hold less (more) bonds and more (less) money. Since security yields vary inversely with security prices this causes yields to fall (if security prices are bid up) or rise (if security prices are bid down). In essence, this assumes a downward-sloping demand curve and an upward-sloping supply curve for securities. The change in interest rates (e.g. a decrease) then has an additional effect (negative) on the availability of credit in areas with higher interest rates which consequently causes interest rates there to fall.[5]

However, in a fractional reserve banking system open market operations (e.g. a purchase) also cause changes (here an increase) in the amount of cash held by the public. Since most of the cash will be held in banks as demand deposits excess reserves will rise which means that more loans can be made at a lower interest rate. As long as there is less than full employment the effect of open market operations will not be inflationary.[6] Samuelson (1972) believes that "the maximum effect of a single open market operation will be reached within one or two quarters."[7]

In summary, neo-Keynesian monetary theory assumes the money supply is exogenously determined and that changes (whether anticipated or unanticipated) in the quantity of money (or in a dynamic context, its rate of growth) have causal significance (in this case both real and nominal effects) on changes in interest rates with the distribution of effects being a function of the level of employment of economic resources.

## 4 Keynesian New View

In contrast to the neo-Keynesian monetary analysis and its implicit assumption of an exogenously determined money supply described above, a "New View" associated with Gurley and Shaw (1960), Tobin (1963), and others, has developed.[8] Essentially, the New View approach treats money as an endogenous variable. Because of this, the Keynesian New View approach differs in several respects from other monetary analyses.

1 It challenges the significance of the distinction between commercial banks and other financial intermediaries.
2 It chooses not to concentrate on money narrowly defined but rather it recognizes that many close substitutes exist.[9]
3 It distinguishes between "inside" and "outside" money.[10]

Of special interest, and the case that will be considered here, is a pure inside money economy. In a pure inside money economy the central bank loses the ability to affect the real rate of interest through its open market operations (whether anticipated or unanticipated) – money is neutral (since the price level can still be affected by central bank open market operations).[11] This result of money neutrality is essentially independent of the way expectations are formed. Rather the change (e.g. an increase) in the quantity of (inside) money is not viewed as additional wealth (which through the real balance effect would induce spending) since it is exactly offset by a corresponding increase in liabilities. That is, in the aggregate inside money is not a net private asset. Tobin appears to indicate that the central bank may exert control over the yields on the securities in which it transacts its open market operations, presumably by manipulating the relative supplies of the securities outstanding.

In summary, the Keynesian New View approach posits money neutrality in a pure inside money economy. If correct, this would suggest that central bank monetary policy actions have, at most, transitory (i.e. security price pressure) effects on changes in real interest rates. The central bank is able to influence the rate of change in absolute prices and, hence, nominal interest rates.

## 5 Neoclassical Monetary Theory

An alternative approach to the derivative Keynesian monetary theories described above is the neoclassical monetary theory associated with Milton Friedman and others.[12] First Friedman distinguishes the interest rate as the price of credit – not money.[13] Friedman then divides the effect of an unanticipated change in the money supply into three effects: (1) the liquidity effect; (2) the income and price-level effect; and (3) the price anticipation effect. Anticipated changes in the money supply generally only have an effect on price anticipations (i.e. the expected rate of inflation or deflation).[14]

Essentially this theory views money (or rather real cash balances) as one asset in a portfolio of assets. In equilibrium the ratio of the marginal utility of a good $i$ to its price $P_i$ is equal to the ratio of the marginal utilities of all other goods to their respective prices including money or real cash balances. If one assumes diminishing marginal utility of real cash balances then for a given change in the quantity of money (e.g. an increase) and for a given set of prices $P$ the marginal utility of real cash balances will fall, causing the ratio $U'_h/p'$ to be less than $h$, the marginal utility of income. This means that individuals may increase their utility by transferring resources out of real cash balances and into goods. This will then cause a greater demand for goods and hence may cause prices to change as well. Initially, the public is assumed to exchange excess real cash balances for additional financial securities. This causes the prices of securities to rise or conversely interest rates to fall. This is the liquidity effect.[15]

The income and price-level effect follows the liquidity effect. The increase in real cash balances that is not exchanged for securities is exchanged for goods which bids up their prices and lowers the interest rate. The initial disturbance of portfolios which caused the interest rate to change (e.g. fall) then induces a change (in this case an increase) in income. This increase in income may be viewed as resulting from either an increase in investment spending following the fall in the interest rate or merely the additional demand for goods precipitated by the portfolio disturbance. With prices constant, the resulting increase in income will cause an increase in demand for loanable funds and for real cash balances which will then cause interest rates to rise. Further Friedman suggests that the rise in interest rates may rise too much or "overshoot."[16]

The price anticipation effect arises from the anticipation that prices will continue to rise (fall) at the present rate. This raises the price of holding money which may under certain conditions also produce a decline in the long-run equilibrium real interest rate.[17] The cost of credit – the interest rate – also rises by the anticipated rise in prices. Anticipations are usually assumed to be formed adaptively in neoclassical monetary theory.[18] It should be noted that, with the possible exception of the liquidity effect, the impact of a change in the money supply (or its rate of growth) on the interest rate is not immediate – *long* and *variable* lags occur due primarily to the structure of expectations formation assumed.[19]

In summary, under neoclassical monetary theory changes in the quantity of money (or, in a dynamic context, its rate of growth) have causal significance on prices and, in the short run, on real returns. Anticipated changes in money (or its rate of growth) have only price-level effects. If one ignores the possibilities of a feedback effect of exogenous disturbances, then the money supply is assumed to be completely exogenously determined. This would mean that the money supply is completely under the control of the monetary authority.

## 6 Neoclassical Monetary Theory with Rational Expectations

If one relaxes the assumption of adaptive expectations to allow expectations to be formed rationally within essentially a quantity theory framework, as Sargent and Wallace (1973) have done then money may be neutral even in the short run. Neutrality of money, of course, implies that changes in the quantity of money (or its rate of growth) will only induce a corresponding and direct effect on the price level. Further, this conclusion is independent of whether the change in the money supply is anticipated or unanticipated.

Essentially the analysis that produces this conclusion is as follows. An aggregate supply curve for real output is posited that is a function of some constant plus the deviation between observed and anticipated prices. The justification for this specification of the aggregate supply function is essentially the product of a desire, by some economists, to produce an explanation for business cycles consistent with rational expectations. Hence, fluctuations in aggregate output are induced by the inability of individuals to distinguish changes in absolute prices from changes in relative prices (which would be indicative of a change in the quantity demanded for a good).[20] Obviously, given the intention implicit in this specification of the aggregate supply function important variables may have been left out. Muthian rationality is assumed to characterize the formation of expectations. Sargent and Wallace then conclude:

> In order for the monetary authority to induce fluctuations in real output, it must induce unexpected movements in the price level by virtue of the aggregate supply curve.... But by virtue of the assumption that expectations about the price level are rational, the unexpected part of price movements is independent of the systematic part of the money supply, as long as the authority and the public share the same information. There is no systematic rule that the authority can follow that permits it to affect the unexpected part of the price level.[21]

It should be emphasized that the theoretical implications of money neutrality depend critically on the assumption that the information set possessed by the public is the same as that possessed by the central bank. If the central bank possesses a larger information set and and is able to control the money supply then the money neutrality result no longer holds. It then becomes possible for the central bank to exert some nonneutral effect on interest rates. While it might be argued that the Federal Reserve naturally possesses a larger information set (since it knows what it is going to do with respect to monetary policy), it is not clear that it does if it follows a systematic monetary rule which is known to the public. A systematic monetary rule means that monetary policy is not erratic; that is, the public by knowledge of the monetary rule can predict the reaction of the central bank to a disturbance. This result holds even if the monetary rule is stochastic rather than deterministic.[22] Whether the Federal Reserve exerts neutral or nonneutral effects on interest rates is an empirical rather than theoretical issue.

The implications of this approach for the present analysis concern the neutrality of money with respect to the interest rate. That is, changes (anticipated or not) in the rate of growth of money will exert only a direct effect on the price level and no effect on the real rate of interest. Further, the relationship with respect to unanticipated changes in the rate of money growth should be characterized by an abscncc of any significant lags.

## 7 The Black Dynamic Equilibrium Model

In contrast to both neo-Keynesian and neoclassical monetary theories Black (1972) has developed an alternative monetary theory. Essentially, his purpose was to formulate a monetary model that could be stated as a dynamic equilibrium model. An equilibrium theory according to Black is "one in which all markets are in continual equilibrium; in which there are never excess demands or excess supplies of any asset, goods or services and in which expectations of future prices are formed in a rational manner." Disequilibrium models are rejected because they embody unexploited profit opportunities which "are inconsistent with the assumption that individuals act to maximize utility and firms act to maximize profits."[23]

Black develops a one-sector model that includes money and bonds. In this model the monetary authority has the option of pursuing either a passive monetary policy (i.e. merely accommodating the demands of the public) or an active monetary policy. The assumption of perfect foresight differs from the specification of the expectations formation process employed in the other theories considered above. It is not, in itself, an unusual assumption. It does, however, obviate the necessity of the distinction between anticipated and unanticipated changes in the money supply. Black finds that for his model there is no way to have *M* (money) exogenous (i.e. an active monetary policy) and have *P* (prices) endogenous and the economy globally stable.[24] However, if *P* is exogenously determined and *M* is endogenous (i.e. a passive monetary policy) then the economy will always be globally stable.[25] Further, he notes that an exogenous *M* is "inconsistent with the usual economic logic describing the effect of monetary policy on the economy."[26] That is, a decrease (increase) in the money supply would be associated with an increase (decrease) in the price level if the money supply were exogenously determined.

Given an active monetary policy in the Black model, stability can only be achieved by relaxing the assumption of continual equilibrium in all markets to allow for "consistent disequilibrium in the goods market or in the bond and money markets" or by assuming "a lag in expectations."[27] The stability so achieved comes, however, at the expense of the introduction of unexploited profit opportunities.[28]

In summary, then, the Black dynamic equilibrium model posits a passive monetary policy and no causal significance associated with changes in the money supply (or its rate of growth) on either the real rate of interest or prices.[29] Rather, the direction of influence flows from changes in prices to changes in the money supply.[30] It might appear that undue attention is being given to the Black dynamic equilibrium model in view of the stature of the other monetary theories in macroeconomics. The unusual implications of the Black model *vis-à-vis* the others, however, warrants its special consideration.

## 8 Unutilized Trade Credit Theory

Laffer (1970) argues that the definition of money as currency and demand deposits should be expanded to include "unutilized trade credit available" as well, when money is considered to be held primarily for purposes of facilitating transactions rather than as an asset in "an efficient wealth portfolio."[31] Essentially, this theory contends that unutilized trade credit available (trade credit less trade debt) is a close if not perfect substitute for demand deposits and currency.[32]

The initiation of trade credit aside, changes in the quantity supplied (demanded) are posited to be a direct (inverse) function of the interest rate.[33] In the first instance, changes in trade credit are entirely reflected in changes in the quantity of unutilized trade credit available *ceteris paribus*; an increase (decrease) in the quantity of unutilized trade credit available has the same effect as an increase (decrease) in the money supply narrowly defined. That is "in the short-run, interest rates will tend to fall and prices and/or employment will tend to rise."[34] Since the quantity of trade credit supplied varies directly (and the quantity demanded inversely) with the interest rate, an automatic tendency to counteract exogenous changes in the narrowly defined money supply is introduced.[35]

The major implication of this theory for the present analysis is perhaps straightforward: changes in the (narrowly defined) money supply initiated by central bank open market operations may be partially or completely offset by changes in the quantity of unutilized trade credit available. Consequently, the broadly defined money supply may be partly and, in the limit, fully endogenously determined. Hence one may expect to observe, at most, a weak or, in the limiting case, an absence of relationship between open market operations or other monetary policy actions and changes in (both real and nominal) interest rates.

## 9 Monetary Approach to the Balance of Payments

In another sphere of economics, an old approach to international trade theory – the monetary approach to the balance of payments (whose revival is due to Mundell, Laffer, and others)[36] – suggests that the money supply may be endogenously determined for small open economies under a regime of fixed exchange rates.[37] This aspect has been largely ignored in the above macroeconomic theories since the economy is assumed (either explicitly or implicitly) to be closed. Also, in the past it has usually been assumed that the US economy may be treated as a closed system owing to (1) the use of the US dollar as a reserve currency and (2) the large size of the US economy relative to the rest of the world.[38]

Laffer (1975) describes the essence of the monetary approach to the balance of payments when he states:

> In the simplest form of the monetary approach, the overall balance of payments represents net flows of reserve money into or out of a country. The monetary approach to the balance of payments views money as an international commodity and not as a nontraded commodity. Under fixed exchange rates the domestic stock of money is, in part, and, in the limiting case, fully endogenous to an individual country. According to this view of the balance of payments the domestic monetary authorities lose control of money since the actions of the Federal Reserve are reversed in part by net movements of money among the countries.[39]

Accordingly, the implications of the monetary approach to the balance of payments in regard to the efficacy of Federal Reserve open market operations are perhaps obvious. The money supply may be primarily or at least partially endogenously determined independent of whether monetary policy is active or passive. Consequently, open market operations and other monetary policy actions may exert little, if any, influence on changes in real or nominal interest rates under a system of fixed exchange rates, if the economy may be characterized as small and open.

## 10 Fama–Tobin Approach

Some of the monetary theories considered above suggest that the money supply should be more broadly defined and indicate that the central bank may not control changes in it. In sharp contrast, Fama (1978) suggests that the appropriate definition of money should be more narrowly defined as currency only. This distinction is similar to one used by Tobin (1963). The antecedents of this approach lie in the "currency school" arguments of the nineteenth century. Under this approach the money supply is exogenously determined and changes in it only affect the price level. That is, money is neutral.

The primary implication of this theory for the present study is that, unless open market operations or other monetary policy actions involve the payment or receipt of currency proper, the relevant money supply is not altered, in which case estimated relationships between changes in interest rates and various monetary policy actions would not be significant.

## 11 Irrelevancy of Open Market Operations

Although monetary economists may differ with respect to the particular monetary theory to which they subscribe, most would contend that open market operations represent the primary transmission mechanism of Federal Reserve monetary policy on the economy. For example, the essence of Metzler's classic article is that the *form* of money creation matters, since open market operations will influence net wealth while monetary changes induced by other means may not, and thus the *real* rate of interest will not be invariant to a monetary change induced by an open market operation.

The efficacy of open market operations as an instrument of monetary policy has itself been questioned by economists who do not necessarily contend that the money supply is endogenously determined. In an interesting paper in the *American Economic Review*, Wallace (1980) demonstrates the conditions under which central bank open market operations are irrelevant with respect to changes in the price level or equilibrium consumption (and hence the real rate of interest), holding fiscal policy constant. The essential argument is that open market operations, like changes in the capital structure of firms, merely represent changes in the portfolio composition of financial assets and, as a consequence, should affect neither the price level nor the real rate of interest.[40] Chamley and Polemarchakis (1984) and Sargent and Smith (1987) present more generalized models. The invariance of the real rate of interest with respect to open market operations is consistent with results obtained by Wood (1980). Wood shows that, when disequilibrium trading is forbidden in Metzler's model, then open market operations influence the real rate of interest only when they are accompanied by changes in taxation.

Put differently, the government cannot create wealth through its open market operations. If it did, real interest rates would be affected. Barro (1974) has argued that government bonds are not net wealth. This would suggest that there should be no effect associated with central bank open market operations. Peled (1985) has also suggested irrelevance theorems for Federal Reserve open market operations.

To others, open market operations play a central role in Federal Reserve monetary policy. Yet, despite these sharply conflicting views, surprisingly little empirical evidence exists on whether Federal Reserve open market operations influence interest rates or prices. The empirical literature has been concerned with the influence of Fed open market operations on primarily stochastic changes in reserves (both total and free) (Bonomo and Schotta, 1969), the determination of the target variable that the Federal Reserve attempts to influence (e.g. free or total reserves) (Bonomo and Schotta, 1970), the separation of "dynamic" and "defensive" open market operations (Lombra, 1971; Lombra and Torto, 1973), and whether the Federal Reserve has proximate short-run control over the money stock (Andersen, 1968). Smith and Webb (1993) report evidence of a small but statistically significant increase in volatility around Fed Time.

## 12 Efficient Capital Markets Theory

As was stated at the outset of this chapter, one may view the issue of whether monetary authority policy actions influence changes in interest rates from two perspectives: macroeconomic or financial economic. In the latter case, interest centers on whether the government securities market is efficient with respect to monetary policy actions given the substantial empirical literature on informational market efficiency.[41]

As explained in chapter 2, when new information enters an efficient capital market prices will fully and correctly adjust to reflect the value of the new information. Trading is not necessary to convey the information. In the absence of unequal access to information due to the presence of inside information or private information production, security prices will fully and correctly reflect the value of available information even in the face of positive information costs or information costs that vary across individual investors. Generally, there should be no significant lagged effect associated with the impact of new information on security prices. The speed with which security prices respond to new information also depends on the model of market equilibrium.

At any point in time, security prices fully and correctly reflect the value of existing information. Consequently, from a financial economics perspective one is principally concerned with the analysis of the impact on security prices associated with the introduction of new information. Concentration on new information allows one to isolate the influence of changes in individual economic variables on speculative prices. Since observed values of economic variables, such as monetary policy actions, may be to some extent anticipated, then only the unanticipated component represents new information – the informational value of the anticipated component is already reflected in speculative prices.[42] Examination of new information also allows one to examine the speed of response of changes in security prices to new information.[43] In this regard, one may wish to use the least temporally aggregated data possible.

It is important to note that the security price pressure effect is a hypothesis about the nonavailability of perfect substitutes for the securities the Federal Reserve transacts in. It is not necessarily inconsistent with the notion of an informationally efficient capital market. It is inconsistent with the view that perfect substitutes exist or can be instantaneously created for the securities in which the Federal Reserve transacts.[44] In this case, the effects of large purchases or sales on security prices are negligible.

Some of the monetary models discussed above are inconsistent with modern financial economic theory in their implications of frequent capital market disequilibrium, the presence of significant lags associated with the full impact of a change in the money supply on interest rates and that Federal Reserve open market operations exert pressure on security prices. Modern financial economic theory is not concerned with the causality of money *per se*, nor with the passivity or activity of monetary policy, but rather that, whether money be causal or not, endogenously or exogenously determined, the influence of money be immediately and fully reflected when changes in its rate of growth become known. Similarly, the question of security price pressure revolves around the empirical issue of the uniqueness of the securities traded in open market operations.

## 13 The Fisher Hypothesis

Several of the monetary theories discussed above suggest that monetary policy actions influence changes in the rate of change of prices (or, loosely speaking, the rate of inflation). In order to test whether monetary policy actions influence the price level when using interest rate data one must first maintain some hypothesis concerning the relationship between interest rates and inflation. One such hypothesis which enjoys wide support in the economic literature is the "Fisher hypothesis." Essentially the Fisher hypothesis posits that nominal interest rates have three principal components: (1) an anticipated real rate of interest component; (2) an anticipated inflation component; (3) a cross-product term. This may be stated formally:

$$i_t = r^* + p^* + r^*p^* \tag{4.1}$$

where $i_t$ is the nominal rate of interest on a given bond at time $t$, $r^*$ is the anticipated real rate of interest on the same bond at time $t$, and $p^*$ is the anticipated rate of inflation for the period until the bond matures. When the expected rate of inflation is low the cross-product term is usually ignored and the (approximate) Fisher effect is expressed as

$$i_t = r^* + p^*. \tag{4.2}$$

That is, the Fisher effect is a statement about the *ex ante* relationship between inflation and interest rates. Simply stated, investors demand compensation for both expected inflation and the time value of money (the risk-free real interest rate). *Ex post*, one can always decompose the nominal interest rate into two components: a real rate and an inflation premium component. It is important to emphasize that the issue of the relationship between interest rates and inflation is logically separate from the issue of the causes of inflation.

If monetary policy actions influence $i_t$ then it must be by influencing either $r^*$ or $p^*$. The speed of any response in interest rates to unanticipated monetary policy actions will, of course, then depend upon whether the capital market is efficient *and* the actual model of capital market equilibrium. The Fisher effect assumes that $r^*$ and $p^*$ are independent.[45] If monetary policy actions influence only price expectations, then one cannot necessarily conclude that the change in the interest rate with respect to a change in expected inflation is unity since the change in the real rate with respect to a change in expected inflation may be nonzero.[46] If they are related, as some observers contend, then interest centers on the direction of the relationship.[47] If the relationship is negative, it may be difficult to discern empirically whether monetary policy actions influence the rate of inflation by using interest rate data alone. This would occur if the change in the real return exactly offset the change in the rate of inflation. Further, such a problem might arise if the observed real return was stochastic and unanticipated monetary policy actions influenced price expectations. This could pose a problem only if the variation in the real return were much larger than the variation in anticipated inflation.

## 14 Summary of Testable Implications

The important point to remember is not the mechanism of transmission of a change in the money supply but rather that a change (whether anticipated or not) in the quantity of money (or its rate of growth) is posited to influence (if it is posited to exert any influence) either the anticipated real rate of interest and/or the price anticipation component of the nominal interest rate.

Although one is interested in examining the impact of both anticipated and unanticipated monetary policy actions on changes in interest rates, unanticipated monetary policy actions have especial importance because of the diversity of testable implications associated with their impact. The essential hypotheses associated with the above theories are summarized below.

If changes in the money supply have causal importance for interest rates and the money supply is exogenously determined (as with the neo-Keynesian and neoclassical models) then one would expect that a change in the money supply (or its rate of growth) should cause either a change in the real rate and/or a change in the price anticipations component of the nominal interest rate. However, it might be argued that the impact may vary depending on the size of the change as well as the period or frequency of the temporal aggregation observed, since small or high frequency changes may represent noise rather than information.

Further, if the market is efficient, one would expect the reaction to occur when the monetary policy actions become known if this precedes the actual change in the money supply. Consequently, lagged monetary policy actions may reveal an absence of relationship with contemporaneous changes in the interest rate. It is possible, however, that lagged monetary policy actions may contain information regarding the path of changes in the rate of change of prices, in which event lagged monetary policy actions may reveal a relationship with contemporaneous changes in interest rates. Further, the omission of relevant variables in the estimation of any relationship may under certain conditions produce a spuriously significant lag.

If the market is not efficient and lags exist then one would expect that lagged monetary policy actions would contribute significantly to determining current changes in prices or real returns. Further, if security price pressure exists as Samuelson and others contend, then one would expect open market operations to have an immediate impact on security prices irrespective of any lagged effect. This is true independently of whether the open market operations are "defensive" or "dynamic."[48]

If the market is efficient and perfect substitutes exist or can be instantaneously created then no security price pressure effect should be discernible. However, if the capital market is efficient and money has causal significance for interest rates, one may have trouble distinguishing between security price pressure *per se* and market reaction to the attempt to change the money supply.

If the money supply is completely endogenously determined (as in the Keynesian New View, Black and limiting cases of the monetary approach to the balance of payments, and the unutilized trade credit theories) then one would expect to find an absence of causal relationship between net open market operations and changes in real returns or in prices. This is true regardless of whether monetary policy actions are anticipated, unanticipated, defensive, or dynamic. Changes in the money supply would not show a causal relationship extending from changes in the money supply to changes in interest rates either. It may be possible to determine whether Federal Reserve open market operations are passively (actively) determined by examining unanticipated "dynamic" open market operations to see whether they lag (lead) changes in interest rates.

It is extremely difficult to distinguish the existence of a weak from a strong effect, especially since none of the theories described above specifies the degree of nonzero relationship to be expected. Consequently, the implications common to both the monetary approach to the balance of payments and the unutilized trade credit theory of a weak effect when the money supply is only partially endogenously determined may not be testable.

One obvious testable implication that would distinguish the monetary approach to the balance of payments from other theories of an endogenously determined money supply (especially the unutilized trade credit theory) would be to compare the influence of monetary policy actions under periods of fixed and floating exchange rates for any differential impact on interest rates.

It should be noted that changes in interest rates may themselves be subjected to some degree of anticipation. To the extent that changes in interest rates are predictable one could subdivide the observed change in interest rates into its expected and unexpected components and relate these components to anticipated and unanticipated open market operations respectively. This issue is primarily empirical in nature.

The security price pressure effect is common to both the neo-Keynesian and neoclassical monetary theories (with the possible exception of the neoclassical monetary theory with rational expectations). This effect is purely mechanical rather than informational and hence is independent of whether open market operations are anticipated or not. The Keynesian New View is ambiguous in regard to whether a security price pressure effect exists.

Anticipated money supply changes exert an influence on the real rate of interest independent of the security price pressure effect in neo-Keynesian monetary theory only if the economy is at less than full employment. Under both of the neoclassical monetary theories and under neo-Keynesian monetary theory in the presence of full employment, anticipated open market operations exert only a pressure on the price level.

Unanticipated money supply changes exert only a price-level effect under both neoclassical monetary theory with rational expectations and neo-Keynesian monetary theory under conditions of full employment. Under conditions of less than full employment of resources, unanticipated money supply changes will affect the real rate of interest according to both neoclassical and neo-Keynesian monetary theory.

In the Black dynamic equilibrium model neither anticipated nor unanticipated open market operations or other monetary policy actions exert any effect on either the real or the nominal rate of interest. The impact of money supply changes (anticipated or unanticipated) on real or nominal interest rates under either the monetary approach to the balance of payments or Laffer's unutilized trade credit monetary theory cannot be easily determined since the effect depends on the extent to which the money supply is endogenous. If the money supply is completely endogenously determined then open market operations or other monetary policy actions will have no effect. Similarly, the effect of anticipated or unanticipated monetary policy actions on real or nominal interest rates depends on whether all money is "inside" money or not. With the possible exception of a security price pressure effect, neither anticipated nor unanticipated monetary policy actions influence changes in the real rate of interest in the pure "inside" money economy of the Keynesian New View. However, anticipated or unanticipated changes in the money supply do affect inflation expectations and with it the nominal rate of interest. Finally, if Wallace is correct and open market operations are irrelevant then open market operations – the primary transmission mechanism of monetary policy in the United States – do not exert an impact on real interest rates and the real economy.

## Appendix 4.1: Rational Expectations and Price Flexibility

Before the decade of the 1980s there was a widespread belief among academics and policymakers that prices and especially wages were "sticky." This was an essentially Keynesian idea which nonetheless had a wide following.

An interesting question in economics is whether the presence of stable or rather "sticky" prices (and wages) in the face of real and monetary shocks is consistent with rational expectations. The importance of this question becomes more acute when one considers the impotency, described by some writers on monetary theory, of monetary policy effects on real economic variables in an economy in which expectations are formed rationally.[49] First, it is necessary to distinguish the empirical question of the existence of stable or "sticky" prices from the purely theoretical question of whether the existence of price "stickiness" is consistent with rational expectations.

To answer the empirical question first, it is commonly believed that prices in some markets (primarily nonauction or nonfinancial markets) frequently exhibit some degree of price "stickiness." Further analyses of some indices of prices such as the consumer price index indicate serial dependence in price changes. It should be noted that the issue of whether prices are slow to adjust is related but distinct from the issue of whether prices adjust slowly *when* they adjust. It should be recognized that to some extent this serial dependence is merely an artifact of the measurement process. Consequently, some of the observed serial dependence in price changes is purely spurious.

To answer the theoretical question various explanations have been advanced in the economic literature that allow the introduction of some element of "stickiness" in wages or prices. The explanations considered here are essentially independent of the way in which expectations are formed; that is, they do not explicitly rely upon the process of expectations formation to generate price "stickiness" or serial dependence in price changes (e.g. by assuming adaptive expectations). Hence these expectations may be consistent with rational expectations. However, in some explanations it appears that the "stickiness" in prices or wages results from the relaxation of rational expectations in some sector or sectors of the economy.

One explanation suggests that observed "sticky" prices result from the attempt of producers to minimize the search costs of consumers. Essentially, the search cost explanation assumes that (in the absence of a widely recognized change in relative prices) consumers may confuse changes in relative prices with price differences among producers, thus inducing search by consumers. In order to minimize these search costs, producers maintain stable or "sticky" prices rather than continuously adjust prices. Barring exceptionally large search costs it is difficult to conceive how this explanation would account for real disturbances that are of any appreciable magnitude.

A second explanation which has received some currency is the implicit contract theory of wages. Essentially this explanation argues that laborers prefer to bear less risk in their wage stream and consequently agree (implicitly contract) with producers to receive a (presumably lower) fixed wage in exchange. Consequently, short-run adjustments are made in employment (quantity) rather than in wages (price). As a result, one obtains short-run wage rigidities. This explanation is not without criticism, however.[50] It is not clear why workers should necessarily prefer a fixed to a variable wage since they could always offset any nonsystematic risk associated with their wage stream by suitably adjusting the rest of their portfolio.[51] That is, workers may diversify for themselves. Similarly, they may also alter the composition of their portfolio to adjust the amount of systematic risk they wish to bear.

A natural question that arises is what criteria does one use to determine whether the observed price "stickiness" or serial dependence in price changes is consistent with rational expectations. One criterion that is frequently employed in the financial economics literature and will be adopted here is whether or not potential unexploited profit opportunities exist *after* adjusting for any transactions costs necessarily incurred in their elimination.

Rational expectations are expectations based on all available information. One potential source of information is the time series of past observations (of price changes) of the variable in question. In the absence of transactions costs, the assumption of rational expectations generally implies the absence of serial dependence in price changes.[52] One measure of the presence of serial correlation is the serial correlation coefficient. It is extremely important, however, for the process to be stationary in order that the serial correlation coefficients can be reasonably interpreted. It should be recognized that correlation is a *linear* measure of association or relationship only; and it is possible (but improbable) to have zero serial correlation with nonlinear serial dependence.[53]

When one considers transactions costs it is possible for the serial correlation to be nonzero without implying an abnormal profit opportunity, as long as it lies within the boundary of transactions costs (expressed in percentage terms). The transactions costs criterion can be generalized to extend to information that arises from sources outside the time series of past observations. Consistency with rational expectations merely requires that no abnormal profit opportunities exist within the transactions costs of exploiting the opportunities. Consequently, one may observe price "stickiness" or serial dependence in price changes *within* transactions costs. Obviously, the presence of a known serial dependence in price changes of a seasonal, cyclical, or other nature would merely be reflected in investor's expectations and would not imply the existence of any unexploited profit opportunities (e.g. see Muth, 1961). Further, it is even possible for the serial correlation in price changes, in this case, to exceed the relevant transactions costs boundary (expressed in percentage terms). This would also be consistent with rational expectations.

Most theories that posit that expectations are formed rationally either implicitly or explictly assume homogeneity of expectations. An ancillary issue concerns whether the relaxation of the assumption of homogeneity of expectations to allow for heterogeneous expectations would vitiate rational expectations. That is, will aggregate or market consensus expectations be consistent with rational expectations (i.e. reflect all available information) if expectations are formed heterogeneously? Further, in regard to the aggregation of expectations does one take the average or marginal expectation? Fortunately, the presence of heterogeneity of expectations does not imply that aggregate or market consensus expectations are necessarily nonrational. Rational expectations in the Muthian sense "are essentially the same as the predictions of the relevant economic theory."[54] Consequently, correct or rational expectations will dominate market expectations; otherwise, exploitable profit opportunities would exist for investors who have knowledge of the "relevant economic theory."[55] The actions of these individuals to eliminate the implied profit opportunities will force the market expectations to be rational.[56] Hence the presence of heterogeneous expectations does not vitiate rational expectations.

## Notes

1 It is necessary to distinguish a perfect capital market where there are no transactions costs from an efficient capital market where positive transactions costs may exist. In the former case there is no reason ever to hold money instead of interest-bearing assets while in the latter case there is, at least, a transaction cost motive for holding money.

2 Some Federal Reserve actions, such as changes in the discount rate or reserve requirements, might cause "announcement effects" which may affect interest rates (see Waud, 1970). Not all uses of the policy tools are for active changes in monetary policy. For example, open market operations may be used to offset any monetary policy impact that changes in reserve requirements might have when changes in reserve requirements are made for nonmonetary policy purposes.

3 Smith (1963, p. 237) states: "Open market operations are firmly established as the fundamental weapon of monetary policy in the United States." Samuelson (1972, p. 560) notes: "The chief weapon of the Federal Reserve in doing all this is its open market purchases and sales of government securities."

It should be pointed out that open market operations are not equivalent to the full change in the money supply which they supposedly induce since the multiple expansion (contraction) in demand deposits has yet to occur. To argue that open market operations are equivalent to a change in the money supply implicitly assumes that the money supply is exogenously determined which may or may not be correct.

4 Samuelson (1972) presents a simple model which is in the spirit of Keynes to illustrate the effects of open market operations on prices, income, and the interest rate.

5 As Samuelson (1972, p. 561) notes:

Whenever anybody bids up or down the yields on Government bonds that automatically has an effect upon the supply and demand bids that determine the pattern of yields on corporate bonds and other securities that are alternatives to Government bonds. There is thus, a direct effect upon the structure of interest rates from open market purchases by the Fed. Such purchases directly lower the yields on the issues bought and (with attenuation) tend to lower the yields on Government securities of other maturities and the yield on corporate bonds. Since bonds are substitutes, albeit not terribly close ones, for other forms of investment such as mortgage loans, the lowering of bond yields tends to channel funds into mortgages and lower their yield.

6 Samuelson (1972, p. 564).

7 Ibid.

8 Tobin shares a belief in the nonuniqueness of money common to other adherents of the New View. However, it would be wrong to attribute to him or appear to make him personify the amorphous set of ideas collectively known as the Keynesian New View. Indeed, his variation of New View theory examines the influence of open market operations on the supply price of capital (the price at which the community is willing to hold the capital stock). The influence of open market operations on the supply price of capital appears to depend upon the degree of substitutability of long-term bonds for capital. The closer the degree of substitutability is, the greater the effect.

9 Tobin (1963, p. 412). Feige (1964) did an empirical study on the substitutability of presumed money substitutes. He concluded that these substitutes were worse substitutes for money than would be predicted from the Keynesian New View theory.

10 Gurley and Shaw (1960, pp. 363–4) define inside and outside money as follows: "Inside money – money based on private domestic primary securities. Outside money – money that is backed by foreign or government securities or gold; or fiat money issued by the government."

11 The reader may wonder, however, in what sense changes in money can induce price-level changes if the money supply is endogenously determined.

12 Patinkin (1969) has argued that Friedman's approach – the modern portfolio approach to the demand for money – "although it has some well known antecedents in the traditional theory can only be seen as a continuation of the Keynesian theory of liquidity preference."

13 Friedman (1972, p. 201) states: "The inverse of the price level is the price of money."

14 Friedman and Schwartz (1976) state: "What these effects will be depends, of course, on whether the change in the quantity of money is anticipated – in which case the first two sets of effects largely disappear — or is unanticipated" (pp. 10–11). In another article Friedman (1972, p. 205) states: "The implicit assumption that, in the first instance, the effect is not likely to be on prices, is consistent with much empirical evidence. The implicit assumption seems correct if the jump (in the rate of increase in the money supply) is an unanticipated jump. If it were announced that the jump was going to occur, it would be more plausible that it would have an immediate effect on prices."

15 As Friedman (1972, p. 201) notes, this effect as described above operates through money stocks; however, it could also operate through flows. If the quantity of money is increased through increasing reserves (e.g. an open market operation) then that increases "the supply of loanable funds"; consequently, interest rates fall. Further he notes the difference between the stock effect and flow effect as follows: "The flow effect would produce a decline in the interest rate which might be expected to happen immediately. As long as prices do not react, the effect through stocks will exert a continuing downward pressure on the interest rate."

16 Friedman (1970).

17 Friedman (1970) states:

> However, equilibrium real output will not be unaffected by this monetary change. The exact effect depends on just how real output is measured, in particular whether it includes or excludes the nonpecuniary services of money. If it includes them, as in principle it should, then the level of real output will be lower after the monetary change than before. It will be lower for two reasons: first the higher cost of holding cash balances will lead producers to substitute other resources for cash, which will lower productive efficiency; second the flow of nonpecuniary services from money will be reduced. ... For both reasons the price level will have to rise more than nominal income. ... It is harder to be precise about the equilibrium rate of growth, since that depends on the particular growth model. What is clear is that the aggregate stock of nonhuman capital, including money, will be lower relative to human capital, but that the aggregate stock of physical (nonmoney) capital will be higher, so that the real yield of capital ... will be lower. The nominal interest rate ... will equal this real yield plus the rate of change in prices, so it will be higher.

18 Under adaptive expectations, individuals may look to the last time a similar event occurred in forming their expectations of what will happen next.

19 As noted above, adaptive expectations models are usually employed in neoclassical monetary theory. It should be noted, however, that adaptive expectations models are not necessarily inconsistent with rational expectations. In an interesting article, Sargent and Wallace (1973) develop a modified version of Cagan's adaptive expectations model for hyperinflation where expectations are rational in the Muthian sense. Muthian rationality ensures that the forecast of price changes from the model governing the formation of expectations of changes in prices cannot be systematically different from the forecast of prices from the model governing the actual change in prices. However, as they note, one essential condition for their model to be rational "is the presence of feedback from inflation to subsequent rates of money creation."

20 Such an explanation necessarily relies on the absence of either a complete and efficient futures market or for that matter an efficient money market. If either exists than it is not clear that one would have difficulty distinguishing between absolute and relative prices. Under this approach rational expectations are introduced but the existence of efficient financial markets is restricted in order to maintain this specification of the aggregate supply function.

21 Sargent and Wallace (1973, p. 249).

22 Sargent and Wallace (1973, p. 249). Fischer (1977) and Phelps and Taylor (1977) argue that it is possible to have short-run real effects induced by monetary policy if there is short-run wage or price stickiness, respectively.

23 Black (1972, p. 801). Presumably, profit opportunities can be exploited instantaneously thus precluding the possibility of temporary disequilibrium.

24 Black (1972, p. 807).

25 In another article Black (1974) investigates whether rational behavior is sufficient to determine a unique "competitive equilibrium" path for the price level assuming that the central bank pursues an active monetary policy. The existence of a unique "competitive equilibrium" path is not confirmed and Black concludes that the presence of multiple equilibrium paths requires that the mechanism of achieving equilibrium be more completely specified.

26 Black (1972, p. 807).

27 Drabicki and Takayama (1978), however, claim to obtain stability in a dynamic growth model with an endogenously determined money

supply. Their model is similar to Black's in several respects, most notably that it is dynamic and assumes perfect foresight.

28 Black (1972, p. 809).

29 However, Black's model leaves largely unexplained a central issue in economics – the theory of absolute prices. Black (1972) notes: "The idea of an exogenous price level is unusual and is simply an indication that the model is incomplete. If monetary policy does not determine the price level, what does?" He suggests that for this model the capital stock and the real quantity of government liabilities may determine absolute prices. Later, Black relaxes the exogeneity assumption to allow absolute prices to be endogenously determined.

In a related article Black (1970) states: "An individual can adjust his portfolio of financial assets by trading with other individuals and by dealing with his bank. If he wants more currency, the bank will give it to him; if he wants less, the bank will take it back. If he wants more demand deposits, the bank will give him a loan (at some interest rate), and if he wants less, the bank will reduce his loans. If the bank will not do these things, other individuals or businesses will. So transactions that affect portfolio composition are purely financial; they have no impact on the real sector or on the price level.

30 Outside the dynamic equilibrium model *per se*, Black offers other reasons why an active monetary policy may not characterize the economy. In a section assessing the significance of then current (1970) Federal Reserve regulatory controls on the banking system and the economy Black (1970) notes in regard to the use of currency as reserves:

> Since our present banking system allows the use of currency as reserves and since we do not observe that banks are willing to pay more than face value for currency (in crediting a bank account), it seems likely that the Federal Reserve Board does not set the maximum quantity of reserves below its natural level. In other words, open market operations must be ineffective. If they were effective in controlling the quantity of reserves, then we would observe a two-price system. The only other possibility is that there is a profit opportunity that banks have not been exploiting, in paying more than face value for currency and central bank deposits.

31 Laffer (1970, p. 239), states: "Virtually all of modern theory views money's role as almost exclusively an asset in a wealth portfolio. An alternative view, referred to here as the classical view considers money's principal role as the most efficient lubricant for present transactions and as an inventory against uncertainty." The inclusion of unutilized

trade credit available in the definition of money is dependent upon the assumption that money is not held as an asset since unutilized trade credit available cannot be held net.

32 Laffer (1970, p. 240) states: "Since unutilized trade credit available is an acceptable means of payment, there is no need to possess an intermediary commodity – demand deposits and currency – in order to acquire goods and services." Laffer recognizes that unutilized trade credit available represents a set of specialized as opposed to generalized purchasing power. However, he contends that this distinction does not affect his analysis.

33 Laffer (1970, p. 245). The incentive to establish trade credit arises whenever the present discounted value of the benefits arising from the (normally mutual) reduction in noninterest-bearing demand deposits and currency exceeds the cost of its establishment.

34 Laffer (1970, p. 245) also notes: "This is accomplished without any reference to the private wealth effect of unutilized trade credit available, for there is none."

35 Laffer (1970, p. 247) further observes that if one accepts the amount of unutilized trade credit available as money then nonbank firms, as well as banks, can issue money (broadly defined).

36 For a series of articles on the monetary approach to the balance of payments see Frenkel and Johnson (1976).

37 As Mundell (1969) notes in regard to each of the three major approaches to international trade (i.e. the elasticity, absorption, and monetary approaches) "It is not meaningful to question the validity of the three approaches. The terms can be defined so that they are all correct and assert identical propositions even if capital movements are included."

38 Evans (1976) concludes that the pre-1914 US economy, at least, behaved as a small and open economy.

39 Laffer (1975, p. 10).

40 The notion that the value of a firm is independent of its capital structure is central to modern corporation finance. It owes its origin to the irrelevance theorems of Modigliani and Miller (1958). Basically, Modigliani and Miller contend that a firm cannot create wealth for its shareholders by altering its capital structure under certain conditions. That is, the capital structure of the firm is irrelevant in the sense of creating value. The reason for this is that individual investors can undo what the firm does.

41 Given that the monetary authority attempts to influence the behavior of short-term interest rates, the question of whether the short-term interest rate market is informationally efficient is especially important.

Roll (1970) reports that the US Treasury bill market is informationally efficient.

42 This is true even if the causal variable changes gradually. In this case, one would observe the change in security prices temporally preceding changes in the causal variable.

43 The speed with which security prices respond to new information also depends on the model of market equilibrium.

44 As noted in chapter 2, Scholes (1972) defines the information effect to be a change in price due to the belief that the large block trader has information not generally available. It may be difficult, in this case, to distinguish the information effect from the security price pressure effect.

45 The reader is referred to Levi and Makin (1978) for a more complete discussion of this issue.

46 Fama (1975) provides evidence in support of the Fisher effect. He reports an approximate one-to-one correspondence between changes in expected inflation and changes in interest rates.

47 Mundell (1963) posits a negative relationship between $r^*$ and $p^*$. Essentially, he argues that a decline in the real rate of interest results from increased savings which follow from the decline in real money balances due to higher inflation. Darby (1975) posits a positive relationship between $r^*$ and $p^*$. Essentially, Darby argues that under a system of taxation on nominal income the real rate changes with changes in inflation as investors attempt to maintain a constant *after-tax* real return.

Hansson and Stuart (1986) advance a model with an *open* economy (and capital markets) to reconcile Darby's hypothesis with the observed (approximate) one-to-one correspondence between changes in nominal interest rates and inflation.

48 Chandler (1969, p. 225). The Federal Reserve also trades in securities issued by US Government agencies for the system open market account. In principle, private securities or real assets could also be used by the Federal Reserve. This would not change the analysis, however. The distinction between defensive and dynamic open market operations is due to Roosa (1956). However, Smith (1963) appears to draw a similar distinction:

> In addition to their use to control credit in the interest of economic stability and growth open market operations are carried on continuously for the purpose of offsetting the short-run effects on member bank reserves resulting from factors outside the control of the Federal Reserve – changes in float, currency

in circulation, gold stock, treasury and foreign deposits at the Reserve Banks and so on.

49 See Sargent and Wallace (1975).

50 Gordon (1977) has pointed out that this explanation suffers from two additional criticisms: (1) the implicit contract theory involves a "deadweight loss" to both employers and employees since the marginal product of labor is not equal to the marginal value of time; (2) workers would be unwilling to accept the potential for unemployment in the absence of governmental transfer payments. However, the existence of government transfer payments would only encourage firms to unemploy additional workers.

51 It is recognized that human capital may comprise most of the assets in many individuals' portfolios. Nevertheless, the remaining assets may offer some room to maneuver. Further, to the extent that changes in occupation may be easily made systematic risk adjustments may occur in this manner.

52 As will be noted later this is not always true. Muth (1961), for example, explained the existence of the hog-price cycle in a framework where expectations are formed rationally.

53 Consequently, one may also wish to consider tests which allow for the presence of nonlinear serial dependence as well.

54 Muth (1961, p. 537).

55 As Muth (1961, p. 550) notes: "If expectations were not moderately rational there would be opportunities for economists to make profits in commodity speculation, running a firm, or selling the information to present owners."

56 In the long run, only those individuals or firms who act according to the predictions of the relevant economic theory will survive.

## References

Andersen, L. C. 1968: "Federal Reserve Defensive Operations and Short-Run Control of the Money Stock," *Journal of Political Economy*, 76, March–April, 275–88.

Barro, R. J. 1974: "Are Government Bonds Net Wealth?," *Journal of Political Economy*, 82 (6), 1095–1117.

Black, F. 1970: "Banking and Interest Rates in a World Without Money," *Journal of Bank Research*, 1, Autumn, 9–20.

Black, F. 1972: "Active and Passive Monetary Policy in a Neoclassical Model," *Journal of Finance*, 27, September, 801–14.

Black, F. 1974: "Uniqueness of the Price Level in Monetary Growth Models with Rational Expectations," *Journal of Economic Theory*, 7, January, 53–65.

Bonomo, V., and C. Schotta, 1969: "A Spectral Analysis of Post-Accord Federal Open Market Operations," *American Economic Review*, 59, March, 50–61.

Bonomo, V., and C. Schotta 1970: "Federal Open Market Operations and Variations in the Reserve Base," *Journal of Finance*, 25, June, 659–67.

Canto, V. A., D. H. Joines, and R. I. Webb 1984: "Taxation, Rational Expectations and the Neutrality of Money," *Journal of Macroeconomics*, 6 (1), Winter, 69–78.

Chamley, C., and H. Polemarchakis 1984: "Assets, General Equilibrium and the Neutrality of Money," *Review of Economic Studies*, 51, 129–38.

Chandler, L. C. 1969: *The Economics of Money and Banking*, 5th edn, New York: Harper and Row.

Darby, M. R. 1975: "The Financial and Tax Effects of Monetary Policy on Interest Rates," *Economic Inquiry*, 3, June, 266–76.

Drabicki, J. Z., and A. Takayama 1978: "Money, Growth, and the Stability of the Steady State Under Myopic Perfect Foresight," *Economic Letters*, 2, 45–8.

Evans, P. 1976: "A Time Series Model of the U.S. Economy: 1879–1915," Mimeo, University of Chicago.

Evans, P. 1978: "Time Series and Structural Analysis of the German Hyperinflation," *International Economic Review*, 19, February, 195–210.

Fama, E. F. 1970: "Efficient Capital Markets: A Review of Theory and Empirical Work," *Journal of Finance*, 25, May, 343–417.

Fama, E. F. 1975: "Short Term Interest Rates as Predictors of Inflation," *American Economic Review*, 65, June, 269–82.

Fama, E. F. 1978: "Banking in a Theory of Finance," Mimeo, University of Chicago.

Feige, E. 1964: *The Demand for Liquid Assets: A Temporal Cross-Section Analysis*, Englewood Cliffs, NJ: Prentice–Hall.

Fischer, S. 1977: "Long-Term Contracts, Rational Expectations and the Optimal Money Supply Rule," *Journal of Political Economy*, 85, February, 191–206.

Frenkel, J., and H. G. Johnson 1976: *The Monetary Approach to the Balance of Payments*, Toronto: University of Toronto Press.

Friedman, M. 1968: "The Role of Monetary Policy," *American Economic Review*, 58, March, 1–17.

Friedman, M. 1970: "A Theoretical Framework for Monetary Analysis," *Journal of Political Economy*, 78, March–April, 193–238.

Friedman, M. 1972: "Factors Affecting the Level of Interest Rates," in John T. Boorman and Thomas M. Havrilesky (eds), *Money Supply, Money Demand, and Macroeconomic Models*, Boston, MA: Allyn and Bacon, pp. 89–97.

Friedman, M. and A. J. Schwartz 1976: "Money and Interest Rates," Mimeo, University of Chicago, January.

Gordon, R. J. 1977: "The Theory of Domestic Inflation," *American Economic Review*, 67, February, 128–47.

Gurley, J. G., and E. G. Shaw 1960: *Money in a Theory of Finance*, Washington, DC: Brookings Institution.

Hansson, I., and C. Stuart 1986: "The Fisher Hypothesis and International Capital Markets," *Journal of Political Economy*, 94 (6), 1330–7.

Kydland, F. E. and E. C. Prescott 1977: "Rules rather than Discretion: The Inconsistency of Optimal Plans," *Journal of Political Economy*, 85, June, 473–91.

Laffer, A. B. 1970: "Trade Credit and the Money Market," *Journal of Political Economy*, 78, March–April, 239–67.

Laffer, A. B. 1975: "Trade Credit and Other Forms of Inside Money," in Ronald J. McKinnon (ed.), *Money and Finance in Economic Growth and Development*, New York: Marcel Dekker.

Levi, M. O., and J. H. Makin 1978: "Anticipated Inflation and Interest Rates," *American Economic Review*, 68, December, 801–12.

Lombra, R. E. 1971: "Federal Reserve Behavior: Identification, Rationale, and Implications," Ph.D. dissertation, Pennsylvania State University.

Lombra, R. E., and R. G. Torto 1973: "Federal Reserve 'Defensive' Behavior and the Reserve Causation Argument," *Southern Economic Journal*, 40, July, 47–55.

Modigliani, F., and M. Miller 1958: "The Cost of Capital, Corporation Finance, and the Theory of Investment," *American Economic Review*, 48 (3), June, 261–97.

Mundell, R. 1963: "Inflation and Real Interest," *Journal of Political Economy*, 71, June, 280–3.

Mundell, R. 1969: "The Balance of Payments," in David Sills (ed.), *International Encyclopedia of the Social Sciences*, New York: Crowell Collier and Macmillan.

Muth, J. F. 1961: "Rational Expectations and the Theory of Price Movements," *Econometrica*, 29, 315–35.

Patinkin, D. 1969: "The Chicago Tradition, the Quantity Theory and Friedman," *Journal of Money, Credit and Banking*, 1, February, 46–70.

Peled, D. 1985: "Stochastic Inflation and Government Provision of Indexed Bonds," *Journal of Monetary Economics*, 15, 291–308.

Phelps, E. S., and J. B. Taylor 1977: "Stabilizing Powers of Monetary Policy Under Rational Expectations," *Journal of Political Economy*, 85, February, 163–90.

Roll, R. 1970: *The Behavior of Interest Rates: Application of the Efficient Market Model to U.S. Treasury Bills*, New York: Basic Books.

Roosa, R. V. 1956: *Federal Reserve Operations in Money and Government Securities Markets*, New York: Federal Reserve Bank of New York.

Samuelson, P. 1972: "Money, Interest and Economic Activity: Their Interrelationship in a Market Economy," in *The Collected Scientific Papers of Paul A. Samuelson*, ed. Robert Merton, vol. 3, Cambridge, MA: MIT Press.

Sargent, T. J., and B. Smith 1987: "Irrelevance of Open Market Operations in Some Economies with Government Currency Being Dominated in Rate of Return," *American Economic Review*, 77(1), March, 78–92.

Sargent, T. J., and N. Wallace 1973: "Rational Expectations and the Dynamics of Hyperinflation," *International Economic Review*, 14, June, 328–50.

Sargent, T. J., and N. Wallace 1975: "Rational Expectations, the Optimal Monetary Instrument, and the Optimal Money Supply Rule," *Journal of Political Economy*, 83, April, 241–54.

Scholes, M. 1972: "The Market for Securities: Substitution Versus Price Pressure and the Effects of Information on Share Prices," *Journal of Business*, 45, April, 179–211.

Smith, D. G., and R. I. Webb 1993: "The Volatility of Eurodollar Futures Prices Around Fed Time," *Journal of Fixed Income*, 2 (4), March, 56–73.

Smith, W. 1963: "The Instruments of General Monetary Control," in John T. Boorman and Thomas M. Havrilesky (eds), *Readings in Money, National Income, and Stabilization Policy*, 3rd edn, Homewood, IL: Irwin.

Tobin, J. 1961: "Money, Capital and Other Stores of Value," *American Economic Review*, 51, May, 26–37.

Tobin, J. 1963: "Commercial Banks as Creators of 'Money.'" in D. Carson (ed.), *Banking and Monetary Studies*, Homewood, IL: Irwin.

Tobin, J. 1970: "Money and Income: Post Hoc Ergo Propter Hoc?," *Quarterly Journal of Economics*, 84, May, 301–17.

Wallace, N. 1981: "A Modigliani–Miller Theorem for Open Market Operations," *American Economic Review*, 70, June, 267–74.

Waud, R. N. 1970: "Public Interpretation of Federal Reserve Discount Rate Changes: Evidence and the Announcement Effect," *Econometrica*, 38, March, 231–50.

Webb, R. I. 1979: "The Impact of Open Market Operations on Treasury Bill Yields," Ph.D. dissertation, University of Chicago.

Wood, J. H. 1980: "Metzler on Classical Interest Theory," *American Economic Review*, 70, March, 135–48.

# 5

# A Review of the Evidence on Monetary Theories

> On the present view the classical view of causality is inverted. Instead of saying that every event has a cause, we recognize that observations vary and regard scientific method as a procedure for analyzing the variation. Our starting-point is to consider all variation as random; then successive significance tests warrant the treatment of more and more of it as predictable, and we explicitly regard the method as one of successive approximation.
>
> (Sir Harold Jeffreys, *Scientific Inference*, p. 81)

## 1 Introduction

The principal objective of this chapter is to review and assess the empirical evidence on the influence of monetary policy actions on changes in speculative prices and expected inflation. In addition, the relationship between asset prices and inflation is considered, as is the issue of whether the central bank exerts control over the short-run *nominal* money stock. The chapter begins with a review of the empirical literature on the influence of money supply announcements on changes in interest and foreign exchange rates and stock prices. We consider the evidence on the influence of money on speculative prices and whether the central bank controls the nominal money stock.

The casual reader may have certain preconceived notions of what linkages have been proven to exist in the macroeconomic literature. Such readers are in for a surprise in the area of monetary economics.

Many widely held beliefs have little support in the empirical economic literature. Other ideas, which are commonly believed to be true by many market participants (such as the existence of a liquidity effect), remain matters of much controversy in the economics profession.

Considerable attention is directed to some of the early empirical literature, much of which is flawed. Nevertheless, given the widespread acceptance as fact by many market participants that changes in the money supply influence changes in speculative prices it is useful to review the often weak foundations for that belief. In this regard, consider, for instance, Gibson's (1970) review of the early literature in this area. After noting that Cagan measured the total effects of a change in money on changes in interest rates, he states:

> Other studies have generally not dealt with the effects of money on interest rates, but some provide evidence on the separate effects .... [Tobin's] evidence for the [liquidity] effect consists of plotting the commercial paper rate against "idle balances" (the quantity of money adjusted for transactions needs), he concluded that the resulting negatively sloped curve supports his hypothesis of a liquidity preference relation. Demand for money studies (Latané, 1954; Friedman, 1959; Meltzer, 1963) now use more complex techniques but give similar evidence on this point holding money income constant, increased money balances will be held only at lower interest rates.
>
> (p. 441)

More rigorous tests of these perceived relationships yield less supportive results for both Keynesians and monetarists. For instance, Pierce (1977) reports an *absence* of relationship between changes in the money supply and many other economic variables including changes in interest rates. Although the methodology employed in his study has been criticized by others for its low power, other studies using different econometric techniques have found evidence consistent with many of his results. These studies will be considered in more detail later. Also much of the early work ignored the implications of informationally efficient capital markets whose importance for testing macroeconomic relationships Mishkin (1978) demonstrates.[1]

## 2 Review of the Empirical Literature

It is not the purpose of this chapter to provide an exhaustive survey of the literature in this area. Rather, the purpose of this chapter is to examine, from both an economic and an econometric perspective, the empirical support (or lack thereof) for various widely held macroeconomic beliefs. Particular attention is directed to ascertaining whether unanticipated changes in the money supply cause unanticipated changes in interest rates and other speculative prices. Simply stated, this chapter attempts to answer the question how important is macroeconomic information on changes in the money supply for financial market participants?

## 3 Money Supply Announcements and Changes in Interest Rates

No discussion of macroeconomic information would be complete without a consideration of the reaction of financial market prices to weekly money supply announcements. Each business Thursday, the Federal Reserve releases data on the money supply for various definitions. At present, the report is released at 4:30 p.m. New York time after most US markets are "closed."[2]

It is difficult today to understand how the weekly money supply announcement could exert such a powerful impact on market prices. Yet, in the not too distant past, the release of the weekly money supply announcement was anxiously awaited by many market participants. Unexpected changes in the weekly number often had a profound impact on speculative prices.

There is a substantial body of literature on the influence of Federal Reserve weekly money supply announcements on interest rates. Much of this work was done in the late 1970s and early 1980s. Not surprisingly, the principal focus of some of the literature, for instance Grossman (1981) and Urich and Wachtel (1981), was whether the Treasury bill market was informationally efficient with respect to Federal Reserve money supply announcements. These studies report evidence that the Treasury bill market was informationally efficient because of the differential and apparently rapid response of interest rates to anticipated and unanticipated money supply announcements. That is, the market responded quickly to unanticipated changes in the money supply contained in the announcements but not at all to anticipated changes (because that information was presumably already reflected in interest rates).

Urich and Wachtel (1981) report evidence of a positive relationship between unanticipated increases in the money supply and changes in interest rates which they attribute to the anticipation by market participants of future contractions of the money supply by the Fed in order to offset the increase. The policy anticipation hypothesis is simply the notion that unexpected increases in the money supply will be offset by decreases in the future causing an increase in the interest rate as liquidity is drained from the system. That is, market participants react to an expected future liquidity effect associated with an expected future Fed-induced change in the money supply. As with other studies, they report a larger effect after the Fed switched to a policy of targeting monetary aggregates.[3]

Several hypotheses have been advanced to explain the observed positive correlation between changes in short-term interest rates and unanticipated changes in the money supply. In addition to the policy anticipations or expected liquidity effect discussed above, two other hypotheses on the influence of money supply announcements on interest rates have received considerable attention. They are the inflation expectations and money demand (or real economic activity) effects.

Basically, the inflation expectations effect suggests that investors interpret an unanticipated increase in the money supply as an indication of higher future inflation. This means higher interest rates (and lower bond prices) if expected nominal interest rates include an expected inflation component. Conversely, an unanticipated decrease in the money supply indicates lower future inflation and lower nominal interest rates.

The money demand effect posits a linkage between money demand and future real economic activity. An unanticipated increase in the money supply is interpreted by investors as an indication of higher future real output and higher real interest rates.[4] Sheehan (1985) provides an extensive review of the empirical literature in this area and concludes that each of the three hypotheses might hold.

Urich and Wachtel (1984) examine the response of interest rates to the release of government economic reports on inflation (both the producer price index (PPI) and the consumer price index (CPI)) in order to distinguish between the policy anticipations and inflation expectations hypotheses. They report an absence of relationship between unanticipated CPI reports and changes in interest rates and a significant positive relationship between unanticipated PPI reports and changes in interest rates. However, the relationship between changes in interest rates and (monthly) PPI reports is weaker than the relationship found for (weekly) money supply announcements. Moreover, Urich and Wachtel find a differential response of the overnight Fed funds rate to the two sources of macroeconomic information. They interpret their results as providing corroborating evidence, of a sort, for the view that the operative effect is the policy anticipation effect.

Urich and Wachtel (1984) report a larger money supply announcement effect after October 6, 1979, than before it. In an examination of preannouncement data, Urich and Wachtel also report evidence of a significant liquidity effect. They state:

> If we move several weeks prior to the announcement, we find the actual money supply change has a significant negative effect on interest rates. This effect corresponds to a liquidity effect or the standard macroeconomic result that an increase in the money supply leads to lower interest rates which takes place when open market operations affect reserves and prior to the actual change in the money supply and its subsequent announcement. The combined liquidity effect in the second to fourth week implies that a one billion dollar money supply increase reduces [short-term] interest rates by about 1 1/2 basis points.
>
> (pp. 1186–7)

Cornell (1983a) provides an analysis that is both more extensive and illuminating in that it is not limited to Treasury bills but also examines other segments of the fixed-income market. This allows Cornell to examine whether money supply announcements have a differential impact on interest rates over the yield curve as the policy anticipation hypothesis would predict. That is, short rates would be affected by expected future liquidity effects while long rates would not. However, if the inflation expectations hypothesis is correct then an increase in the future rate of inflation could affect both short and long rates. Cornell uses both time series models and survey data to develop proxies for the expected component of money supply announcements.

Cornell reports positive correlation between unexpected changes in the money supply and both short- and long-term interest rates for both methods of determining expectations.[5] Moreover, Cornell reports more significant results for the post October 6, 1979, period than for the preceding period.

Cornell also investigates the money demand effect. He rejects this explanation because the observed variation in interest rates due to money supply announcements exceeds variation in the expected real rate of interest reported in other studies. Cornell states:

> Is it reasonable for investors to conclude that the *ex ante* real rate will be higher over the next 30 years on the basis of 1 week's money supply announcement, only to reverse their conclusion the following week? Such behavior seems particularly irrational in the light of the fact that the capital stock, time preferences, and investment opportunities, factors to which Fama and Gibbons attribute variation in the *ex ante* real rate, are known to evolve slowly over time....
>
> (p. 18)

Cornell rejects the inflation expectations hypothesis as unconvincing. He concludes:

> [We are left] with no explanation of why the market participants react so violently to short-term announcements. It hardly seems rational for an investor to adjust his long-run inflation expectations significantly on the basis of 1 week's announcement. One possible explanation for this apparently irrational behavior is that the announcement of October 6, 1979, had a far greater influence on investors than has been realized....
>
> (p. 21)

Part of the explanation for the market's seemingly irrational reaction to weekly money supply reports may lie in the confusion of many market participants between changes in the money supply and changes in the rate of growth of the money supply. An unexpected change in the money stock is relevant information to market participants only if that change is expected to affect the *permanent* rate of growth of the money supply.[6]

Roley and Walsh (1985) also examine the response of both long-term bonds and short-term money market securities to the unanticipated component of money supply announcements. Essentially, they try to reconcile the observed large response of long-term bonds to unanticipated changes in the money supply (reported by Cornell) with the policy anticipations hypothesis. They contend that the large response of long-term bonds reflects shocks to money demand that persist over time and a Fed policy of counteracting such shocks over time.

Many of the commonly cited empirical studies of the impact of the money supply announcement on changes in speculative prices have been criticized for their use of Money Market Services (MMS) expectations data. Clark, Joines, and Phillips (1988) have argued that MMS survey respondents overlooked a monthly seasonal component of the *seasonally adjusted* money supply which is induced by social security payments. As a result, MMS forecasts of the money supply contain systematic errors and this may explain the observed negative correlation between changes in interest rates and the anticipated money supply. Deaves, Melino, and Pesando (1987) disagree with this explanation. Using both US and Canadian data they report evidence which suggests that adjusting for the systematic bias in consensus expectations of money supply data does not eliminate the negative relationship between anticipated changes in the money supply and changes in interest rates.

The question naturally arises why the reaction to the unanticipated component of the money supply has decreased since the early 1980s. Clark, Joines, and Phillips (1988) advance two potential explanations for this phenomenon: a shift in Fed operating strategy, or that money supply announcements simply contain less information. The latter might reflect a change in the accounting system for reserves. In February 1984, the Fed switched from a policy of lagged reserve accounting to contemporary reserve accounting. As Clark, Joines, and Phillips note this meant that potential information on reserve imbalances was no longer revealed. They state:

> According to this second hypothesis, the switch to contemporaneous reserve accounting from lagged reserve accounting resulted in the elimination of important information from weekly money supply announcements. Absent this information, financial markets no longer react in a systematic fashion to the release of money stock estimates. This hypothesis is consistent with the trivial estimated cefficients on unexpected money changes since February 1984....
>
> (p. 276)

In order to separate the influences of money demand and money supply on interest rates, Hardouvelis (1987) examines the relationship between reserve announcements and changes in interest rates.[7] Given that the Federal Reserve controls reserves, unanticipated changes in reserves could be interpreted as an indication about Fed-intended changes in the money supply. That is, one can ignore the money demand hypothesis. Hardouvelis reports the evidence in support of a liquidity effect. He concludes:

> The unanticipated components of nonborrowed and borrowed reserves reflected surprises about *Fed supply behavior*. Thus, hypotheses that originate in real business-cycle models and attempt to explain a correlation outside the sphere of discretionary monetary policy are not potential candidates for the observed interest rate reactions to announced changes in reserves. This is why we can claim that the expected change in the real rate of interest is due to an *expected* liquidity effect.
>
> (p. 421)

Cornell (1983b), in contrast, fails to find a relationship between unanticipated changes in high-powered money (i.e. the monetary base) and changes in interest rates. He concludes:

> The regression coefficients confirm, therefore, that innovations in the monetary base have little impact on interest rates. This is somewhat surprising in light of Fama's [1982] finding that the base is more highly correlated with inflation.
>
> (p. 21)

Joines (1991) reports similar results to Cornell's. *A priori* one would expect to observe a closer relationship between changes in the monetary base and changes in interest rates if those theories which posit an exogenously determined money supply are correct.

Joines (1991) examines a variant of the real economic activity hypothesis using a model advanced by Siegel (1985) in which money is neutral and prices are perfectly flexible. While he reports an absence of relationship between unanticipated changes in the monetary base and changes in interest rates, Joines is unable to provide statistical support for two other testable implications of the model.

## 4 Money Supply Announcements and Changes in Other Speculative Prices

The question naturally arises as to what is the influence of money supply announcements on other asset prices. How do changes in the money supply affect stock prices and exchange rates for instance?

Ito and Roley (1987) present evidence of a differential impact on the yen–dollar exchange rate of the unanticipated component of US and Japanese money supply announcements and other sources of macroeconomic data. They report greater responsiveness to US macroeconomic data and indicate a positive relationship between money supply surprises and the foreign exchange value of the dollar. This is explained as the dollar responding to higher real interest rates (i.e. the expected liquidity effect).

Engel and Frankel (1984) note that the inflation expectations hypothesis suggests a negative relationship between the foreign exchange value of the dollar and unanticipated changes in the money supply. Given that they report evidence that the dollar is positively correlated with money announcement surprises they reject the inflation expectations hypothesis in favor of the hypothesis that the real rate of interest rose.

Barnhart (1988) examines the influence of money supply announcements and other economic reports on commodity futures prices in order to distinguish between the inflationary expectations and policy anticipation hypotheses. He reports evidence in support of the policy anticipation hypothesis.

Both Sheehan (1985) and Cornell (1983b) provide a summary of the effects of money supply announcements on various classes of speculative prices for each of the major hypotheses that have been advanced to explain the phenomena. In addition, Cornell advances a fourth hypothesis, which he calls the risk premium hypothesis, to explain observed relationships.

Data on money supply announcements have also been used to ascertain whether information on money supply changes influences changes in stock returns. Studies by Berkman (1978), Lynge (1981) and Pearce and Roley (1983) all suggest the existence of a significant negative relationship between changes in the money supply and changes in stock prices or returns. Further, the Berkman and Pearce and Roley articles suggest that it is the unanticipated change in the money supply which exerts the impact on stock prices. This finding is consistent with what one would expect in an informationally efficient capital market where new information is immediately impounded into asset prices. It is also superficially consistent with the view that an unanticipated increase in the rate of growth in the money supply is inflationary.

Contrary to the findings reported in many of the above studies concerning the magnitude of unexpected changes in the money supply on the fixed-income market, Vance and Roley do not detect a statistically significant difference in the influence of unexpected money supply changes on common stock prices in the pre- and post-October 6, 1979, period. Not only does this result have implications for the Lucas hypothesis about economic relationships being sensitive to policy shifts, it also raises the question of why bonds behaved differently in these two periods and stocks did not.

## 5 Changes in the Money Supply and Interest Rates

Mishkin (1982) examines the relationship between unanticipated changes in the rate of growth of the money supply and unanticipated changes in short-term nominal interest rates. Mishkin's purpose is to determine the efficacy of monetary policy in an informationally efficient capital market. Mishkin examines data covering the period 1959–76. He reports evidence of a statistically significant positive coefficient for the unanticipated changes in the rate of growth of money. These results lead Mishkin to reject the notion of a Keynesian liquidity effect.

In a similar study, Mishkin (1981) examines the relationship between unanticipated changes in the growth rate of the money supply (both $M_1$ and $M_2$ were employed) and the unanticipated change in long-term nominal interest rates. Although Mishkin reports positive coefficients for unanticipated changes in the $M_1$ growth rate they are not statistically significant at the 5 percent level. Mishkin notes that even if the variables were statistically significant the magnitude is sharply lower than certain well-known Keynesian structural econometric models would predict. In conclusion, Mishkin states that (subject to methodological caveats):

> *There is little empirical support here for the view that increases in the money stock are negatively correlated with changes in long-term interest rates. ...*
>
> (p. 50; emphasis in original)

In an interesting study, Litterman and Weiss (1985) examine the influence of changes in the money supply on changes in interest rates, inflation, and output in order to ascertain the importance of money in explaining business cycles. According to many monetary theories money exerts an influence on the real economy through changes in the real rate of interest. Thus, the question naturally arises as to whether the real rate of interest is exogenous with respect to money and other variables. Litterman and Weiss present evidence that the real rate of interest is exogenous with respect to money, prices, and output. They interpret their finding as "cast[ing] strong doubt on the Keynesian notion that monetary policy has affected output through changes in the real rate of interest" (p. 136). Exogeneity of the real rate also has adverse implications for the rational expectations model advanced by Lucas (1972) in which unanticipated changes in the money supply alter perceived real returns among *individual* economic agents.

Moreover, Litterman and Weiss suggest that unanticipated changes in the real rate of interest do not explain much of the variation in future output. Indeed, they note that unanticipated changes in the nominal interest rate or in expected inflation explain a greater portion of the variance of output than unanticipated changes in the real rate of interest. They state:

> This striking change in the variance decomposition means that while an unexpected increase in nominal interest rates, given current values for output and money, implies a major revision in the forecast of output, an unexpected increase in the real rate signals essentially no change in the prospect for output. ...
>
> (p. 144)

This result suggests that even if the central bank controlled changes in the real rate of interest such control would not have a discernible impact on output.[8]

Sims (1980) examines the role of money on economic activity in the United States. He finds that unanticipated changes in the money supply are not important in explaining changes in industrial production and prices when unanticipated changes in the short-term interest rate are included in tests.[9] Indeed, Sims (1980) states:

> When a short interest rate is added to the vector autoregression, the remarkable similarity in dynamics between [the postwar and interwar] periods persists, but the central role of the money stock surprises [i.e. unexpected changes] evaporates for the postwar period. While there are potential monetarist explanations for such an observation, ... [a] nonmonetarist explanation of the dynamics, based on the role of expectations in investment behavior, seems to fit the estimated dynamics better. That this explanation, which is consistent with a passive role for money, could account for so much of the observed postwar relation between money stock and income may raise doubts about the monetarist interpretation even of the interwar data.
>
> (p. 250)

Sims advances a model where rapid adjustments in the capital stock are costly to explain the observed relationships noted above. Essentially, Sims suggests that expected decline in the future real marginal product of physical capital causes both the amount and price of investments to fall. This, in turn, causes the interest rate to rise in an environment where the price of capital goods declines slowly over some time interval. Sims argues:

> This theory explains the similarity in response to interest shocks across [the interwar and postwar] periods by similarity in the short-run supply elasticity for capital goods and similarity in short-run yield

> elasticities of savings. This seems more plausible to me than the similarity of persistent patterns of monetary policy errors which the monetary theories seem to require. The theory does not directly explain why price responses to interest and to money-stock innovations should be different .... For monetarist theories, the absence of price response to a change in money stock following an interest-rate surprise does seem a problem.
>
> (p. 256)

In a fascinating paper that received much criticism, Pierce (1977) reports a virtual absence of relationship between a number of important economic variables. By prewhitening economic time series, Pierce is able to relate the relevant components from a financial economics perspective (i.e. the unanticipated components).[10] He reports an astonishingly low degree of relationship for many economic time series. Of most interest for present purposes is his finding of an absence of relationship between changes in the money supply and changes in interest rates. It should be noted that the econometric technique (cross correlation of the residuals from economic times series) that Pierce employs is controversial. Hsiao (1977), for instance, contends that the Granger–Sims tests of econometric exogeneity have little power.

In a different sphere, Evans (1978) examines whether the money supply was endogenously or exogenously determined during the German hyperinflation of the 1920s. He concludes that the evidence is consistent with an endogenously determined money supply.

## 6 The Behavior of Real Interest Rates

As noted above, changes in the real rate of interest represent the principal means by which the monetary authority influences the real economy. If expected inflation and the *ex ante* real interest rate are related (as both Mundell and Darby contend) then monetary policy on inflation may also impact the real economy through its impact on inflation.[11] Indeed, one could argue that one measure of the influence of active monetary policy is reflected in the observed variation of short-term interest rates.[12]

In his classic article on monetary policy, Friedman (1970) contends that the real interest rate, empirically speaking, has been relatively constant over time in the United States at least.[13] Further, given the mobility of capital across national markets, this would suggest that the real rate of interest has been constant across countries, for otherwise exploitable arbitrage opportunities would arise.

The equity premium puzzle of Mehra and Prescott (1985) which was discussed in chapter 3 prompted Siegel (1992) to examine the behavior of real interest rates in the UK and the United States over a longer time period. Siegel reports higher real rates of interest outside the period of Mehra and Prescott's sample but finds that the return on equity was essentially unchanged. This leads Siegel to suggest that the large equity premium observed by Mehra and Prescott may not persist.

In his study of short-term nominal interest rates as predictors of expected inflation, Fama (1975) reports that virtually all of the variation in short-term interest rates is attributable to variation of expectations of inflation. That is, the real interest rate is approximately constant. Fama finds that, on average, changes in nominal interest rates vary with changes in observed inflation as measured by the CPI. The Fama study supports the Fisher hypothesis of a one-to-one correspondence between changes in expected inflation and changes in expected real interest rates.

The findings of Fama are controversial. The notion of constancy in the real rate of interest is disturbing because the hypothesis is stated with respect to the *before-tax* real interest rate. Frequent changes in marginal tax rates in the United States suggest the potential for significant changes in the expected after-tax real interest rate. Put differently, if Friedman and Fama are *both* correct (with respect to the constancy of real interest rates), then this would suggest that both fiscal and monetary policy actions exert little, if any, influence on the behavior of the real interest rate. That is, one implication of a constant real rate of interest is that there should be no discernible liquidity effect.

Empirical tests of the behavior of the *ex ante* real interest rate are impeded by the fact that the expected real rate of interest is difficult to ascertain. Similar comments apply to expected inflation.

Joines (1977) suggests that Fama's results may be due to the choice of the CPI rather than the wholesale price index (the predecessor to the PPI). Nelson and Schwert (1977) dispute Fama's contention that the real interest rate is constant.

Fama and Gibbons (1982) present evidence that changes in the real rate follow a random walk. Fama and Gibbons also report evidence of a negative relationship between inflation and expected interest rates.

Litterman and Weiss (1985) reject Fama's (1975) finding of constancy of the real interest rate. However, Litterman and Weiss provide some evidence in support of Fama and Gibbons' assertion that changes in the real rate of interest follow a random walk.

## 7 The Early Literature on Money Supply and Interest Rates

The nature of scientific inquiry is that the apparent validity of various propositions changes when conflicting evidence emerges. Consequently, there are articles in the empirical economics literature which purport to provide evidence of the existence of the interest rate effects predicted by the various monetary theories discussed in chapter 4. These articles helped to persuade an earlier generation of economists that a strong relationship between changes in the money supply and interest rates existed. It is instructive to consider some of that literature in more detail.

Gibson (1970) attempts to assess the differential effects of monetary policy on interest rates during the period 1947–66. It is hypothesized that the total effect of money on interest rates may be divided into three separate effects: (1) liquidity, (2) income, and (3) price expectations. Gibson attempts to measure these separate effects through regression analysis. Regressions, in seriatim, of the Treasury bill rate, the Treasury bond rate, and the rate on AAA corporate bonds on coincident and past values of the growth rate in the narrowly defined money supply $M_1$ (and, in turn, in the more broadly defined money supply $M_2$) were run on the levels and in first-difference form. Using seasonally adjusted monthly and quarterly data for both interest rates and money supply series, Gibson concludes: "The estimates obtained here show that a change in the money stock produces an immediate negative liquidity effect on market interest rates, also produces (only a little later) positive effects which tend to offset the initial negative influence."[14]

In reviewing Gibson's evidence one finds high adjusted $R^2$s accompanied by extremely low Durbin–Watson (DW) statistics for the regressions on the levels (e.g. $R^2 = 0.883$ and DW = 0.074) corresponding to a dramatic decrease in the $R^2$s and an increase in the DW statistics for the regressions in first-difference form (e.g. the $R^2$ and DW of the previously reported regression in first-difference form are 0.103 and 1.429 respectively). From an economic perspective, the appropriate specification of the regression equation would, in this case, be in first-difference form.[15] That is, economic interest centers on the effect of a change in the growth rate of money on the change in interest rates and not on the relation between the growth rate of money and the level of the interest rate.

Further, one would be primarily interested in the effect of an unanticipated change in the money supply on the change in the interest rate. One possible source of information useful in predicting future values of the monetary growth rate is contained in the past sequence or time series of the monetary growth rate. Thus, the anticipated monetary growth rate would be one that fully exploits all information contained in the time series of past values of the monetary growth rate. In addition, information outside that contained in the past time series of the monetary growth rate might be used to forecast future values of the monetary growth rate if the appropriate model which investors use to forecast future values of the monetary growth rate were known. In the absence of such knowledge, prediction of future monetary growth rates based solely on the information contained in the past time series provides a "weak-form" test. From a purely econometric perspective, it is important to remove any autocorrelation present in either series prior to relating them in a regression framework in order to avoid the spurious regression phenomenon noted by Granger and Newbold (1974). The presence of autocorrelated errors in regression analysis leads to inefficient estimates of the regression coefficients, suboptimal forecasts using the regression and invalid $t$ and $F$ ratios.[16] In fact, Gibson's evidence may be largely explained by his failure to account adequately for the serial correlation in the data.

The DW statistic is a measure of first-order autocorrelation only. First-differencing the levels sometimes is sufficient to remove the autocorrelation present in the series *if* it is primarily of first order. It is obvious that the process of first-differencing did not remove all of the autocorrelation present in the series in view of the low DW statistics for the regression equations in first-difference form. It should be noted that Gibson does not obtain individually significant *t* statistics for the coefficients of past values. The cumulative value is significant, however. Gibson's argument for a lagged effect of monetary growth rates on interest rates centers on a "significant" *F* statistic for the subset of past values. However, the presence of autocorrelated errors invalidates the significance of the *F* statistic anyway. Further, the omission of relevant variables from the regression equation might induce an apparent lagged relationship.[17] Temporal aggregation of the monthly data to a quarterly basis yields higher $R^2$s and lower DW statistics throughout. However, the increase in $R^2$ is purely mechanical and occurs anytime one temporally aggregates data that have positive autocorrelation.[18] Further, Gibson's use of seasonally adjusted data (both the interest rate and money supply scrics are seasonally adjusted) casts doubt on his results. The perils of the use of seasonally adjusted data in general and the money supply in particular have been pointed out by Plosser (1976) and Laffer and Miles (1977) respectively. From the evidence Gibson presents it appears likely that the regression equations are misspecified. In summary, Gibson's evidence for the presence of a significant liquidity, income, or price-level effect associated with a change in the quantity of money is weak at best, since the estimates are not measured very precisely, and nonexistent at worst.

Cagan and Gandolfi (1969) attempt to infer the lag in monetary policy through examination of the dependence of the coincident change in the interest rate on coincident and lagged changes in the values of the monetary growth rate. Monthly data on the commercial paper rate and monetary growth rate (presumably $M_2$) covering the period 1910–65 are used. The regression equation is specified in first-difference form. In a regression containing 38 lagged values of the change in the monetary growth rate they report that 19 of the first 23 coefficients are significant at the 5 percent level although a weak overall relationship is indicated by the low $R^2$ of 0.081. They conclude that a change in the monetary growth rate affects a change in the interest rate with a long lag.

Unlike Gibson's study referred to above, Cagan and Gandolfi employ the correct specification of the regression equation (i.e. in first-difference form). They mistakenly argue, however, that this is equivalent to relating the unanticipated change in the money supply to the change in the interest rate. Ignoring sources of information other than that contained in the past time series of observations of the monetary growth rate for the moment, the first-difference form yields an unanticipated change only if the first differences themselves follow a white noise process.

Unfortunately, Cagan and Gandolfi do not report a DW statistic in their study. If, as in Gibson's study, there is serial correlation present in the monetary growth rate series then one must conclude that Cagan and Gandolfi were unsuccessful in their attempt to relate "unanticipated" changes in the monetary growth rate to changes in the interest rate. Further, the presence of serially correlated errors in the regression equation would invalidate the significance of the *F* statistic (which incidentally was also not reported but at least can be calculated from the information provided) for the regression as a whole. Of course, if there are sources of information useful in predicting future values of the monetary growth rate outside that contained in the past time series alone, then even the complete absence of autocorrelation in the series may not produce unanticipated values in the first differences. Once again, the presence of significant lags could be the result of omitted variables.

Even if one accepts Cagan's and Gandolfi's interpretations as evidence of a significant lagged effect of the growth rate of money on changes in interest rates one would be surprised by the negligible economic impact they report. For instance, a 1 percentage point change in the monetary growth rate leads to an initial *decline* of the interest rate of approximately *two* basis points. The net effect over 38 *months* is an *increase* in the interest rate of about *two* basis points.[19]

To emphasize this last point, suppose one believes the Cagan and Gandolfi evidence. Then in order for the Federal Reserve to lower interest rates by 1 percentage point it would have to increase the rate of growth of the money supply from *x* percentage points to *x* percentage points plus 50 percentage points.[20]

Neoclassical monetary theory is fundamentally a theory of absolute prices which posits that a change in the money supply leads to a roughly proportional change in prices (holding both output and the demand for money constant). Recall that these are regressions on changes in the nominal interest rate and consequently should accurately reflect assessments of future changes in the purchasing power of money associated with a change in the money supply (if the capital market is efficient and changes in the money supply have a causal influence on prices). Even if one assumes that the entire net increase in interest rates associated with an increase in the monetary growth rate is solely attributable to an increase in prices then Cagan's and Gandolfi's evidence would suggest a negligible impact on prices over a period as long as 38 months.

## 8 The Empirical Relationship Between Money and Stock Returns

Monetary policy actions are presumed to affect changes in speculative prices besides interest rates. A fairly extensive literature exists, which purports to present evidence indicating a relationship between changes in the money supply and stock prices or stock returns.[21] With the exception of two studies that will be considered here, most of the empirical studies in this area have presented evidence of a lagged effect of money on stock prices. These studies have been previously examined in detail by both Cooper (1971, 1974) and Rozeff (1974) and were found wanting from both an economic and econometric perspective and consequently will not be re-examined here.

Cooper (1971) recognizes the disparity between the implications of neoclassical quantity theory concerning the influence of lagged values of money on stock returns and the implications of efficient capital market theory. He then advances a model, which he calls SQ-EM, which is consistent with both the simple quantity theory of money and efficient capital markets. Cooper examines the relationship between money supply changes and stock returns using cross-spectral analysis. The evidence he presents appears to indicate that stock returns lead changes in the money supply over low frequencies; however, over high frequencies the reverse is true (albeit with a very short lag). Cooper interprets this as evidence of causality flowing from changes in the money supply to stock returns. This dichotomy is essential to Cooper's inference that high frequency data are noise while low frequency relationships represent what is predictable since it allows him to distinguish the SQ-EM model from the case of an endogenous money supply. To support this interpretation, Cooper examines the relationship between past, future, and coincident changes in the money supply and stock returns using regression analysis. Using temporally aggregated data $R^2$ rises from 0.07 at the monthly level to 0.16 at the quarterly level to 0.52 at the annual level. Cooper concludes: "The very low $R^2$ from both regressions indicate little correlation between [stock] returns and money changes for monthly data. The spectral results indicated that most of the correlation between money and returns is in the low frequency range."

In a similar study, Rozeff (1974) investigates whether significant lags exist between the change in the money supply and stock returns. Rozeff distinguishes between a monetary model (which he calls "the predictive model") where only lagged changes in money influence changes in stock prices and a monetary model ("the nonpredictive model") where only contemporaneous changes in money influence changes in stock prices. The latter is consistent with efficient capital market theory while the former is not. Rozeff uses regression analysis (and monthly data) to distinguish between the two models.

Rozeff finds (as did Cooper) that lagged changes in money are not significant and consequently rejects the predictive monetary model. However, in a regression of the coincident and future values of a prewhitened monetary growth rate series Rozeff finds only two significant coefficients, both of which are future values. Rather than conclude that this is evidence of causality flowing from stock returns to changes in the monetary growth rate, he argues that this is evidence of market efficiency (where information in addition to that contained in the past time series of the monetary growth rate is utilized) with an endogenously determined money supply. Rozeff concludes (on the basis of this and other regressions) that the "nonpredictive" model is supported by the evidence he presents. Further, it appears that Rozeff views his results as a reconciliation of efficient capital market theory and neoclassical monetary theory.

The reconciliation is incomplete, however. From an economic perspective one must question the significance of Rozeff's results. As was previously noted, neoclassical monetary theory is above all a theory of absolute prices – which essentially posits that an increase in the money supply results in a roughly proportional increase in the price level (assuming output and the demand for money remain constant). If the capital market is efficient and investors are compensated for expected inflation then the increase in prices induced by an increase in the money supply should be fully, correctly, and immediately reflected in the expected return on equity. Thus, a 1 percentage point increase in the rate of change in prices should correspond to a 1 percentage point increase in the expected return on equity.[22] However, Rozeff's results imply that a 1 percentage point increase in the money supply results in, at most, an increase of from 3 to 10 basis points in the return on equity rather than 100 basis points.

Assuming that expectations are formed in a rational manner then the low value that Rozeff obtains leaves one to consider the reconciliation as incomplete. Either a new theory of absolute prices is needed or the capital market is not efficient in assessing future rates of inflation with respect to stock returns.[23] Evidence by Fama (1975) appears to indicate that the capital market assesses future inflation rates fairly well at least for short-term interest rates.[24] Asymmetry in the assessments of future rates of inflation is, of course, possible although *a priori* it would appear unlikely.

## 9 Short-Run Control of the Nominal Money Stock

In order to exert effective control over short-term interest rates the central bank must exercise short-run control over the nominal money stock.[25] This means, in terms of the cross-spectrum, that a strong low frequency relationship between the monetary base and the money supply is not sufficient to indicate effective short-run control of the nominal money stock by the central bank. Rather, there must also be a strong high frequency relationship between the monetary base and the money supply for the central bank to have proximate control of the money stock. Similarly, the presence of a strong relationship between monetary base and $M_1$ or $M_2$ at both high and low frequencies may nevertheless be consistent with an endogenously determined money supply if the appropriate measure of the money stock is some higher level monetary aggregate which is not under the control of the central bank. Alternatively, if the money supply is more appropriately defined as only currency, as Fama (1978) and Tobin (1963) appear to argue, then a strong relationship between other (noncurrency) components of the monetary base and $M_1$ would not necessarily be indicative of central bank influence over the nominal money stock.[26] Or, of course, there simply may not be a causal relationship between changes in the money supply (however defined) and changes in either interest rates or the rate of change of prices.[27]

A brief review of the literature on this topic is presented below. Several previous studies have empirically examined the issue of Federal Reserve control over the nominal money stock (e.g. Andersen, 1968; Fand, 1972; Rutner, 1975). In general, these studies have indicated that the Federal Reserve appears to exercise control over the nominal money stock although the relevant horizon of control (i.e. short run or long run) remains a point of controversy. Of especial interest to this chapter are the study by Andersen which examines this question using data on Federal Reserve security holdings and the study by Rutner.

Andersen investigates whether the Federal Reserve has effective short-run control over the nominal money stock given the presence of significant stochastic disturbances of a seasonal and nonseasonal nature in both total and free reserves. Using both weekly and monthly data on changes in Federal Reserve security holdings and changes in free and total reserves for the period 1954–65, Andersen finds that the Federal Reserve through its "defensive" open market operations has reduced the variation in both total and free reserves. Further, he finds that the direction of correlation (–0.92 and –0.96), timing, and magnitude of defensive open market operations support the conclusion that the Federal Reserve was successful in offsetting short-run variations in reserves (both total and free). Andersen then interprets his results as evidence of a "high degree" of short-run control over the money stock by the Federal Reserve.

The central problem with Andersen's article is that he does not adequately account for the serial correlation present in the series under examination, and consequently the reported correlations may be entirely spurious.

Rutner examines the relationship between changes in a "whitened" monetary base series (both adjusted and unadjusted) and changes in a "whitened" money stock series (both $M_1$ and $M_2$). The purpose of prewhitening is of course to remove that part of each time series which is predictable from knowledge of its past alone. This is necessary in order to avoid any spurious correlation that might result from the fact that both series have "upward trends" in *both* the levels and the first differences. Rutner employs both regression analysis and cross-spectral analysis in relating the monetary base and the money supply. Using regression analysis he finds an extremely weak relationship between changes in the logarithm of each series (after each has been "detrended"). For example, the adjusted $R^2$ for a regression between the unadjusted base and $M_2$ is only 0.0508. This compares with a much stronger relationship indicated between the two series when the common trend has not been adequately taken into account (i.e. only first differencing). In the example noted above, the adjusted $R^2$ is 0.4853 in this case. Using cross-spectral analysis, Rutner reinforces the interpretation of an absence of relationship at high frequencies but does find the presence of a high degree of coherence at low frequencies, Rutner concludes: "[I]n the short-run there is no significant relationship between the money stock and either the adjusted or unadjusted monetary base. For intermediate time lengths, though, money is highly correlated with both the adjusted and unadjusted base" (p. 9).

Although Rutner prewhitens each series (presumably) using different filters and performs a regression he does not conduct a modified Sims test since he fails to include future values as well as past and coincident values. Rutner employs a high-order autoregressive filter to whiten the monetary base and money supply series rather than some lower order mixed autoregressive integrated moving average process. Unfortunately, he does not reveal the order of the autoregressive filter that he employs nor whether the underlying data are adjusted for any seasonality present in the series. It is not clear that a high order autoregressive model represents the most parsimonious process, however. Other studies, for example Cooper (1971) and Rozeff (1974), have indicated that a third-order autoregressive process seems to govern the seasonally adjusted narrowly defined money supply. However, Zellner and Palm (1975) find that a (313) model is more appropriate for the log of $M_1$ than a (310) model when a likelihood ratio test is employed. Further, using the same procedure to decide among alternative models for the log of the monetary base they find that "a random walk model (010) performs as well as more complicated models on the basis of the large sample $\chi^2$ tests ...." Unfortunately, a more detailed analysis of Rutner's paper is impeded by the fact that he only reports the $R^2$ in his regression analyses and the coherency (with an abbreviated report on lead–lag relationships at various cycle lengths) in his spectral analyses.

Zellner and Palm (1975) report that the monetary base appears to follow a random walk with drift and that the drift parameter appeared to have changed in 1963. The question naturally arises as to whether Federal Reserve monetary policy was random during this period. Similarly, Plosser (1976) reports that the seasonally and otherwise *un*adjusted monetary base appears to follow an IMA(1) process.

Keep in mind that monetary theories contend that the central bank exercises *short-run* control over the nominal money stock. That is, the principal mechanism of transmission of monetary policy on the economy is by changing the supply of high-powered money. If the Fed does not have short-run control over high-powered money how can it exercise control over short-term interest rates? In terms of the effect(s) of changes in the money supply on interest rates, long-run control over the nominal money supply is tantamount to no effect on short-term interest rates.

## 10 Conclusions

There is a substantial amount of evidence (both casual and scientific) that significant changes in speculative prices were frequently associated with the release of weekly money supply figures during the period from October 1979 to February 1984. The evidence of significant announcement effects on changes in speculative prices prior to October 6, 1979, is mixed. Unanticipated changes in the money supply were positively correlated with changes in nominal interest rates and the foreign exchange value of the US dollar, and negatively associated with changes in stock prices. The explanation for the observed announcement effects on changes in interest rates remains controversial.[28] Similarly, the literature fails to explain satisfactorily the general absence of response of speculative prices to unanticipated changes in the money supply since 1984 nor why long-term bonds should react so much to weekly money supply announcements.[29]

Unlike the evidence of significant announcement effects on changes in speculative prices associated with unanticipated changes in the money supply, the evidence of the influence of changes in the money supply on changes in interest rates, prices, and output is less clear-cut when somewhat more temporally aggregated data are used. Indeed, many widely held beliefs among market participants concerning the effects of changes in the money supply on changes in speculative prices have surprisingly little support in the empirical economics literature. In particular, there is little evidence that unanticipated changes in the money supply affect unanticipated changes in real interest rates. That is, there is little evidence of a liquidity effect. This result is consistent with the evidence in the financial economics literature that most of the variation in the real rate is small relative to variation in expected inflation.

There is also little evidence that innovations in the monetary base explain unanticipated changes in the interest rate. Indeed, it appears that changes in the monetary base follow a random walk with drift. This raises a question of whether the Fed actually controls the money supply. A passive monetary policy is consistent with the evidence Sims (1980) presents that unanticipated changes in the money supply do *not* explain changes in real output or prices. Not surprisingly, the influence of money on changes in interest rates, prices, and output remains controversial.

The apparent simultaneous existence of announcement effects on changes in interest rates associated with unanticipated changes in the money supply coupled with a dearth of evidence that changes in the money supply explain changes in real interest rates over the same period is puzzling. One potential explanation is that market participants are responding more to noise than to information. This suggests that an examination of the response of speculative prices to other Federal Reserve monetary policy actions and other sources of Fed macroeconomic information might be instructive. The market's response to Federal Reserve monetary policy actions is the subject of the next chapter.

## Appendix 5.1: The Effect of Omitted Variables on the Lag Structure

Before evaluating empirical analyses on the influence of changes in the money supply on changes in interest rates or other speculative prices, it is important to consider explicitly whether the reduced form equations in the model to be empirically examined are misspecified, i.e. whether relevant variables are ignored. In particular, should one expect changes in interest rates to be determined primarily by changes in the quantity of money (or more correctly its rate of growth) or are there other important variables that also act to determine changes in interest rate that have been omitted from the analysis?[30] If so, what is the effect of this omission on subsequent analysis?

Suppose one posits that changes in interest rates may be expressed as the output from a discrete dynamic linear transfer function model,[31] where open market operations and another (unspecified) variable represent the relevant inputs. This "true" relationship may be expressed as follows:[32]

$$\theta(L)y_t = \phi(L)x_{1t} + \phi(L)x_{2t} + a(L)u_t \tag{5.1}$$

In addition, let $x_{1t}$ and $x_{2t}$ be respectively described by the autoregessive integrated moving average models in the following equations:

$$\phi_3(L)x_{1t} = \phi_4(L)a_t \tag{5.2}$$

$$\phi_5(L)x_{2t} = \phi_6(L)a_{2t} \tag{5.3}$$

where $\theta$ and $\phi_i$, $i = 1, ..., 6$, are polynomials in the lag operator $L$, $y_t$ equals the change in the interest rate at time $t$, $x_{1t}$ equals open market operations (the change in Federal Reserve security holdings) at time $t$, $x_{2t}$ equals the omitted variable and $a_{1t}$, $a_{2t}$, and $u_t$ represent white noise. Further $a_{1t}$ and $a_{2t}$ are uncorrelated with each other.

Assuming the polynomials are invertible, one may solve equation (5.3) for $x_{2t}$ to obtain

$$x_{2t} = \phi_5^{-1}(L)\phi_6(L)a_{2t}. \tag{5.4}$$

Now substituting equation (5.4) into equation (5.1) yields

$$\theta(L)y_t = \phi_1(L)x_{1t} + \phi_2\phi_5^{-1}(L)\phi_6(L)a_{2t} + a(L)u_t. \tag{5.5}$$

Multiplying equation (5.5) by $\phi_5$ gives

$$\phi_5\theta(L)y_t = \phi_5\phi_1(L)x_{1t} + \phi_2\phi_6(L)a_{2t} + \phi_5 a(L)u_t. \tag{5.6}$$

If one estimates equation (5.6), then it is apparent that unless $\phi_5(L)$ is of degree zero the effect of omitting the variable $x_{2t}$ will be to increase the observed lag independent of the actual lag. The implications of the above result should be emphasized: (1) observed significant lags in the effect of changes in the money supply (or, for example, open market operations) on interest rates may be spurious, owing to the omission of important independent variables;[33] (2) in estimating equation (5.6) (or any equation where one has reason to believe that important variables may have been omitted) it is doubly important to allow for an adequate lag structure. It is important to note that if $a_{1t}$ and $a_{2t}$ are correlated with each other, then this will induce a correlation between $x_{1t}$ and the error term in equation (5.6) $x_{1t}$ would then appear as an "endogenous" variable.

## Notes

1 For instance, the relevant relationship in an informationally efficient capital market is often between unanticipated changes in economic variables and changes in speculative prices.

2 The report used to be released after the fixed income markets had closed but before the equity markets closed. At one point the weekly money supply announcements were made on Fridays instead of Thursdays. The release date was switched to Fridays on February 8, 1980, and subsequently switched back to Thursday a short time later.

The report is released after most US financial markets are closed in order to avoid disturbing them. Given that some US Treasury securities are traded around the clock this argument has lost some of its validity.

3 Urich and Wachtel (1981) state:

> Importantly, this variation [in the size of the announcement effects] is consistent with changes in the operating procedures of the Federal Reserve System. Larger announcement effects are found, as expected, when policy has emphasized the monetary aggregates and when the money supply deviates from target bands....
>
> (p. 1072)

4 Nichols, Small, and Webster (1983) advance a model with this result. Fama's (1982) article provides some empirical support for a money demand effect.

5 Cornell reports that when time series processes were used to determine expectations the 30 year bond index moved slightly less than half as much as the three month Treasury bill rate in response to an unanticipated change in the money supply.

6 Assuming, of course, that changes in the money supply affect changes in interest rates.

7 Friedman (1986) has argued that both the monetary base and $M_2$ are better measures for determining changes in the money supply than is the monetary aggregate, $M_1$.

8 Litterman and Weiss report a strong negative relationship between unanticipated changes in the real rate and unanticipated changes in the rate of inflation.

9 This result might understate money's influence if changes in the money supply had a significant influence on changes in the interest rate. Aware of this potential objection, Sims reports evidence of little

relationship between unanticipated changes in the money supply and unanticipated changes in interest rates.

10 This assumes, of course, that the prewhitening technique represents an effective way of separating anticipated and unanticipated information.

11 Canto, Joines, and Webb (1984) demonstrate that, under a system of progressive taxation on nominal income, money may not be neutral as inflation pushes individuals with higher nominal (but not necessarily real) incomes into higher tax brackets.

12 This assumes, of course, that the monetary authority does not pursue a policy of stabilizing short-term interest rates over time.

13 Friedman argues that monetary policy can exert an impact on real interest rates for short periods of time.

14 Gibson (1970, p. 453).

15 This statement should not be construed as suggesting that differencing always yields the appropriate specification of the regression equation or is somehow required to achieve a stationary series. Hendry (1977) observes that differencing "is not a universal panacea (no mechanical procedure ever is in econometrics)" (p. 195). Further, it is plausible to conceive of cases where one is interested in examining the relationship between the levels of the interest rate and the money supply.

16 Granger and Newbold (1974, p. 111).

17 See the appendix to this chapter for an illustration of the effects of omitted variables on lags.

18 See Zellner and Montmarquette (1971).

19 Unfortunately, Cagan and Gandolfi do not report a standard error so it is not possible to construct a prediction interval.

20 The implications of monetary theories such as the neoclassical theory might seem more compatible with the empirical evidence if the economy were at less than full employment. However, such theories do not usually admit the possibility of long-term unemployment of economic resources.

21 There is also a fairly extensive financial economics literature which examines the relationship between inflation and stock prices. Basically, it finds that stock prices are poor hedges against either anticipated or unanticipated inflation.

Just as changes in the money supply are believed to affect stock prices, changes in stock prices are believed to affect the quantity of money demanded. Using quarterly data, Friedman (1988) presents evidence showing that the real quantity of money demanded is a function of the levels of both lagged and contemporaneous real stock prices.

22 It is possible that a proportional increase in the money supply may represent a less than proportional increase in the price level owing to some type of "supply response" by holders of capital (i.e. they may accumulate more capital). It is likewise possible that it may represent a more than proportional response due to the taxation of nominal income. Darby (1975) advances such an argument.

23 It should be recognized that the capital asset pricing model and the arbitrage pricing theory are partial equilibrium rather than general equilibrium models. This is because such models assume that the risk-free interest rate evolves deterministically or is somehow exogenously determined. Fama (1977) observes that uncertainty in the evolution of the risk-free rate is inadmissible in the context of the capital asset pricing model of Sharpe and Lintner.

24 Fama and Schwert (1977) present some evidence that stock returns are negatively correlated with anticipated inflation.

25 Recall that neoclassical monetary theory suggests that the real money stock is endogenously determined.

26 If one accepts Tobin's (1963) distinction between "bank credit" created money (demand deposits) and "printing press" created money (fiat currency) then it is possible that there may be a relationship between changes in the supply of currency and prices or interest rates but not one between changes in some broader measure of the money supply (such as $M_1$ or $M_2$) and changes in prices or interest rates.

27 Sims (1972) and Pierce (1977) argue that the econometric exogeneity tests employed above may result in the observed absence of a "causal" relationship when one exists or reverse the apparent direction of "causation" in the presence of certain closed-loop control policies.

28 Sheehan (1985) concludes that there is evidence in support of the policy anticipations, inflation expectations, and money demand hypotheses.

29 Joines's (1991) argument that money supply figures contain less information after the switch to contemporaneous reserve accounting is plausible but not convincing.

30 During some periods Friedman (1972) has found that changes in money account for over half of the fluctuations in the nominal interest rate.

31 A discrete dynamic linear transfer function model is discrete in the sense that observations of both the input and output variables are recorded at discrete points in time, dynamic in the sense that the response of the output to the input may be delayed rather than immediate. The interested reader is referred to chapters 10 and 11 of Box and Jenkins (1976) for an extended discussion of transfer function analysis.

32 I am indebted to Professor Arnold Zellner for this example.

33 This may have some obvious implications for previous analyses in monetary economics that have claimed to have found extremely long significant lags.

## References


Andersen, L. C. 1968: "Federal Reserve Defensive Operations and Short-Run Control of the Money Stock," *Journal of Political Economy*, 76, March–April, 275–88.

Barnhart, S. W. 1988: "Commodity Futures Prices and Economic News: An Examination Under Alternative Monetary Regimes," *Journal of Futures Markets*, 8 (4), 483–510.

Berkman, N. G. 1978: "On the Significance of Weekly Changes in $M_1$," *New England Economic Review*, May–June, 5–22.

Box, G. E. P., and G. M. Jenkins 1976: *Time Series Analysis: Forecasting and Control*, San Francisco, CA: Holden-Day.

Cagan, P. and A. Gandolfi 1969: "The Lag in Monetary Policy as Implied by the Time Pattern of Monetary Effects on Interest Rates," *American Economic Review*, 59, May, 277–84.

Canto, V. A., D. H. Joines, and R. I. Webb 1984: "Taxation, Rational Expectations and the Neutrality of Money," *Journal of Macroeconomics*, 6 (1), Winter, 69–78.

Clark, T. A., D. H. Joines, and G. M. Phillips 1988: "Social Security Payments, Money Supply Announcements, and Interest Rates," *Journal of Monetary Economics*, 22, 257–78.

Cooper, R. Y. L. 1971: "Money and Stock Returns," Ph.D. dissertation, University of Chicago.

Cooper, R. Y. L. 1974: "Efficient Capital Markets and the Quantity Theory of Money," *Journal of Finance*, 29, June, 115–46.

Cornell, B. 1982: "Money Supply Announcements, Interest Rates, and Foreign Exchange," *Journal of International Money and Finance*, 1, August, 201–8.

Cornell, B. 1983a: "Money Supply Announcements and Interest Rates: Another View," *Journal of Business*, 56 (1), 1–23.

Cornell, B. 1983b: "The Money Supply Announcements Puzzle: Review and Interpretation," *American Economic Review*, 73, September, 644–57.

Darby, M. R. 1975: "The Financial and Tax Effects of Monetary Policy on Interest Rates," *Economic Inquiry*, 3, June, 266–76.

Deaves, R., A. Melino, and J. Pesando 1987: "The Response of Interest Rates to the Federal Reserve's Weekly Money Announcements: The Puzzle of Anticipated Money," *Journal of Monetary Economics*, 19, 393–404.

Engel, C., and J. Frankel 1984: "Why Interest Rates React to Money Announcements: An Explanation from the Foreign Exchange Market," *Journal of Monetary Economics*, 13, January, 31–9.

Evans, P. 1978: "Time Series and Structural Analysis of the German Hyperinflation," *International Economic Review*, 19, February, 195–210.

Fama, E.F. 1975: "Short Term Interest Rates as Predictors of Inflation," *American Economic Review*, 65, June, 269–82.

Fama, E. F. 1977: "Risk-Adjusted Discount Rates and Capital Budgeting Under Uncertainty," *Journal of Financial Economics*, 5, August, 3–24.

Fama, E. F. 1978: "Banking in a Theory of Finance," Mimeo, University of Chicago.

Fama, E. F. 1982: "Inflation, Output and Money," *Journal of Business*, 55, April, 201–32.

Fama, E., and M. Gibbons 1982: "Inflation, Real Returns and Capital Investment," *Journal of Monetary Economics*, 9, May, 297–323.

Fama, E. F., and G. W. Schwert 1977: "Asset Returns and Inflation," *Journal of Financial Economics*, 5, November, 113–45.

Fand, D. 1972: "Can the Central Bank Control the Nominal Money Stock?," in John T. Boorman and Thomas M. Havrilesky (eds), *Money Supply, Money Demand, and Macroeconomic Models*, Boston, MA: Allyn and Bacon, pp. 89–97.

Friedman, M. 1959: "The Demand for Money: Some Theoretical and Empirical Results," *Journal of Political Economy*, 68, August, 327–51.

Friedman, M. 1968: "The Role of Monetary Policy," *American Economic Review*, 58, March, 1–17.

Friedman, M. 1970: "A Theoretical Framework for Monetary Analysis," *Journal of Political Economy*, 78, March–April, 193–238.

Friedman, M. 1972: "Factors Affecting the Level of Interest Rates," in John T. Boorman and Thomas M. Havrilesky (eds), *Money Supply, Money Demand, and Macroeconomic Models*, Boston, MA: Allyn and Bacon, pp. 89–97.

Friedman, M. 1986: "$M_1$'s Hot Streak Gave Keynesians a Bad Idea," *Wall Street Journal*, September 18, A32.

Friedman, M. 1988: "Money and the Stock Market," *Journal of Political Economy*, 90 (2), 221–45.

Gibson, W. 1970: "Interest Rates and Monetary Policy," *Journal of Political Economy*, 78, May–June, 431–55.

Granger, C. W. J., and P. Newbold 1974: "Spurious Regressions in Econometrics," *Journal of Econometrics*, 2, 111–20.

Grossman, J. 1981: "The Rationality of Money Supply Expectations and the Short-Run Response of Interest Rates to Monetary Surprises," *Journal of Money, Credit and Banking*, 13, November, 409–24.

Hardouvelis, G. A. 1984: "Market Perceptions of Federal Reserve Policy and the Weekly Monetary Announcements," *Journal of Monetary Economics*, 14, September, 225–40.

Hardouvelis, G. A. 1987: "Reserve Announcements and Interest Rates: Does Monetary Policy Matter?" *Journal of Finance*, 42 (2), June, 407–22.

Hendry, D. F. 1977: "Comments on Granger and Newbold's 'Time Series Approach to Econometric Model Building' and Sargent and Sims' 'Business Cycle Modeling without Pretending to Have Too Much A Priori Economic Theory,'" in *New Methods in Business Cycle Research: Proceedings from a Conference*, Minneapolis, MN: Federal Reserve Bank of Minneapolis.

Hsiao, C. 1977: "Money and Income Causality Detection," Mimeo, University of California at Berkeley, April.

Ito, T., and V. Roley 1987: "News from the U.S. and Japan: Which Moves the Yen/Dollar Exchange Rate?," *Journal of Monetary Economics*, 19, 255–77.

Jeffreys, H., Sir 1973: *Scientific Inference*, 3rd edn, London: Cambridge University Press.

Joines, D. H. 1977: "Comment: Short-Term Interest Rates as Predictors of Inflation," *American Economic Review*, 67, June, 476–7.

Joines, D. H. 1991: "Money Supply Announcements and Real Economic Activity," *Journal of Monetary Economics*, 28, December, 391–410.

Laffer, A. B., and M. A. Miles 1977: *Factors Influencing Changes in the Money Supply Over the Short Term*, Boston, MA: Wainwright.

Latané, H. A. 1954: "Cash Balances and the Interest Rate: A Pragmatic Approach," *Review of Economics and Statistics*, 36, November, 456–60.

Litterman, R. B., and L. Weiss 1985: "Money, Real Interest Rates, and Output: A Reinterpretation of Postwar U.S. Data," *Econometrica*, 53 (1), January, 129–56.

Lucas, R. E. Jr 1972: "Expectations and the Neutrality of Money," *Journal of Economic Theory*, 4, April, 103–29.

Lynge, M. J. Jr 1981: "Money Supply Announcements and Stock Prices," *Journal of Portfolio Management*, 8, Fall, 40–3.

Mehra, R., and E. C. Prescott 1985: "The Equity Premium: A Puzzle," *Journal of Monetary Economics*, 15, 145–61.

Meltzer, A. H. 1963: "The Demand for Money: The Evidence from the Time Series," *Journal of Political Economy*, 71, June, 231–4.

Mishkin, F. S. 1978: "Efficient Markets Theory: Implications for Monetary Policy," *Brookings Papers on Economic Activity*, 3, 424–38.

Mishkin, F. S. 1981: "Monetary Policy and Long-Term Interest Rates: An Efficient Markets Approach," *Journal of Monetary Economics*, 7, 29–55.

Mishkin, F. S. 1982: "Monetary Policy and Short-Term Interest Rates: An Efficient Markets–Rational Expectations Approach," *Journal of Finance*, 37 (1), March, 63–72.

Nelson, C. R., and G. W. Schwert 1977: "On Testing the Hypothesis that the Real Rate of Interest is Constant," *American Economic Review*, 67, June, 478–86.

Nichols, D. A., D. H. Small, and C. Webster 1983: "Why Interest Rates Rise When an Unexpectedly Large Money Stock is Announced," *American Economic Review*, 73 (3), June, 383–8.

Pearce, D. K., and V. Roley 1983: "The Reaction of Stock Prices to Unanticipated Changes in Money: A Note," *Journal of Finance*, 38 (4), September, 1323–33.

Pierce, D. A. 1977: "Relationships – and the Lack Thereof – Between Economic Time Series with Special Reference to Money and Interest Rates," *Journal of the American Statistical Association*, 72, March, 11–22.

Plosser, C. 1976: "Time Series Analysis and Seasonality in Econometric Models with an Application to a Monetary Model," Ph.D. dissertation, University of Chicago.

Roley, V., and C. Walsh 1984: "Unanticipated Money and Interest Rates," *American Economic Review*, May, 49–54.

Roley, V., and C. Walsh 1985: "Monetary Policy Regimes, Expected Inflation, and the Response of Interest Rates to Money Announcements," *Quarterly Journal of Economics*, 100, Supplement, 1011–1103.

Rozeff, M. 1974: "Money and Stock Prices: Market Efficiency and the Lag in Effect of Monetary Policy," *Journal of Financial Economics*, 1, January, 245–302.

Rutner, J. L. 1975: "A Time Series Analysis of the Control of Money," *Monthly Review of the Federal Reserve Bank of Kansas City*, 60, January, 3–9.

Sargent, T. J., and N. Wallace 1973: "Rational Expectations and the Dynamics of Hyperinflation," *International Economic Review*, 14, June, 328–50.

Sheehan, R. G. 1985: "Weekly Money Announcements: New Information and Its Effects," *Federal Reserve Bank of St Louis Review*, 67, August–September, 25–34.

Siegel, J. 1985: "Money Supply Announcements and Interest Rates: Does Monetary Policy Matter?" *Journal of Monetary Economics*, 15, 163–76.

Siegel, J. 1992: "The Real Rate of Interest from 1800–1990," *Journal of Monetary Economics*, 29, 227–52.

Sims, C. R. 1972: "Money, Income and Causality," *American Economic Review*, 62, September, 540–52.

Sims, C. A. 1980: "Comparison of Interwar and Postwar Business Cycles: Monetarism Reconsidered," *American Economic Review*, 70 (2), 250–7.

Tobin, J. 1963: "Commercial Banks as Creators of 'Money,'" in D. Carson (ed.), *Banking and Monetary Studies*, Homewood, IL: Irwin.

Tobin, J. 1970: "Money and Income: Post Hoc Ergo Propter Hoc?," *Quarterly Journal of Economics*, 84, May, 301–17.

Urich, T., and P. Wachtel 1981: "Market Response to the Weekly Money Supply Announcements in the 1970s," *Journal of Finance*, 36 (5), December, 1063–72.

Urich, T., and P. Wachtel 1984: "The Effects of Inflation and Money Supply Announcements on Interest Rates," *Journal of Finance*, 39 (4), September, 1177–88.

Walsh, C. 1984: "Unanticipated Money and Interest Rates," *American Economic Review*, 74, May, 49–54.

Webb, R. I. 1979: "The Impact of Open Market Operations on Treasury Bill Yields," Ph.D. dissertation, University of Chicago.

Zellner, A., and C. Montmarquette 1971: "A Study of Some Aspects of Temporal Aggregation Problems in Econometric Analyses," *Review of Economics and Statistics*, 53, November, 335–42.

Zellner, A., and Palm, F. 1975: "Time Series and Structural Analysis of Monetary Models of the U.S. Economy," *Sankhya, Indian Journal of Statistics*, 37, 12–56.

# 6

# Federal Reserve Monetary Policy

> A prediction is never in the form "so and so will happen." At the best it is in the form "it is reasonable to be highly confident that it will happen." This may be disappointing, but in the last resort that is all we can say.
>
> (Sir Harold Jeffreys, *The Theory of Probability*)

## 1 Introduction

In the minds of many financial market participants, central banks often exert an enormous influence on changes in speculative prices. As a result, the monetary policy actions of central banks, in general, and the Federal Reserve, in particular, are closely watched by participants in financial markets. This is especially true in the fixed-income securities markets where the demand by traders for forecasts and interpretations of Fed monetary policy actions has made Fed-watching a cottage industry of sorts. A discount rate change, for instance, or, in years past, a money supply announcement by the Fed can have a substantial impact on changes in speculative prices.

Anticipations of changes in Fed monetary policy also play a central role in understanding the market's reaction to the release of various economic reports. As was noted previously, market participants often interpret economic data from the perspective of whether the data provide the Fed with sufficient rationalization to "ease" or "tighten" the money supply. For example, a sharp reaction of fixed-income security prices to the release of the monthly employment report may reflect, in large part, speculation among market participants about the direction of Fed monetary policy in light of the report.

In a sense, Fed monetary policy is also intimately intertwined with the market reaction to the periodic release of economic reports. Fed governors often purport to watch economic data for clues to the present state and future direction of the US economy as a means of guiding their monetary policy actions. Some Fed governors, for instance, have been portrayed in the financial press as individuals very much concerned with the minutiae of economic data. This raises a parallel question to one raised in chapter 1, namely, what are the apparent macroeconomic beliefs of monetary policymakers? How similar are they to the macroeconomic beliefs of market participants?

There are other important sources of macroeconomic information about Fed monetary policy or financial market transactions besides changes in the discount rate or money supply announcements. Some of this information is released to the public and some is not. These include regular open market operations, including bill or coupon passes; changes in the target Fed funds rate; currency market interventions; changes in reserve requirements; comments by Fed governors in speeches, interviews, and testimony before Congressional committees; and the release of the Beige Book which summarizes economic conditions around the nation. The principal objective of this chapter is to examine these sources of macroeconomic information for speculative markets in more detail. The chapter begins with a description of the Federal Reserve System and its principal instruments of monetary policy. Much institutional detail is provided to give the reader an understanding of the environment in which the Fed operates and potential macroeconomic information is released.

## 2 The Federal Reserve System

The Federal Reserve System serves as the central bank of the United States. It was established by Act of Congress in 1913 in order to ensure an "elastic" money supply (i.e. one that would grow with the needs of the economy).[1] It was also thought that the Federal Reserve could eliminate the seasonal variation in interest rates evident at the turn of the century. In this regard, Clark (1986) states:

> Many financial experts at the turn of the century considered the seasonal variation of interest rates to be extremely dangerous. These men were convinced that the probability of the outbreak of a financial panic was much greater in those months when interest rates were seasonally high than in the remainder of the year.... Since these conditions were presumed to exist during the autumn months when the demands for currency and credit were normally most vigorous, the financial system was thought to be especially vulnerable to the outbreak of panics during that time of year.... This notion influenced the framers of the Federal Reserve Act to stipulate that one of the principal responsibilities of the Federal Reserve System was "to furnish an elastic currency." ...
>
> (p. 77)[2]

During the 1940s and early 1950s the Federal Reserve pursued a policy of pegging interest rates on selected government securities. Because it quickly became the almost exclusive transactor in such markets, it is doubtful that the Federal Reserve actually succeeded in pegging the *market* rate of interest.

Unlike other central banks, the Federal Reserve was purposely decentralized in its organization. The Federal Reserve System was divided into 12 district Reserve banks located in various regions of the United States and a Board of Governors located in Washington, DC. This division reflected political concerns at the time that the central bank be responsive to the needs of the individual economic regions and not become a creature of the large New York City banks.[3]

When the Fed was established it was envisioned that the district Reserve banks would dominate policymaking in the Federal Reserve System. In practice, Fed policymaking is dominated by the Board of Governors with the Chairman exercising influence far beyond what his single vote would suggest. This is not to say that the district Reserve bank presidents do not exercise influence in shaping Fed monetary policy. They do. However, the influence of the district Reserve bank presidents (with the exception of the President of the New York Fed) is clearly secondary to the influence of the members of the Board of Governors.

In addition to its monetary policy role, the Federal Reserve performs other functions. For instance, virtually all US currency consists of Federal Reserve notes.[4] The central bank also exercises many regulatory responsibilities over member banks.

## 3 Political Dimensions of Fed Policy

Although the Fed was established to be independent of Congress and the Administration Fed monetary policy is often perceived (correctly or incorrectly) as responding to the political needs of Congress or, more frequently, the Administration. In part, this reflects the fact that the terms of the seven members of the Board of Governors are staggered to ensure that the President will always be able to nominate members of the Board of Governors. Nominees to the Fed must be confirmed by the United States Senate. With the exception of the Chairman, members of the Board of Governors are elected for terms of 14 years. The Fed Chairman is elected to a four year term which does not coincide with the President's term. This ensures that any President of the United States who serves his full term of office will always have the opportunity to nominate a Fed Chairman.

In years past, the Chairman of the Federal Reserve System was loath to share meaningful information in his periodic testimony before Congressional committees. Not surprisingly, this led to laws requiring more detailed information about the direction of Fed monetary policy. Under the Humphrey–Hawkins Full Employment Act, the Chairman of the Fed is required to testify before Congress twice each year to discuss Fed monetary policy in general and monetary targets in particular. Nevertheless, information on Fed intentions is often difficult to discern and the information provided may not be meaningful. For instance, if one compares actual and forecast monetary growth rate targets the Fed does not appear to be very proficient at forecasting changes in the money supply which it supposedly controls.[5]

## 4 Fed Monetary Policy

The Fed was originally established to play a *passive* role in the economy. It was envisaged that additional demand for credit would be met by having member banks sell or "discount" debt to the district Reserve Banks. The proceeds from discounting securities to the Fed could then be lent out to other customers. In this way, the money supply would grow or fall as business conditions warranted. It would also make financial crises less likely. Needless to say, the passive role of the Federal Reserve System soon gave way to an *active* policy stance.

Monetary policy is determined by the Federal Open Market Committee (FOMC). The FOMC comprises the seven members of the Board of Governors and five district Reserve bank presidents one of whom is always the President of the New York Fed. The FOMC meets approximately eight times per year to discuss monetary policy. General policy actions are determined at these meetings. Implementation of these decisions, however, is relegated to the trading desk of the New York Federal Reserve Bank. The minutes of the FOMC meetings are released to the public on a delayed basis.[6]

The Fed's task is complicated by stochastic fluctuations in banking system reserves which, if left unchecked in a fractional reserve banking system, would cause stochastic changes in the money supply. This, in turn, complicates interpreting Fed monetary policy actions.

The Fed can "target" or attempt to control either the money supply or short-term interest rates. It cannot do both at the same time. If the Federal Reserve targets the money supply the question naturally arises as to the correct definition of money. There are a number of monetary aggregates to choose between.[7] Financial deregulation and innovations have blurred traditional measures of the money supply. Belongia and Chalfant (1989), for instance, present an empirical analysis which supports the use of the narrowest measure of money supply $M_{1A}$.

## 5 Monetary Policy Instruments

The Fed attempts to alter the money supply in order to influence changes in interest rates, prices, or output. In a fractional reserve banking system (such as exists in the United States) this can be accomplished by changing reserves. The Fed has three principal monetary policy instruments at its disposal: (1) changes in reserve requirements; (2) changes in the discount rate; and (3) open market operations. Although changes in the discount rate were the primary transmission mechanism of Fed monetary policy on the economy in years past, open market operations are probably the most important (and most frequently used) monetary policy instrument today.

The relative importance of the three principal instruments of Fed monetary policy is illustrated in table 6.1. As is readily apparent, open market operations are by far the most frequntly used instrument of monetary policy. During the three year period November 25, 1987, through October 31, 1990, there were 408 interventions by the Federal Reserve in the open market (excluding any bill or coupon passes the Fed undertook during this period). In contrast, the discount rate was changed seven times during this interval while reserve requirements were not changed. Table 6.1 understates Fed monetary policy actions slightly because it does not include periodic changes in the Fed Funds rate during the aforementioned period.

**Table 6.1** Frequency of use of Fed monetary policy instruments (November 1, 1987, through October 31, 1990)

| Policy tool | Frequency |
|---|---|
| Discount rate changes | 7 |
| Changes in reserve requirements | 0 |
| Open market operations | 408 |

*Sources*: Board of Governors of the Federal Reserve System; Chicago Mercantile Exchange, *Daily Information Bulletin*

## 6 Changes in Reserve Requirements

Commercial banks which are members of the Federal Reserve system are required to maintain a portion of their total assets in cash or in noninterest-bearing deposits with the Federal Reserve. This is tantamount to a tax to the extent that required reserves exceed what the bank would have maintained in the absence of the requirement. The amount of the tax is equal to the interest income the bank is forced to forgo.[8] An *increase* in reserve requirements means that more funds must remain idle and hence reduces the potential size of the money supply in a fractional reserve banking system. Conversely, a *decrease* in reserve requirements would increase the potential size of the money supply as previously idle funds could be lent out.

The infrequent use of changes in reserve requirements as a monetary policy instrument means that market participants do not necessarily know how to react to an announcement of a change. Consequently, the speed of adjustment may be longer than for other policy tools. For instance, in February 1992, the Federal Reserve lowered the reserve requirements for the first time in several years. Yet, judging from the initial and subsequent reactions of market prices it is apparent that participants in the stock market, at least, did not appreciate the implications of the Fed action. The initial reaction of market prices to the news was a nonevent. Two days later, a rally in bank stock prices was attributed to the cut in the reserve requirement. Investors perceived the change in reserve requirements as representing a change in the apparent tax rate on member commercial banks. Other things equal, a reduction in the reserve requirements should increase the profitability, and hence the stock prices, of affected commercial banks.

## 7 Changes in the Discount Rate

Like changes in reserve requirements, changes in the Federal Reserve discount rate are also a relatively infrequently used instrument of monetary policy. The discount rate is the rate the Federal Reserve charges on loans to member banks. Borrowing from the Federal Reserve is considered to be a privilege rather than a right in order to discourage its overuse. This is necessary because the Fed has invariably set the discount rate *below* the market rate of interest. That is, the discount rate is not a penalty rate. Changes in the discount rate represent a change in the cost of borrowing from the Fed and a signal to market participants as to where the Fed would like to see interest rates go.

By encouraging bank borrowing from the Fed a reduction in the discount rate causes the money supply to increase. Conversely, an increase in the discount rate reduces the amount borrowed from the Fed by member banks and reduces the money supply. As noted above, in the early years of the Federal Reserve System, changes in the discount rate were the principal monetary policy instrument. This is still the case for the central banks of many other nations.

Table 6.2 lists the dates and approximate release times of changes in the discount rate over the period May 1985 through June 1993. The sample size is too small to draw meaningful inferences. Nevertheless, it would appear that the Fed favors Fridays to announce changes in the discount rate. There is also an apparent change in the timing of announcements of changes in the discount rate. The Fed under the chairmanship of Alan Greenspan is more willing than in years past to make discount rate change announcements while the US financial markets are open.

## 8 Market Reaction to Discount Rate Changes

Casual empiricism suggests that stock and bond prices often react sharply to changes in the discount rate. Waud (1970) reports significant "announcement effects" associated with discount rate changes for speculative prices. Some academicians contend that the reaction of speculative prices is a function of the operating procedures that the Federal Reserve employs. For instance, Pearce and Roley (1985) report a significant negative response in stock returns after October 1979 (when the Fed switched to a policy of targeting a monetary aggregate) and no discernible influence before that time (when the Fed targeted interest rates). Similarly, Roley and Troll (1984) report a differential impact of discount rate changes on interest rates depending on the operating policy the Fed pursues. Unlike the negative relationship found for stock prices, Roley and

**Table 6.2** Approximate release times of Federal Reserve discount rate changes (May 1, 1985, through December 15, 1993)

| Date | Day of week | Change in rate | Time of day |
|---|---|---|---|
| May 17, 1985 | Friday | Decrease | 4:50 p.m. |
| March 7, 1986 | Friday | Decrease | 9:00 a.m. |
| April 18, 1986 | Friday | Decrease | 4:50 p.m. |
| July 10, 1986 | Thursday | Decrease | 4:40 p.m. |
| August 20, 1986 | Wednesday | Decrease | 4:35 p.m. |
| September 4, 1987 | Friday | Increase | 9:34 a.m. |
| August 9, 1988 | Tuesday | Increase | 9:47 a.m. |
| February 24, 1989 | Friday | Increase | 9:00 a.m. |
| December 18, 1990 | Tuesday | Decrease | 3:25 p.m. |
| February 1, 1991 | Friday | Decrease | 9:22 a.m. |
| April 30, 1991 | Tuesday | Decrease | 9:30 a.m. |
| September 13, 1991 | Friday | Decrease | 9:30 a.m. |
| December 20, 1991 | Friday | Decrease | 8:34 a.m. |
| July 2, 1992 | Friday | Decrease | 9:17 a.m. |

All times are New York time.

*Sources:* Release time data are from Dow Jones News Service, Reuters and courtesy of Reid Thunberg, First Boston, and J. C. Bradford

Troll report a positive relationship between changes in the discount rate and interest rates.[9]

Financial economic theory suggests that speculative prices should react only to the extent that the discount rate change is unanticipated. Rather than treating discount rate changes as completely unexpected (and hence new information) as the above studies did, Smirlock and Yawitz (1985) distinguish between expected ("technical") and unexpected ("nontechnical") changes in the discount rate. Another reason for doing so is to address the issue of whether changes in the discount rate are endogenously determined. As

Smirlock and Yawitz state:

> If discount rate changes are endogenous, then the existence of announcements effects is difficult to explain within the context of market efficiency....
>
> (p. 1142)

Smirlock and Yawitz report evidence supporting the hypothesis that only unexpected changes in the discount rate exhibit an announcement effect. Further, they report evidence that interest rates and stock returns react quickly to the new information contained in a "nontechnical" discount rate announcement. Moreover, Smirlock and Yawitz's results are consistent with the idea advanced by Roley and Troll and Pearce and Roley that the impact of changes in the discount rate also depends on which operating policy the Fed pursues. One puzzle that emerges from the analysis by Smirlock and Yawitz, Roley and Troll, and Pearce and Roley is why Waud found significant announcement effects associated with discount rate changes during a period (i.e. pre-1979) when the Fed supposedly pursued a policy of targeting short-term interest rates.

There is some evidence that discount rate changes also impact changes in commodity prices. For instance, Barnhart (1988) reports a significant *negative* response in certain commodity futures prices to Fed discount rate changes during the 1977–9 period. It should be noted that this significant negative response in commodity futures prices occurred at the same time that the Federal Reserve was pursuing a policy of targeting the Fed funds rate. This cast doubt on the argument that switches in the Fed's operating strategy explain the differential response of interest rates to discount rate changes.

The market's reaction to changes in the discount rate, while often dramatic, are sometimes inconsistent even when expectations are taken into account. Consider, for instance, the reaction of the financial markets to news of the large discount rate cut of Friday, December 20, 1991. The magnitude of the discount rate cut (1 full percentage point) was unusually large. It is likely that both the magnitude of the discount rate cut and probably the timing as well caught the market by surprise. Yet, there was a minimal reaction in the stock market when it opened on Friday even though the discount rate cut occurred at 8:34 a.m. (New York time).[10] On the following Monday, in contrast, the stock market soared. The rally was attributed in the financial press to a delayed reaction to the discount rate cut. This was followed by a rally in stocks for the rest of December all of which was presumably ignited by the Fed discount rate cut. There was a similar reaction in the bond market which was open when the discount rate cut was announced and did not have the excuse of options expiration to confuse the response.

## 9 Fed Open Market Operations

As table 6.1 suggests, the most frequent source of information about Fed monetary policy is the Fed's open market operations. However, information on Fed open market operations is not released in the same fashion as money supply announcements. As explained below, key elements of the information, such as Federal Reserve monetary policy *intentions*, are not disclosed and hence are the subject of much speculation by market participants.

Open market operations are intended to alter banking system reserves in order to influence the economy, principally by inducing changes in the Fed funds rate and other short-term interest rates.[11] The choice of which securities to transact in is largely a matter of convenience. In practice, the Fed has chosen to transact in government securities and banker's acceptances. Theoretically, the Fed could transact in real assets or other financial securities as Metzler (1951) points out. In any event, a purchase of financial securities or real assets increases the money supply while a sale of financial securities or real assets decreases the money supply. The effect on interest rates depends on one's view of the linkage between changes in the money supply and changes in interest rates.

It should be pointed out that banking system reserves may change independently of monetary policy actions by the Federal Reserve for seasonal and technical reasons among others. Fluctuations in reserves may occur due to both stochastic and deterministic variations in (1) the float; (2) the currency in circulation; and (3) the amount of government deposits. In addition, fluctuations in banking system reserves may arise from (4) shifts of deposits between time and demand accounts and (5) shifts of deposits between city and country banks if differential reserve requirements exist among account or bank classifications. There is also a seasonal component to changes in the money supply. For instance, the amount of currency in circulation typically increases around holidays.

One consequence of these stochastic and deterministic fluctuations in reserves is the need of Federal Reserve policy actions to offset *undesired* changes. Open market operations designed to counter the unwanted portion of reserve fluctuations are called *defensive*. In contrast, open market operations designed to change the reserve position of the banking system are called *dynamic*.[12] As a result, net open market purchases (sales) will not always be indicative of an expansionary (contractionary) monetary policy. Most open market operations are defensive in nature.

In years past, the Federal Reserve would engage in outright purchases and sales of government securities and banker's acceptances to change the money supply. An open market operation designed to increase the money supply would be accomplished through the purchase of securities by the Federal Reserve. Since payment is made by check or wire transfer, this action increases the excess reserves of the banking system and under a fractional reserve banking system causes a multiple expansion in demand deposits and hence causes $M_1$ to increase. If the Federal Reserve sells securities usually receiving payment by check or wire transfer, banking system reserves fall, causing a multiple contraction in demand deposits and causing $M_1$ to fall as well.

Outright security transactions are no longer as extensively used as they once were. Instead repurchase agreements (repos or RPs) and matched-sale purchase agreements (matches, reverses or MSPs) are more frequently employed. Indeed, outright purchases and sales of securities are relatively rare and usually occur outside of the Fed's usual intervention period.[13] Morever, because most outright transactions are not settled the same day there is usually little effect on either reserves or interest rates.[14]

The Federal Reserve may conduct transactions for its own account (System Open Market Account) or for the account of its customers. Distinctions are drawn between *system* repos (i.e. RPs done for the System Open Market Account) and *customer* repos (i.e. RPs conducted for Fed customers). Both system and customer repos exert the same impact on the money supply. However, there are some differences in the amount of information which accompanies their execution. This may result in different announcement effects associated with the two types of repo transactions. In particular, the Fed never specifies the size of system RPs that it wishes to conduct when it announces its intention to intervene. In contrast, the Fed notes the approximate size of customer RPs that it wishes to conduct. In practice, the Fed uses customer RPs to inject a small amount of reserves. Thus, system RPs are always larger than customer RPs.

As the name suggests, in a repo transaction, one party sells a security to another with the promise to repurchase it later. Essentially, repos are really nothing more than collateralized loans. As noted earlier, outright purchase or sale transactions by the Fed are fairly time consuming while both repos and matched-sale purchase agreements can be executed fairly quickly. Repos enjoy another advantage over outright transactions, namely repos can be unwound without re-entering the market. This is especially advantageous in executing defensive open market operations.

Repos differ by maturity. Most repos are entered into on an *overnight* basis or for just a few days (e.g. a weekend repo). Repurchase agreements which cover a longer period than just a few days are called *term* repos. Essentially, repos consist of two simultaneous transactions: (1) borrowing money and (2) lending securities. A reverse repo is simply a repo transaction viewed from the perspective of the counterparty. That is, it consists of two transactions: (1) lending money and (2) borrowing securities. Because Fed open market operations are always viewed from the perspective of the primary government securities dealers with whom the Fed transacts, the announcement that "the Fed is doing repos" really means that the primary government securities dealers are doing repos with the Fed. That is, the Fed is injecting money into the banking system. Conversely, the announcement that the "Fed is doing reverses or matches" means that the Fed is draining money from the banking system.[15]

The Fed conducts an auction among primary government securities dealers when it transacts in the repo market. Dealers submit bids of the amount that they will do at a given repo rate. The Fed then ranks the bids received from lowest to highest. Because a repo transaction is equivalent to lending money and borrowing securities,

**Table 6.3** Distribution of Federal Reserve open market operations by type and by day of the week for the period November 25, 1987, to October 31, 1990

| | System RP | Customer RP | Matched-sales | No Fed | Total |
|---|---|---|---|---|---|
| Monday | 23 | 41 | 18 | 50 | 132 |
| Tuesday | 26 | 40 | 19 | 67 | 152 |
| Wednesday | 31 | 29 | 20 | 73 | 153 |
| Thursday | 23 | 37 | 22 | 69 | 151 |
| Friday | 12 | 43 | 24 | 72 | 151 |
| Total | 115 | 190 | 103 | 331 | 739 |

Twenty-one Federal holidays were observed during this period, of which 20 were observed on a Monday, one was observed on a Tuesday, one was observed on a Wednesday, three were observed on a Thursday, and four were observed on a Friday.

*Source:* Chicago Mercentile Exchange, *Daily Information Bulletin*; reprinted with permission of the *Journal of Fixed Income*

the Fed takes the amount offered at the highest rate first and then continues taking amounts at lower repo rates until it has finished. The lowest rate at which the Fed does a repo is called the *stop-out rate*.

The relative frequency of customer repos, system repos, and matches during the period November 25, 1987, to October 31, 1990, is illustrated in table 6.3. Table 6.3 also indicates the number of days in which the Fed did not intervene (i.e. "No Fed") in the securities markets during this period. As is readily apparent, the most common Fed open market operation during this period were customer repos. Notice also the large number of days when the Fed did not transact in the open market. There appears to be a minor day of the week effect.

## 10 Fed Time

The execution of open market operations is a highly structured process. According to Meek (1982, 1985), each trading day starts with a meeting between officers from the trading desk of the New

York Federal Reserve Bank and representatives from selected primary government security dealers. An internal review of market developments follows. In addition, there is a regularly scheduled discussion with Treasury officials concerning probable Treasury department balances at Reserve banks. This leads to the development of a recommended course of action; a regularly scheduled discussion with members of the FOMC or staff; and the implementation of the decisions arrived at. Meek (1982) describes the process as follows:

> When the [regularly scheduled conference] call [to FOMC members or staff] ends, a bit after 11:30 a.m., the officers [of the trading desk] usually carry out the program [of open market operations] outlined fairly quickly. To emphasize the break with the Federal funds rate operating strategy, the [trading] desk concentrates most of its reserve management operations between 11:30 a.m. and 12:15 p.m. This approach seeks to assure market participants that open market operations are directed at reserve objectives, rather than at maintaining the Federal funds rate within any particular band. On rare occasions, usually when an unusual rise or fall in the Federal funds rate suggests the reserve estimates are substantially in error, the desk may operate outside the normal time, but they are the exceptions that prove the rule....
>
> (p. 138)

The Fed conducts its open market operations within a fairly short time period during the trading day. This period is commonly called "Fed time." It is the period during the trading day when the Fed is most likely to transact in the security markets.[16] Although Meek states that open market operations are typically conducted within a 45 minute period (i.e. 11:30 a.m. to 12:15 p.m.), in practice Fed security transactions in the open market are conducted within an even shorter time interval. Fed time is generally regarded to be 11:30–11:45 a.m. New York time.

Table 6.4 illustrates how most Federal Reserve open market operations are clustered during Fed time. It is immediately apparent that open market operations are not evenly spread out. Smith and Webb (1993) from whose article tables 6.3 and 6.4 are reproduced state:

> [A]lmost 57% of all Fed open market operations occurred during the five minute period 10:37am–10:41am [Chicago time], and 71% of all Fed open market operations occurred within the seven minute interval 10:36am–10:42am.
>
> (p. 61)

**Table 6.4** Distribution of Federal Reserve intervention time as reported by major news vendors for the period November 25, 1987, to October 31, 1990

| Time (Chicago) | Number of interventions 25 Nov 1987 to 8 Nov 1988 | Number of interventions 9 Nov 1988 to 10 Nov 1989 | Number of interventions 13 Nov 1989 to 31 Oct 1990 | Total number of interventions 25 Nov 1987 to 31 Oct 1990 |
|---|---|---|---|---|
| Before 10:30 | 4 | 6 | 1 | 11 |
| 10:30 | 0 | 1 | 0 | 1 |
| 10:31 | 0 | 0 | 0 | 0 |
| 10:32 | 2 | 0 | 0 | 2 |
| 10:33 | 3 | 1 | 0 | 4 |
| 10:34 | 5 | 2 | 2 | 9 |
| 10:35 | 7 | 7 | 0 | 14 |
| 10:36 | 11 | 11 | 6 | 28 |
| 10:37 | 29 | 9 | 9 | 47 |
| 10:38 | 25 | 18 | 4 | 47 |
| 10:39 | 23 | 9 | 13 | 45 |
| 10:40 | 16 | 24 | 15 | 55 |
| 10:41 | 9 | 15 | 13 | 37 |
| 10:42 | 7 | 10 | 15 | 32 |
| 10:43 | 5 | 4 | 6 | 15 |
| 10:44 | 4 | 4 | 7 | 15 |
| 10:45 | 0 | 3 | 7 | 10 |
| 10:46 | 0 | 3 | 4 | 7 |
| 10:47 | 0 | 3 | 3 | 6 |

**Table 6.4** Continued

| Time (Chicago) | Number of interventions 25 Nov 1987 to 8 Nov 1988 | Number of interventions 9 Nov 1988 to 10 Nov 1989 | Number of interventions 13 Nov 1989 to 31 Oct 1990 | Total number of interventions 25 Nov 1987 to 31 Oct 1990 |
|---|---|---|---|---|
| 10:48 | 0 | 2 | 1 | 3 |
| 10:49 | 0 | 2 | 3 | 5 |
| 10:50 | 0 | 2 | 6 | 8 |
| 10:51 | 0 | 0 | 2 | 2 |
| 10:52 | 0 | 0 | 2 | 2 |
| 10:53 | 0 | 2 | 0 | 2 |
| 10:54 | 0 | 0 | 3 | 3 |
| 10:55 | 0 | 0 | 1 | 1 |
| After 10:55 | 0 | 3 | 4 | 7 |
| Total | 140 | 141 | 127 | 408 |

Reprinted with permission of the *Journal of Fixed Income*.

Table 6.4 also indicates that in 1989 and 1990 several open market operations occurred after Fed time "ends" at 11:45 a.m. Relative to the rest of Fed time the percentage of transactions occurring after Fed time is relatively minor. Nevertheless, it illustrates that Fed time is not a rigid "official" intervention period.

Because the Fed concentrates most of its open market operations in the short time interval called Fed time recurrent patterns in the volatility of speculative prices might be observed during that period. These volatility patterns could result from market participants' reaction to the perceived new information contained in the Fed's security transactions in the open market or noise. Smith and Webb (1993) examine the volatility of Chicago Mercantile Exchange Eurodollar futures prices around Fed time. They report evidence which suggests an observable (albeit small and short-lived) increase in volatility of Eurodollar futures prices around Fed time. The volatility patterns are more pronounced on certain days of the week and for certain types of Fed security transactions. These results are depicted in figures 6.1, 6.2, and 6.3 which are reproduced from their article.

Figure 6.1 shows the average number of prices in intervals around Fed time. This serves as a proxy for volatility, the essential argument being that the more volatile the market the greater the number of price changes. As is readily apparent, there are more price changes during Fed time than during the surrounding periods. Smith and Webb also used other measures of volatility to ascertain whether recurrent patterns in the volatility of Eurodollar futures prices existed around Fed time. They report similar results when other measures of volatility are used.

The question naturally arises whether the observed patterns in the volatility of Eurodollar futures prices around Fed time vary by the day of the week or the type of Fed open market transaction. These questions are answered in figures 6.2 and 6.3. Figure 6.2 depicts the volatility of Eurodollar futures prices in five minute intervals for a two hour period around Fed time by day of the week for the time period November 25, 1987, through October 31, 1990. The figure indicates that the greatest volatility, on average, in the two hour period around Fed time occurred on Fridays.

Figure 6.3 depicts the volatility of Eurodollar futures prices in five minute intervals for a two hour period around Fed time by type of Federal Reserve open market operation during the period November 25, 1987, through October 31, 1990. The figure indicates that the greatest volatility occurred with matched-sale purchase transactions. Viewed from the perspective of an informationally efficient capital market, this would seem to indicate that there is more information in matches than in customer or system repos.

It should be pointed out that Federal Reserve open market operations are often shrouded in needless mystery. Rather than simply announce its monetary policy intentions to market participants in a clear and unambiguous fashion, the Fed seemingly prefers to signal its intentions to market participants in ways that may be occasionally misunderstood. The net result of this approach is the creation of additional uncertainty about the correct interpretations of individual Fed monetary policy actions (or inaction). In particular, market participants are often left wondering whether a specific action (or for that matter inaction) represents a change in monetary policy. Many market participants measure Fed monetary policy actions by watching the Fed funds rate. By refusing to share the

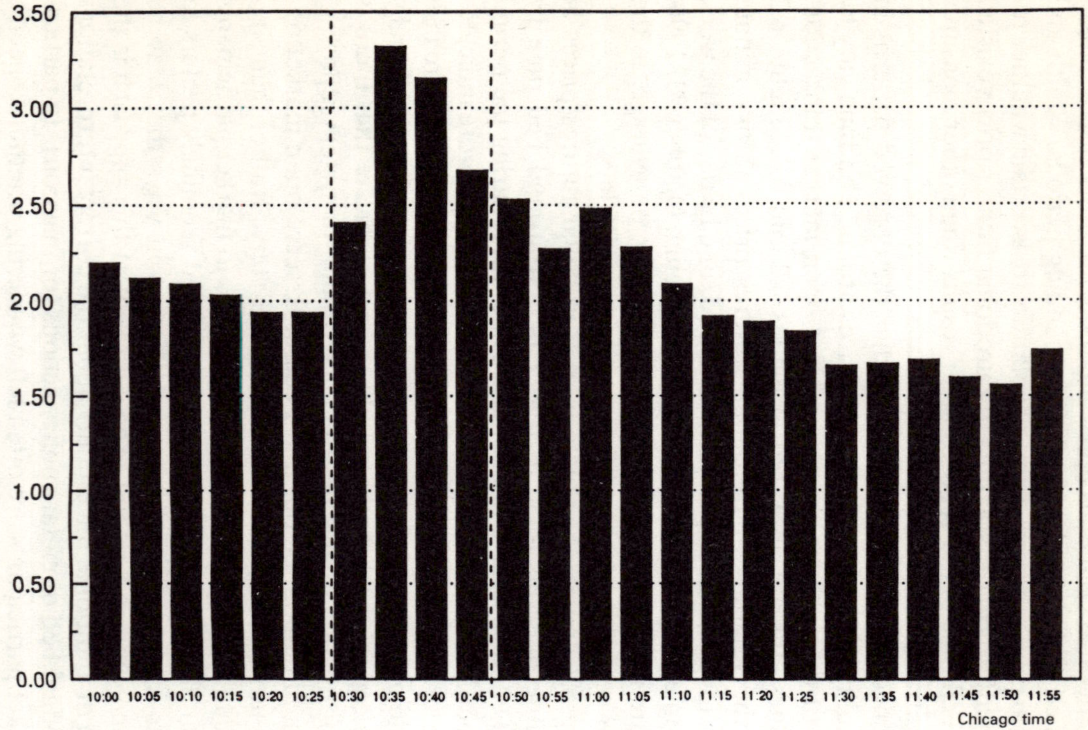


**Figure 6.1** Average number of prices in intervals around Fed time, front month, CME Eurodollar futures contracts: November 25, 1987, to October 31, 1990. Reprinted with permission of the *Journal of Fixed Income*

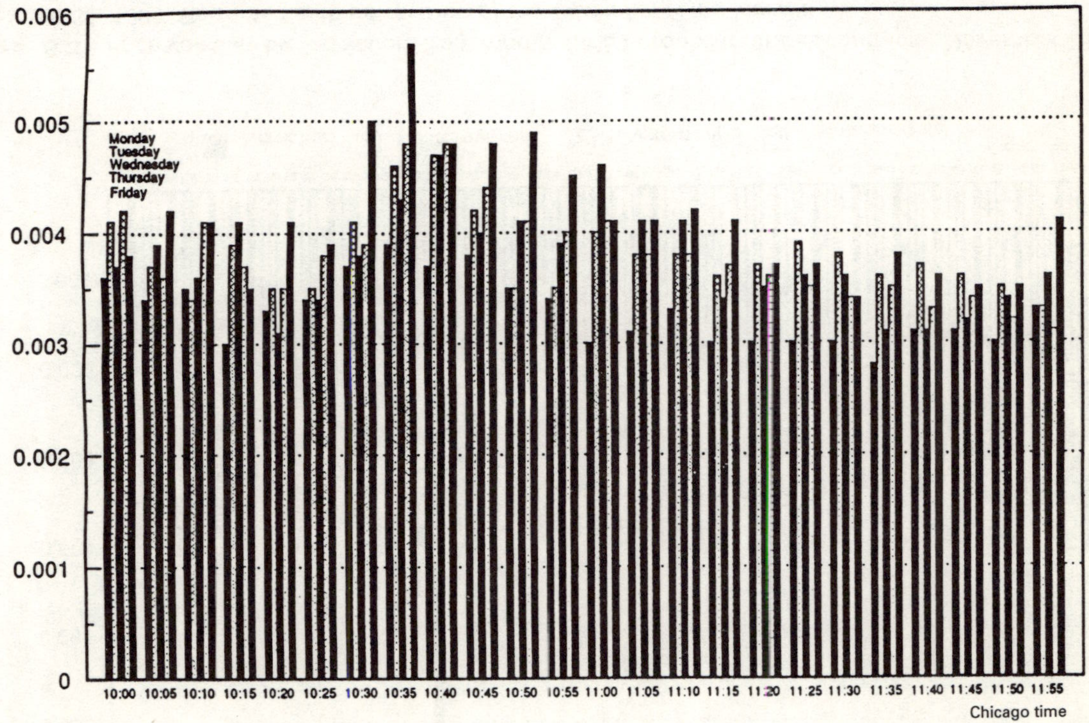


**Figure 6.2** Price volatility by day of the week, front month, CME Eurodollar futures contracts: November 25, 1987, to October 31, 1990. Reprinted with permission of the *Journal of Fixed Income*

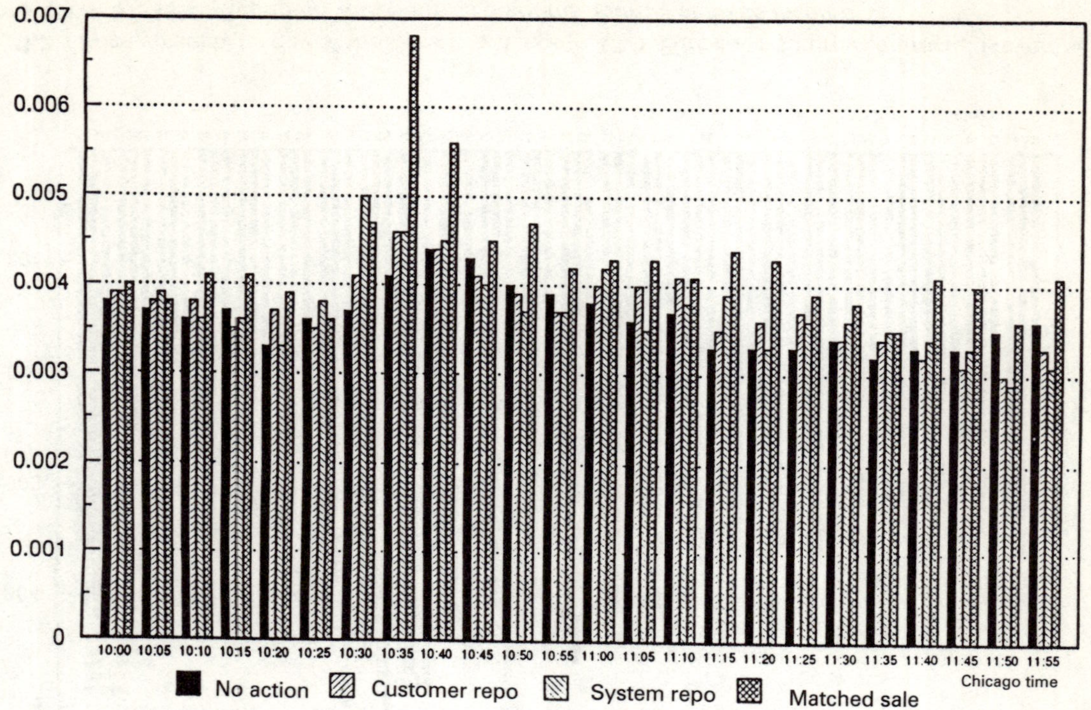


**Figure 6.3** Price volatility by Fed action, front month, CME Eurodollar futures contracts: November 25, 1987, to October 31, 1990. Reprinted with permission of the *Journal of Fixed Income*

reasons motivating its security transactions in the open market with market participants in a timely fashion, the Fed unnecessarily exacerbates uncertainty over its intentions.[17] It should be noted that some observers (see for example Stein, 1989) have argued that this ambiguity over Fed intentions is necessary if the Fed is to exercise any influence on the economy.

As the earlier quote from Meek suggests, the Fed occasionally enters the market early to make its intentions clear to market participants. A case in point is the reaction of many market participants to Fed open market operations around Thanksgiving 1989. The early intervention of the following Monday was meant to dispel any doubts that the Fed had eased.

For instance, on Tuesday, November 28, 1989, the *Wall Street Journal* reported:

> Most interest rates rose yesterday after the Federal Reserve startled bond traders by sending a clear signal that it didn't ease credit after all.... Traders said the [early] timing [of the intervention] made it especially clear that the Fed hasn't changed credit policy, contrary to what most forecasters had thought....[18]

The policy of concentrating its security transactions to a narrow period during the trading day is relatively recent. It arose in large part as a means of convincing market participants that the Fed had switched from a policy of targeting the Fed funds rate to a policy of targeting reserves. As noted earlier, the Fed changes from one operating strategy to another somewhat frequently. Consequently, the Fed still conducts most of its open market operations during Fed time even though the Fed has returned to a policy of targeting the Fed funds rate recently.

It should be noted that the Federal Reserve does not have to conduct large dynamic open market operations. Relatively small but consistent open market operations may be all that is required to achieve the monetary aggregate growth rate objective. It is the forecasting error of reserves that is responsible for large open market operations. For instance, Meek (1982) points out:

> In 1981, less than $50 million a week had to be added to member bank reserves to achieve a six percent annual rate of growth. But

> the average error in forecasting reserves at the beginning of the statement week was about ten times as large. The size of the forecast error gives zest to the game....
>
> (p. 116)

## 11 Expected Federal Reserve Open Market Operations

Information on expected Fed open market operations for a given day are readily available to market participants from major electronic news vendors. Each day major news vendors survey a small sample of Fed watchers as to their views on the open market operations for the day. The consensus view is then published electronically (usually with a brief analysis) and is immediately available to interested subscribers of the news vendors. An element of Fed open market operations is readily predictable using simple time series models. Webb (1991) reports the presence of significant runs in the data on Fed open market operations. This reduces the potential information content of open market operations to market participants.

## 12 Bill and Coupon Passes

Closely related to regular open market operations are the bill and coupon passes that the Fed sometimes engages in. As noted above, bill and coupon passes are usually conducted outside Fed time. A bill pass refers to a transaction where the Fed indicates that it will buy an unspecified quantity of Treasury bills at a given yield. Treasury bills of any maturity may be submitted. A coupon pass refers to the announcement by the Fed that it will buy an unspecified quantity of Treasury coupon securities at a given yield. Again, Treasury securities of any maturity may be submitted for consideration. In both cases, the announcement typically precedes the time when the Fed will actually decide which securities to purchase by a couple of hours. Treasury bill and Treasury coupon passes provide an excellent means for the primary government security dealers to clear their inventories of less liquid off-the-run Treasury securities.[19]

A bill or coupon pass has the same effect on the money supply as any other outright purchase of securities by the Fed. That is, both types of transactions increase the money supply. The announcement of a coupon or bill pass often drives up fixed-income prices as dealers vie to unload their unwanted securities on the Fed. The overall price impact is typically very slight and often short-lived. Sometimes, bill or coupon passes can exert a larger price impact. For instance, on Wednesday, June 3, 1992, the *Wall Street Journal* reported:

> An unexpected purchase of Treasury securities by the Federal Reserve drove up bond prices yesterday. Long-term Treasury bonds, which slumped in the morning, ended with gains of about 1/4 point or $2.50 for each $1,000 face amount.... Early in the session, Treasury bond prices fell more than 3/8 of a point in reaction to further signs that the economy is rebounding.... But the Fed maneuver, known in bond jargon as a "coupon pass," helped change the market's tune. Traders agreed that the Fed action didn't indicate any change in monetary policy. Instead, the Fed was moving to inject new money into the banking system to offset technical factors that were draining reserves....

The article also noted that the exact size of the coupon pass was uncertain. One element of the article deserves special emphasis: namely, the comment that bond prices rallied even though traders understood the Fed action was "to offset technical factors that were draining reserves" rather than indicative of a change in monetary policy, i.e. interest rates respond to a Fed action even though the Fed action is not perceived as changing the money supply or its rate of growth. Possible explanations for this behavior (assuming the article is correct) would include the existence of a security price pressure effect (arising from the Fed bidding up the prices of fixed-income securities); the liquidity effect arising from the temporary expansion in the money supply that the coupon pass induced; a reaction to other information which arrived in the market at the same time; or the reaction of traders to noise. One must be careful not to read too much into the above anecdotal evidence given the small sample size.

## 13 Operating Strategy

The Fed can pursue an operating strategy of either controlling some short-term interest rate such as the Fed funds rate or controlling some monetary reserve aggregate. Despite the misleading impression Fed officials often leave with the public, it cannot do both at the same time. Over the years the Fed has switched from one operating strategy to another. Further, when the Fed has pursued an operating strategy of targeting reserves it has changed the reserve aggregate it is focusing on. Not surprisingly, the Fed often remains somewhat fuzzy about the operating strategy it is currently pursuing which is undoubtedly a source of confusion to market participants.

After Saturday, October 6, 1979, the Fed switched from a policy of targeting the Fed funds rate to targeting a reserve aggregate. The question quickly arose as to which reserve aggregate is most appropriate. *Total* reserves can be dichotomized into *borrowed* reserves (reserves borrowed from the Fed through the discount window) and *nonborrowed* reserves. Another possible decomposition of total reserves is to divide total reserves into *excess* reserves and *required* reserves. Other ways of classifying reserves are possible. For instance, *free* reserves simply represent the positive difference between excess reserves and borrowed reserves while *net borrowed* reserves represent the negative difference between excess reserves and borrowed reserves.

Which monetary aggregate the Fed concentrates on influences how unexpected changes in reserves are viewed. For instance, suppose the Fed targets nonborrowed reserves. This means that if total reserves increase (decrease) borrowed reserves are forced up (down). And due to the presumed reluctance of banks to borrow from the Fed, upward pressure on borrowings coincides with a higher Fed funds rate as the rate for *free* reserves (excess reserves less borrowed reserves) is bid up.

Even when the Fed was pursuing an operating strategy of targeting reserves the Fed appeared to focus on other factors including the likely behavior of the Fed funds rate. Consequently, some observers contended that the Fed did not abandon interest rate targeting as an operating strategy.[20] If correct, this raises a question about the empirical evidence showing a differential effect associated with unanticipated changes in the money supply on changes in speculative prices during the pre-October 1979 and post-October 1979 periods.

At present, the Fed appears to be pursuing an operating strategy of controlling the Fed funds rate. When the Federal Reserve pursues an operating strategy of targeting the Fed funds rate, changes in the Fed funds rate become a significant information event. For instance, there was a considerable reaction in speculative prices to the news that the Fed had cut the Fed funds rate by 25 basis points on Thursday, April 9, 1992.

As noted in the previous chapter, the empirical economic literature reports evidence of significant positive correlation between unanticipated money supply changes and unanticipated changes in interest rates in the October 1979 to February 1984 period. The lack of a significant relationship prior to this period is attributed to the Fed following an operating strategy of targeting the Fed funds rate instead of a monetary aggregate as it did after 1979. To the extent that the Federal Reserve has returned to an operating strategy of targeting the Fed funds rate instead of a monetary aggregate this would suggest that one would not observe a significant response to weekly money supply announcements.

Given that the Fed may yet return some day to an operating strategy of targeting reserves, the question arises as to why the Fed does not focus on some monetary aggregate such as $M_1$ instead of reserves in the conduct of its daily open market operations. Essentially, the changing definition of *money*, the instability of money demand (contrary to what Milton Friedman has argued), strong seasonal factors, etc. make the choice of reserves targeting preferable to targeting a broader monetary aggregate directly. As others have noted, the seasonal component in the money supply numbers is quite strong.[21]

There is little argument that the Fed could control high-powered money if it decides to pursue an active monetary policy. Federal Reserve control over higher level monetary aggregates is less clear, however. In this regard, the question naturally arises as to what is the proper definition of money. Over the years, various definitions of the money supply have been advanced. Some of the distinctions are quite silly as a look at past definitions reveals.[22] The essential point is that the more broadly the money supply is defined the less likely it is that the Fed can control it and the more likely that the money supply is endogenously determined.

The Fed currently imposes a system of contemporaneous reserve requirements on its member banks. It would seem that under such a system precise forecasting of nonborrowed reserves would be a fairly easy task. However, a number of problems such as float and unexpected change in Treasury balances arise. Float is the difference between funds credited for checks received and the actual amount of funds collected. Essentially, it is a credit from the Federal Reserve system. Its existence means that banking system reserves are larger than desired. Float may arise, for example, due to inclement weather which interferes with the physical transfer of checks. Over the years, the Federal Reserve has made changes in the check processing system in order to reduce the economic incentives for float.

## 14 Other Sources of Fed Policy Impact

Reading the Fed's tea leaves in order to anticipate its future monetary policy actions has a long history on Wall Street. It was noted earlier that the FOMC sets monetary policy at the Federal Reserve. The minutes of their meetings are released on a delayed basis, once again denying timely information about Fed monetary policy to the market. Not surprisingly, a news story leaking the contents of the minutes may prompt a market reaction. A case in point is the market's reaction to a report which appeared in the *Wall Street Journal* on Thursday, May 21, 1992, indicating that the Fed had decided not to ease any time soon. On Friday, May 22, 1992, the *Wall Street Journal* reported:

> Discouraged investors bid stock and bond prices lower in the wake of the Federal Reserve's apparent decision to hold the line against further interest rate cuts. The dollar rose. [stocks fell].... A report in this newspaper yesterday said Fed policy-makers decided earlier this week against any immediate reduction in short-term interest rates and also eliminated a bias toward lower rates. That's a sign rates won't be reduced for at least several weeks, if then....
>
> (p. C1)

Lest the casual reader think that the minutes of the FOMC meetings contain vast insights with free-wheeling discussions this is unfortunately not the case.

Market reactions sometimes arise from the testimony, speeches, or interviews of members of the Federal Reserve Board of Governors.[23] Yet, another source of information is released by the Chairman of the Fed when he testifies before Congress. The Beige Book (also known as the "tan" book) can sometimes prompt a reaction. It should not be surprising that market participants look at these numbers closely because the Fed often does too.

## 15 Fed Currency Transactions

In addition to transactions in the open market which are primarily designed to influence the economy by changing the rate of interest, the Fed also intervenes in the currency markets. It does so at the direction of the US Treasury which is responsible for determining the exchange rate policy. These interventions are relatively infrequent and often coordinated with currency interventions by other central banks. Not surprisingly, interventions by the Fed in the foreign exchange rate markets are closely watched especially by participants in the foreign exchange markets.

The purchase of a foreign currency by the Fed is equivalent to selling dollars. The sale of a foreign currency by the Fed is equivalent to buying dollars. The underlying premise behind currency interventions is the mistaken belief that central banks can influence the exchange rate through large purchases or sales of currency (which exert buying or selling pressure, respectively, on prices). That is, it is at essence a security price pressure argument. For instance, the sale of dollars to buy Deutschemarks by the Fed is interpreted by many market participants as an attempt to lower the value of the dollar or raise the value of the Deutschemark. Conversely, the sale of Deutschemarks to purchase dollars is viewed as an attempt to raise the value of the dollar or lower the value of the Deutschemark. The size of central bank interventions in the currency markets is miniscule compared with the massive total volume of currencies traded each day. Consequently, while there may be transitory effects on exchange rates associated with central bank interventions in the foreign exchange market, casual empiricism suggests that central bank interventions in the foreign exchange market are rarely effective in the long term.[24]

Foreign exchange market interventions by the Fed also have potential implications for the prices of fixed-income securities. The reason for this is that currency interventions change the US money supply. From an economic perspective, it does not matter whether the money supply was altered due to an open market operation or a foreign currency transaction by the Fed. The effects should be the same. Because currency policy is determined by the Treasury rather than the Fed, the Fed attempts to *sterilize* its foreign currency transactions, i.e. neutralize the impact of Fed currency transactions on the money supply by offsetting it with open market operations. This practice suggests that Fed currency market interventions should only have, at best, a transitory price pressure effect on foreign exchange rates.

## 16 Monetary Policy Actions of Foreign Central Banks

Although the primary focus of this chapter is on the actions of the US central bank similar comments might be made about the influence of other central banks on changes in speculative prices. While central banks frequently share the same objectives, however, the tools employed to implement monetary policy may differ.

For instance, although open market operations are the primary instrument of Fed monetary policy this is not always the case in other countries. Nevertheless, central bank intervention in the fixed-income securities markets is closely watched even in countries where central bank security transactions are not the principal instrument of monetary policy. For instance, the June 28, 1990, *Financial Times* reports:

> The West German bond market suffered from a bout of profit-taking yesterday after the Bundesbank's regular weekly tender of repurchase agreements had indicated a slightly tighter than expected monetary policy. The fact that the tender was DM1.2 bn below market expectations was taken as a sign that the Bundesbank wants to take a tight stance ahead of next Monday's monetary union between

> the two Germanys. The Bundesbank's action pushed bond futures down almost a full point and the market was still in decline in after-hours trading late yesterday....
>
> (p. 22)

The above excerpt indicates that the intentions of the Bundesbank, like the Fed, must often be inferred from its monetary policy actions. In general, the Fed releases minimal *timely* information on its policy actions or intentions. This lack of complete information on the Fed's policy actions is itself a source of uncertainty to market participants and makes correct interpretation of Fed actions (or lack thereof) more difficult.

## 17 Conclusions

In assessing the prospects for changes in Fed monetary policy, traders have a number of potential sources of Fed information to respond to. These include changes in the discount and Fed funds rates; regular open market operations; bill and coupon passes; and changes in reserve requirements. Changes in these variables are widely perceived to have a direct impact on changes in speculative prices and provide clues about the future course of monetary policy. Interpreting the implications of various Fed actions for the future course of monetary policy is exacerbated by the Fed's policy of not releasing information on its monetary policy intentions in a timely fashion.

The empirical literature reports significant announcement effects associated with unanticipated changes in the discount rate in the post-October 1979 period. Other Fed actions frequently have less impact. For instance, open market operations are the primary transmission mechanism of Fed monetary policy. Although Fed open market operations (which are concentrated during Fed time) increase volatility, the increased volatility in Eurodollar futures prices is slight and short-lived. In addition, for many participants in speculative markets, much of the interest in other sources of macroeconomic information (such as periodic economic reports) centers on the potential clues it provides on the course of future monetary policy.

## Notes

1 As noted earlier the Fed was also formed to remove apparent seasonality in short-term interest rates. Clark (1986) argues that the disappearance of seasonality in interest rates after the formation of the Fed was a worldwide phenomenon and not the result of Fed monetary policy.

2 The Federal Reserve is widely credited with eliminating interest rate seasonals in the United States. Clark (1986) presents evidence contrary to that belief. He concludes:

> The similarity of the behavior of interest rates in the United States and other countries suggests that the disappearance of interest rate seasonals was a worldwide phenomenon attributable to common causes.... When currency and high-powered money were investigated, it was found that the seasonal movements alleged to have brought an end to interest rate seasonals did not commence until the latter part of 1917 [although Clark contends that interest rate seasonals disappeared in 1914]....
>
> (p. 120)

3 Political considerations also explain why there are two Federal Reserve banks located in the state of Missouri.

4 Technically, there are 12 currencies in the United States which are legal tender. Each of the District Federal Reserve Banks issues its own currency. Of course, the "currency" of each District Reserve Bank has a fixed exchange rate of unity with the currencies of each of the other District Reserve Banks.

5 The failure of the Fed to accurately forecast the money supply growth rate a few quarters ahead suggests that the Fed may not be able to control the money supply.

6 The minutes of the FOMC represent another potential source of macroeconomic information.

7 Friedman has long argued that the Fed should pursue a policy of letting the money supply grow at a constant rate, say 3 percent per year. Which monetary aggregate the Fed targets is less important than that the Fed chooses one monetary aggregate and attempts to control that measure.

8 This is true only if the Federal Reserve does not fully compensate member banks for the opportunity cost of the reserve requirements in some other fashion.

9 This provides some empirical support for those monetary theories which posit an inverse relationship between changes in the money supply and interest rates.

10 The discount rate cut happened to occur on the same day that many options on equity securities or indices expire. This is commonly known as a triple witching Friday because of the perceived impact that option expirations can have on the volatility of the underlying securities.

11 It should be pointed out that the Fed can also change the money supply by engaging in private security transactions with its customers (principally foreign central banks and US government agencies). These *nonmarket* security transactions have the same effect on banking system reserves as open market operations. The principal disadvantage of these transactions is that they occur at the discretion of the counterparties rather than when the Fed wants to transact. That is, these transactions would limit the Fed to playing a passive role of reacting to the needs of its customers. As a result, nonmarket security transactions are less frequently used than security transactions in the open market. Incidentally, these transactions are not disclosed immediately upon execution. Rather, the transactions are released a couple of weeks later.

12 This distinction is due to Roosa (1956).

13 The principal reason for this is the time-consuming nature of cash market transactions where the Fed is forced to choose which maturity of which security it wants to transact as well as ascertain that it will do so at the best price available. Meek (1982) states:

> Outright transactions in either bills or coupon securities are more time-consuming, both because dealers contact a large number of customers and because a larger number of bids or offers have to be priced and recorded. Choosing among the propositions is also more complicated because a yield curve involves more choices than the single interest rate comparison typical of RPs and MSPs. Generally an hour or more is required for a go-around in Treasury bills. A similar operation in Treasury coupon securities or Federal agency issues can easily require two hours, largely because of the increased number of maturities and the operational time required by desk personnel to compare offering yields relative to the yield curve.
>
> (p. 139)

Friedman (1982a, b, 1993) has criticized the use of repo transactions by the Fed in the conduct of its monetary policy. He has characterized such transactions as "churning" the Fed's portfolios and has advocated that the Fed be prohibited from engaging in repo transactions.

14 In this regard, Meek (1982) observes:

> In conducting outright transactions, the [trading] desk frequently buys or sells securities during the afternoon for delivery a day or two later. These transactions have no immediate impact on reserve availability or the Federal funds rate; often the reserve effect takes place in a subsequent statement week.
>
> (p. 138)

15 Technically, the Fed cannot engage in reverse repo transactions because legally it cannot borrow money. Matches, which are economically equivalent to reverse repos, allow the Fed to circumvent that restriction.

16 This excludes bill and coupon passes (which are discussed below) and foreign exchange interventions which usually occur outside Fed time.

17 Melton (1985) comments:

> To many, the Fed funds rate is quite simply the cutting edge of monetary policy. But with the Fed controlling the rate less tightly than it did prior to October 6, 1979, it is easy to become confused about the direction of policy. That is a large problem for the securities dealers most of all, since their high leverage makes them quite vulnerable to being left behind in the race to anticipate near-term interest rate movements....
>
> Another striking feature of the funds market is the way the Fed systematically withholds information that might potentially reduce the day-to-day volatility of the funds rate and make other money market rates less erratic.... [T]he funds market labors under significant uncertainty concerning reserve supplies and the degree to which they are being affected by factors only the Fed has (sometimes incomplete) knowledge about. When policy is changing, it is obviously appropriate for interest rates to respond. It is unfortunate when they react because of a lack of information about float or some similar influence on the availability of reserves.
>
> (p. 124)

18 *Wall Street Journal*, Tuesday, November 28, 1989, p. C23.

19 Treasury securities which are *not* the most recently issued Treasury securities in a particular maturity class are called "off-the-run." This

Treasury securities in a particular maturity class, i.e. "on-the-run." Off-the-run Treasurys are invariably less liquid than their on-the-run counterparts.

20 Concerning the incomplete abandonment of interest rate targeting when the new operating procedures were adopted by the Fed, Melton (1985) states:

> This convoluted procedure was anathema to monetarists though ironically enough it was Allen H. Meltzer, a leading monetarist who (as far as the author has been able to determine) first proposed operating procedures similar to those adopted. In essence, the new system was simply funds-rate targeting reborn with a semiautomatic pilot that promptly revised the target funds rate in response to deviations of money growth from its target rate.
>
> (p. 51)

21 For instance, Melton (1985) has noted:

> Inadequate seasonal adjustment of the money stock data provides bread and butter for quite a few market participants. Specifically, almost all Fed watchers routinely prepare forecasts of weekly money stock changes. Almost without exception, their forecasts are based solely and exclusively on their subjective corrections of the Fed's seasonal factors. In other words, fancy stuff like income, employment, inflation, and interest rates has virtually no role in forecasting the weekly money number. It's a seasonal adjustment game....
>
> (p. 89)

22 For instance, for a long time $M_1$ was defined as the sum of currency in circulation plus demand deposits. That is, a legalistic view was taken over the definition of money. For instance, $M_1$ did not include travelers checks outstanding. $M_2$ included savings (time) deposits which in many communities could be withdrawn immediately like demand deposits. $M_3$ included broader savings accounts etc.

23 The Friday, July 23, 1993, issue of the *Wall Street Journal* provides an example in this regard in an article detailing the comments of Fed Chairman Greenspan on the future course of interest rates (p. A2).

24 With the possible exception of the Bank of France, the impotency of central bank interventions in the foreign exchange market was demonstrated for several European central banks during the currency crisis of September 1992.

## References

Barnhart, S. W. 1988: "Commodity Futures Prices and Economic News: An Examination Under Alternative Monetary Regimes," *Journal of Futures Markets*, 8 (4), 483–510.

Belongia, M. T., and J. A. Chalfant 1989: "The Changing Empirical Definition of Money: Some Estimates from a Model of the Demand for Money Substitutes," *Journal of Political Economy*, 97 (2), 387–97.

Clark, T. A. 1986: "Interest Rate Seasonals and the Federal Reserve," *Journal of Political Economy*, 94 (1), 76–125.

Friedman, M. 1982a: "Monetary Policy: Theory and Practice," *Journal of Money, Credit and Banking*, February, 98–118.

Friedman, M. 1982b: "Reply to Levin and Meulendyke," *Journal of Money, Credit and Banking*, August, 406.

Friedman, M. 1993: "End the Fed's Fine-Tuning," *Wall Street Journal*, September 15, A22.

Meek, P. 1982: *U.S. Monetary Policy and Financial Markets*, New York: Federal Reserve Bank of New York.

Meek, P. 1985: *Open Market Operations*, New York: Federal Reserve Bank of New York.

Melton, W. C. 1985: *Inside the Fed: Making Monetary Policy*, Homewood, IL: Dow-Jones Irwin.

Metzler, L. A. 1951: "Wealth, Saving, and the Rate of Interest," *Journal of Political Economy*, 59, April, 103–29.

Pearce, D. K., and V. Roley 1985: "Stock Prices and Economic News," *Journal of Business*, 58 (1), 49–68.

Roley, V. V., and R. Troll 1984: "The Impact of Discount Rate Changes on Market Interest Rates," *Federal Reserve Bank of Kansas City Economic Review*, 69, 27–39.

Roosa, R. V. 1956: *Federal Reserve Operations in Money and Government Securities Markets*, New York: Federal Reserve Bank of New York.

Smirlock, M., and J. Yawitz 1985: "Asset Returns, Discount Rate Changes, and Market Efficiency," *Journal of Finance*, 40 (4), 1141–58.

Smith, D. G., and R. I. Webb 1993: "The Volatility of Eurodollar Futures Prices Around Fed Time," *Journal of Fixed Income*, 2, March, 56–73.

Stein, J. C. 1989: "Cheap Talk and the Fed: A theory of Imprecise Policy Announcements," *American Economic Review*, 79 (1), March, 32–42.

Waud, R. N. 1970: "Public Interpretations of Federal Reserve Discount Rate Changes: Evidence and the Announcement Effect," *Econometrica*, 38, March, 231–50.

Webb, R. I. 1979: "The Impact of Open Market Operations on Treasury Bill Yields," Ph.D. dissertation, University of Chicago.

Webb, R. I. 1991: "Using Consensus Expectations in Assessing Federal Reserve Security Transactions," *Economic and Financial Computing*, 1 (1), 39–48.

# 7

# The Reaction of Speculative Prices to Macroeconomic Information

> [T]he ideas of economists and political philosophers, both when they are right and when they are wrong, are more powerful than is commonly understood. Indeed the world is ruled by little else. Practical men who believe themselves to be quite exempt from any intellectual influences, are usually the slaves to some defunct economist....
>
> (John Maynard Keynes, *The General Theory of Employment, Interest, and Money*, p. 383)

## 1 Introduction

Most of the preceding chapters considered the behavior of speculative prices in response to the arrival of new macroeconomic information largely from the perspective of macroeconomic and financial economic theory. This chapter takes a different perspective. It examines the behavior of speculative prices in response to the arrival of new macroeconomic information from the perspective of traders in speculative markets. As such, rigorous econometric tests of alternative hypotheses are eschewed in favor of the simpler and more straightforward approach of examining changes in speculative prices at various time intervals following the release of macroeconomic information. This simplicity comes at a cost. Namely, the inferences are suggestive rather than conclusive. Ultimately, however, financial economic and (where appropriate) macroeconomic theory must explain the actual time series behavior of changes in speculative prices which traders see.[1]

The principal objective of this chapter is to examine the actual behavior of speculative prices in response to new macroeconomic information in order to glean insights on the apparent macroeconomic beliefs of traders; the informational efficiency of the market; the possible validity of various macroeconomic models; and the manner in which new information is incorporated into speculative prices. In particular, this chapter examines the response of US Treasury bond futures prices to the information contained in the release of selected government economic reports.

An ancillary objective of this chapter is to consider briefly the influence on changes in speculative prices of fiscal, debt management and exchange rate policies and other aperiodic sources of macroeconomic information. Some anecdotal evidence is presented.

Interpreting the new macroeconomic information contained in economic reports correctly sometimes poses its own set of challenges. Information conflicts sometimes arise between component parts of the report. In addition, the overall report may be distorted due to a single factor (e.g. increased exports of aircraft may reduce the merchandise trade deficit); an exogenous event; or the manner in which the data are collected, estimated or analyzed. Consequently, some knowledge of the composition of the report is potentially valuable to traders.

Similarly, a detailed understanding of the institutional details of the economic reports is occasionally advantageous. The operative word here is *occasionally*. Consequently, one should not make too much of this from a trader's perspective. Not surprisingly, the task of deciphering the true meaning of economic reports is typically relegated to economists in the employ of large financial firms and the financial press.

Extensive information on the Employment and Earnings Report is presented in appendix 7.1 to illustrate some of the institutional details underlying economic reports in general and the Employment and Earnings Report in particular.[2] It is not apparent that having a better understanding of the "real" information content in an economic report necessarily provides traders with a valuable *short-term* information advantage, on average.

The reaction of speculative prices to the release of the information in economic reports provides a measure of how well or poorly market participants predict macroeconomic information.

Significant changes in speculative prices are an indication that market participants are unable to forecast the information content of economic reports very well. As has been stressed in earlier chapters, speculative prices change only in response to the arrival of new information in an informationally efficient capital market. Information on the reaction of speculative prices to perceived forecast errors is presented for selected economic reports. Potential econometric problems associated with the use of time series of "consensus" forecasts of economic data from periodic surveys (where the size and composition of the sample varies over time) are also discussed.

## 2 Government Economic Reports

This chapter analyzes the reaction of US Treasury bond futures prices to a number of monthly government economic reports.[3] These include reports on employment and earnings; the merchandise trade balance (i.e. the trade deficit); producer prices; consumer prices; durable goods; retail sales; and gross national product. Other economic reports are released by the government (e.g. housing starts, business inventories, personal income and consumption expenditures) but are (as of this writing) considered of secondary importance. Occasionally, one of these secondary economic reports exerts a significant influence on speculative prices.

The perceived importance of economic reports to market participants often changes over time. As noted in chapter 1, the money supply was considered very important in the late 1970s and early 1980s, yet it is currently virtually ignored by market participants. Similarly, the merchandise trade balance (which was arguably the most important economic report during 1987–8) has lost much of its former importance in recent years.

All of the above economic reports are released at 8:30 a.m. (Washington DC time) on various business days according to a previously announced schedule. Consequently, the trading community is well aware of the scheduled release times of those periodic government economic reports of interest to it.[4] Because the release dates of forthcoming economic reports are known, surveys of individual forecasts (of the information content) of forthcoming economic reports are often conducted and the associated "consensus expectations" are calculated. Sometimes more than one important economic report is released simultaneously. This complicates the process of analyzing the individual reaction of speculative prices to the arrival of macroeconomic information especially when the individual reports have conflicting implications for changes in interest rates.

In addition, the economic reports typically contain both the preliminary data of interest to market participants and a revision from the previous month. One difficulty in analyzing the information content of economic reports is determining how much weight to assign to the revision. Casual empiricism suggests that the revised data are ignored more frequently than one would expect to observe.

Economists may quarrel over the correct interpretation of an economic report. However, to the extent that an economic report contains relevant information for speculative prices, the trading community, as a whole, must determine how much speculative prices should change in response to the information. Put simply, the trading community must collectively answer the question how much a given piece of new macroeconomic information is worth (in terms of the prospective change in speculative prices).

## 3 Consensus Expectations

As was noted in chapter 2, an informationally efficient capital market suggests a sequence of price equilibria. In contrast, much of the literature in chapter 3 suggests the presence of noise or the effect of noninformational factors on changes in speculative prices and hence price disequilibria. It is useful initially to consider some economic forecasting issues within the context of an informationally efficient capital market. One implication of market efficiency is that speculative prices reflect the *consensus* expectation.

Consensus expectations can be viewed from two perspectives. First, from an econometric perspective the issue is to what extent the consensus forecast combines forecasts in an optimal fashion (e.g. minimizes mean square error). Second, from a financial economics perspective the consensus forecast reflects the beliefs of market participants weighted by the value of their security holdings.

Surveys of expectations of the information content of many economic reports are conducted on a regular basis and the resultant consensus (i.e. mean or median) forecasts are widely disseminated to market participants via electronic (and sometimes print) news vendors. However, the composition and size of the sample from which the consensus forecast is determined often vary considerably for a given economic report over time. The question naturally arises as to the most appropriate way to determine the consensus forecast from such survey data. Zarnowitz (1992) argues that potentially significant aggregation errors may result from the use of the mean or median as the measure of the consensus forecast under such conditions. In an empirical study comparing the accuracy of individual and group mean forecasts of respondents to National Bureau of Economic Research (NBER) quarterly surveys on the rates of change in four economic variables Zarnowitz concludes that the group mean forecasts were more accurate, on average, than most individual forecasts.

In essence, the issue is one of whether and how to combine forecasts. Palm and Zellner (1992) explicitly address the issue of combining forecasts. As they note, while there has been a substantial literature in this area since Bates's and Granger's (1969) classic article, significant questions remain unanswered. Palm and Zellner state:

> Among the issues that have not yet been completely resolved are questions such as: Does it always pay to combine? Should one combine an unbiased forecast with one that is heavily biased? Should one obtain the optimal weights as suggested by Bates and Granger [1969] or should one simply average the individual forecasts, a combining procedure that has worked well in practice.... The question of whether to combine forecasts or to combine information sets in the presence of model uncertainty has not been completely resolved either....
>
> (p. 688)

There is a parallel (albeit inexact) between the issue of combining forecasts and diversification (i.e. combining securities into portfolios). As is well known, diversification reduces portfolio risk by reducing the influence of risks specific to individual securities on the risk of the overall portfolio. Diversification works any time that securities which are less than perfectly positively correlated with each other are combined into a portfolio. In a perfectly diversified portfolio individual security risk is entirely eliminated.

Not surprisingly, similar comments apply to combinations of forecasts when the individual forecasts are measured with error. Put differently, the forecast error for the consensus forecast may be decomposed into two components: individual forecast error (which can be diversified away), and overall forecast error which cannot.

*A priori*, one would expect deviations from consensus expectations to exert more of an impact the greater the dispersion in the forecasts. Thus, knowledge of the dispersion of individual forecasts may be valuable to individual traders when there is a significant deviation from the consensus expectation.[5]

Jeffreys (1973) has argued that all observations are measured with error.[6] This applies to the information released in economic reports as well. One might think that this would suggest that market participants should only respond to statistically meaningful deviations from expectations when there is general agreement over the expected value of the information in an economic report and the probability distribution of the data is known. Put differently, traders should behave as if there is a confidence interval around the various point estimates released in economic reports. This is not necessarily true, however. Whether an individual responds to a deviation from expectations depends upon other factors as well, including his loss function and the importance of what is being forecast.

The question naturally arises as to whether the irrationality in survey data on exchange rate forecasts noted by Ito (1990) is present in other series. And if so, how, if at all, does it affect the consensus forecast. It was noted in chapter 5, that Clark, Joines, and Phillips (1988) report that the forecasters of the weekly money supply series ignored an interest rate seasonal induced by monthly social security payments that was present in the *seasonally adjusted* measures of the money supply. As Zarnowitz (1992) points out, individual economic forecasts may be irrational while the consensus or market forecast may be rational.

## 4 US Treasury Bond Futures Price Data

Time and sales data on US Treasury bond futures prices were obtained from the Mid-America Commodity Exchange for the period April, 1987, to December 1988.[7] Similar data were obtained from the Chicago Board of Trade for periods after November 1988 although the material is not presented here. Price changes on the front month bond futures contract were used.[8] The minimum price change on a futures contract is called a "tick." In the case of the bond futures contracts traded on the Chicago Board of Trade and the Mid-America Commodity Exchange the tick is a thirty-second. This translates into \$31.25 and \$15.63 for a one-tick move for each bond futures contract on the Chicago Board of Trade and the Mid-America Commodity Exchange, respectively. A one point (32/32) move corresponds to a gain or loss of \$1,000 on one Chicago Board of Trade bond futures contract and \$500 on the Mid-America Commodity Exchange bond futures contract. It is not unusual for market participants to have a significant number of futures contracts outstanding.

Another aspect of the bond futures price data should be noted: namely, the time and sales data report new *transaction* prices only. That is, a price is reported only when there has been a change from the previous transaction price. Associated volume data for each transaction are not available. Casual empiricism suggests that there is greater trading volume around the release of important economic reports. However, the absence of volume data means that it is not possible to control for any security price pressure effects associated with increased trading volumes.

As with any market there is a bid–offer spread at any moment in time in the bond futures market. Transactions arise when individuals sell at (i.e. "hit") the bid or buy at (i.e. "take") the offer. The apparent size of the bid–offer spread in the Chicago Board of Trade bond futures market is one tick; however, the effective size of the bid–offer spread may be narrower if individuals are able to buy at the bid or sell at the offer part of the time. This means that fluctuations of a single tick may merely reflect market-making activity instead of a response to the arrival of new information.

One question that arises from observing changes in bond futures prices is why there are not more jumps in prices. This phenomenon is not unique to bond futures prices either. Webb and Smith (1994) report that virtually all of the changes in Eurodollar futures prices are for a single tick (the minimum price increment). This would suggest that the adjustment process is less rapid than it might be. Do profit opportunities result? That is difficult to determine. The answer depends, in part, on when a futures position is entered. The fact that a transaction occurred at a particular price does not mean that a customer can necessarily transact at that price especially in a fast market. Fast markets typically follow the release of economic reports.

## 5 Employment and Earnings Report

Perhaps no economic report exerts as much impact on speculative prices (especially bond prices), or is as closely followed by participants in speculative markets, as the Labor Department's monthly Employment and Earnings Report. The report is generally released at 8:30 a.m. on the first Friday of the month with appropriate exceptions made for government holidays.[9] The report contains a variety of statistical data which are updated monthly. Of principal interest to bond market participants, however, is information on the overall unemployment rate and the number of new jobs created outside of agriculture (i.e. nonfarm payrolls).

Each month sample data are gathered on employment and earnings in the United States. Two surveys are used: a survey of households and a survey of business establishments. The two surveys are intended to supplement one another and, as such, emphasize different information. In particular, the household survey collects data on the demographic characteristics of the eligible population, namely the civilian noninstitutional population aged 16 and over. In contrast, the survey of business establishments collects information on industry classifications. The household survey is part of the current population survey conducted by the Bureau of the Census.

Although the data from the two surveys are designed to supplement one another differences sometimes arise.[10] For instance, one source of potential discrepancy between the two surveys lies in the fact that the household survey includes both agricultural and nonagriculatural workers while the establishment survey is limited to nonagricultural workers only. Table 7.1 summarizes some of the similarities and differences between the two surveys.

The question naturally arises whether the information contained in the employment and earnings report can be obtained from other sources. Simply put, how much new information is in the report. One potential source of similar information is contained in data on new claims for unemployment insurance. The principal problem in using these data are that the number of new claims for unemployment insurance represents a subset of the set of all unemployed individuals. The reason for this is that the household survey on the unemployed includes those who do not qualify for unemployment insurance. One only needs to be jobless and searching for employment to be counted as unemployed according to the household survey. This includes those who no longer qualify for unemployment insurance (because benefits have run out); new entrants to the labor force (who hence do not qualify for unemployment insurance); and those who are no longer employed at positions for which there was no unemployment insurance (e.g. the self-employed). It should also be pointed out that in some cases individuals can be counted as employed for purposes of the household survey and yet still be entitled to unemployment insurance (e.g. those in part-time employment).

Given the emphasis on the concept of "full" employment in some macroeconomic theories, the question naturally arises as to what constitutes full employment. The full employment rate has changed over time. In the 1960s full employment was thought to be 3–4 percent. By the 1980s full employment was thought to be closer to 5–6 percent. In the standard Keynesian model of macroeconomic theory, when full employment is reached further increases in wages are inflationary. Not surprisingly, when the US economy reached "full" employment in the late 1980s there was much concern about the supposed inflationary pressures associated with that milestone.

As was stressed in the preceding chapters, the behavior of speculative prices in response to the arrival of new macroeconomic information depends, in part, on how market participants perceive the Fed responding to the new macroeconomic information. For instance, if market participants believe that Fed governors believe that the economy is at "full" employment and will increase interest rates to reduce the potential inflationary pressure of higher wages,

**Table 7.1** A comparison of the household and business establishment (or payroll) employment surveys

| | Household | Establishment |
|---|---|---|
| Sample size | Approximately 60,000 households | Over 300,000 establishments |
| Noninterview rate | 4–5% | n.a. |
| Employment status as of | Calendar week including 12th of month | Calendar week including 12th of month |
| Survey conducted by | Bureau of the Census | Bureau of Labor Statistics |
| Survey method | Direct interviews | Mail questionnaires |
| Survey frequency | Monthly | Monthly |
| Principal focus of market participants | Unemployment rate | Change in nonfarm payrolls (i.e. the net number of new jobs created) |
| Ancillary focus of market participants | 1 Number of discouraged workers | 1 Average hours worked<br>2 Earnings<br>3 Source of new jobs (e.g. services, manufacturing, construction, government) |
| Definition of employment (full or part-time) | 1 Wage and salary workers<br>2 Self-employed<br>3 Unpaid workers at family-run firms working 15 hours or more per week<br>4 Members of armed forces stationed in the United States | 1 Wage and salary workers at nonagricultural firms only |
| Multiple positions | Individuals employed at more than one job are counted once | Individuals employed at more than one job may be counted more than once |

**Table 7.1** Continued

| | Household | Establishment |
|---|---|---|
| Employees on leave without pay | Counted as employed | Not counted as employed (if on unpaid leave throughout payroll period) |
| Hours worked | Counts only hours employees actually worked | Counts hours employers paid for (including for example those for employees on paid leave) |
| Employee earnings | Measures median earnings across occupations and industries | Measures average earnings in production construction, mining, and private service sector |
| Release time | 8:30 a.m. New York time (usually the first Friday in the month) | 8:30 a.m. New York time (usually the first Friday in the month) |
| Unique information | Demographic characteristics | Industrial classifications |

*Source:* US Department of Labor, *Employment and Earnings*, May 1990, pp. 153–4

traders may react accordingly (thus doing the Fed's job for it) even if most market participants do not believe in Keynesian macroeconomic theory.

Most bond traders would interpret a greater than expected increase in the unemployment rate as indicating that the economy is weakening and that interest rates may fall as a result of the weak economy or Fed easing. Conversely, most bond traders would interpret a greater than expected decrease in the unemployment rate as indicating a strengthening economy and that interest rates may rise as a result of growing demand for funds or Fed tightening.

Similarly, most bond traders would regard a greater than expected increase in the number of nonfarm payrolls as indicating a growing economy and higher interest rates due to economic growth or Fed tightening in the future. Conversely, most bond traders would regard a smaller than expected increase (or a greater than expected decrease) in nonfarm payrolls as indicating a weakening economy which may cause interest rates to fall and provide the excuse for the Fed to ease monetary policy.

Figures 7.1 and 7.2 depict the average absolute change in Mid-America Commodity Exchange US Treasury bond futures prices after the employment report was released for the period April 1987 to December 1988 (excluding April 1988). Figure 7.1 shows that within the first 20 seconds of the report's release bond prices had changed, on average, by 2.5/32 up or down. Within a minute, bond futures prices were about 8/32 away from where they were before the report's release. Bond futures prices had changed, on average, by approximately 11.6/32 within a minute and a half of the report's release and by about 13.5/32 within two minutes of the report's release. Notice that the vast bulk of the response in bond futures prices comes very quickly as one would expect in an informationally efficient capital market. Although the bond continues to change after the first two minutes of trading the change is approximately absorbed by the bid–offer spread.

Figure 7.2 suggests that the initial "trend" established immediately after the report's release tends to persist, on average, with the bond futures contract changing approximately a whole point by 2:00 p.m. the same day. None of this should be misconstrued as suggesting that a profitable strategy would be to buy (sell) the bond futures contract if bond futures prices rose following the release of the Employment and Earnings Report and dispose of the position around 2:00 p.m. For instance, the subsequent "trend" in bond futures prices may simply represent a response of bond futures prices to the arrival of other information later in the day.

Figure 7.3 shows the incremental change from the previous time interval during the first four minutes of trading. As is readily apparent, the largest incremental change occurs during the second half of the first minute of trading. The second largest incremental change occurs between 60 and 90 seconds after the report's release.

The two principal components of the Employment and Earnings Report of interest from a bond trader's perspective (i.e. the unemployment rate and the nonfarm payrolls number) sometimes present conflicting information.[11] How does one interpret the conflicting information? Such a situation occurred on May 6, 1988, when both the unemployment rate and nonfarm payrolls were lower

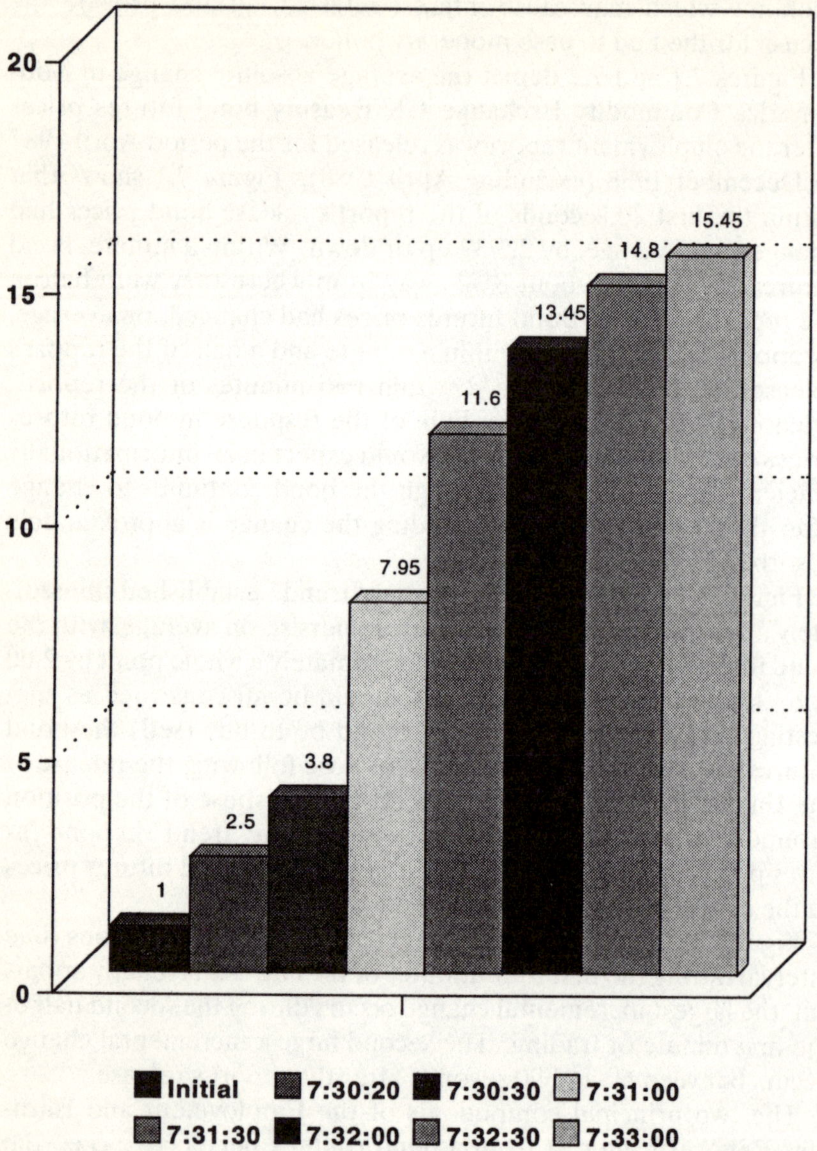


**Figure 7.1** Average absolute change in bond futures prices after the employment report is released: period April 1987 to December 1988, Mid-America Commodity Exchange, in thirty-seconds (excludes April 1988 due to holiday)

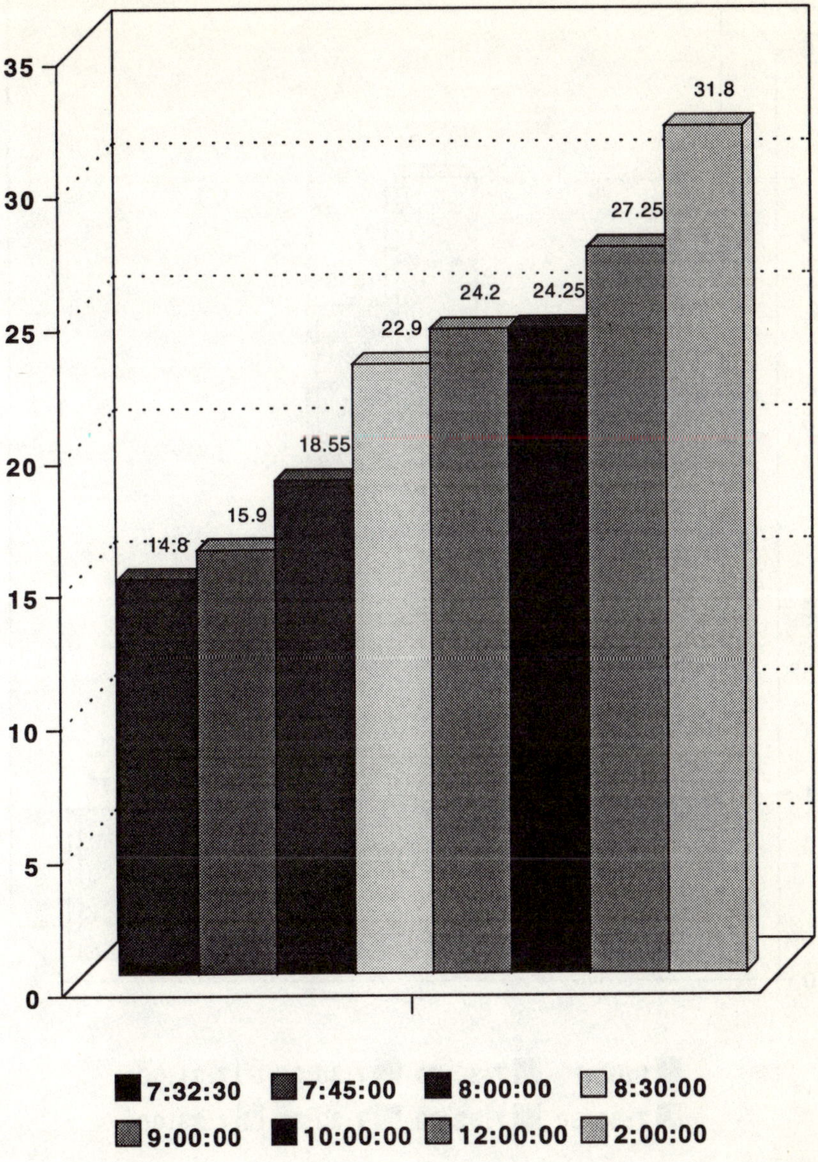


**Figure 7.2** Average absolute change in bond futures prices after the employment report is released: period April 1987 to December 1988, Mid-America Commodity Exchange, in thirty-seconds (excludes April 1988 due to holiday)

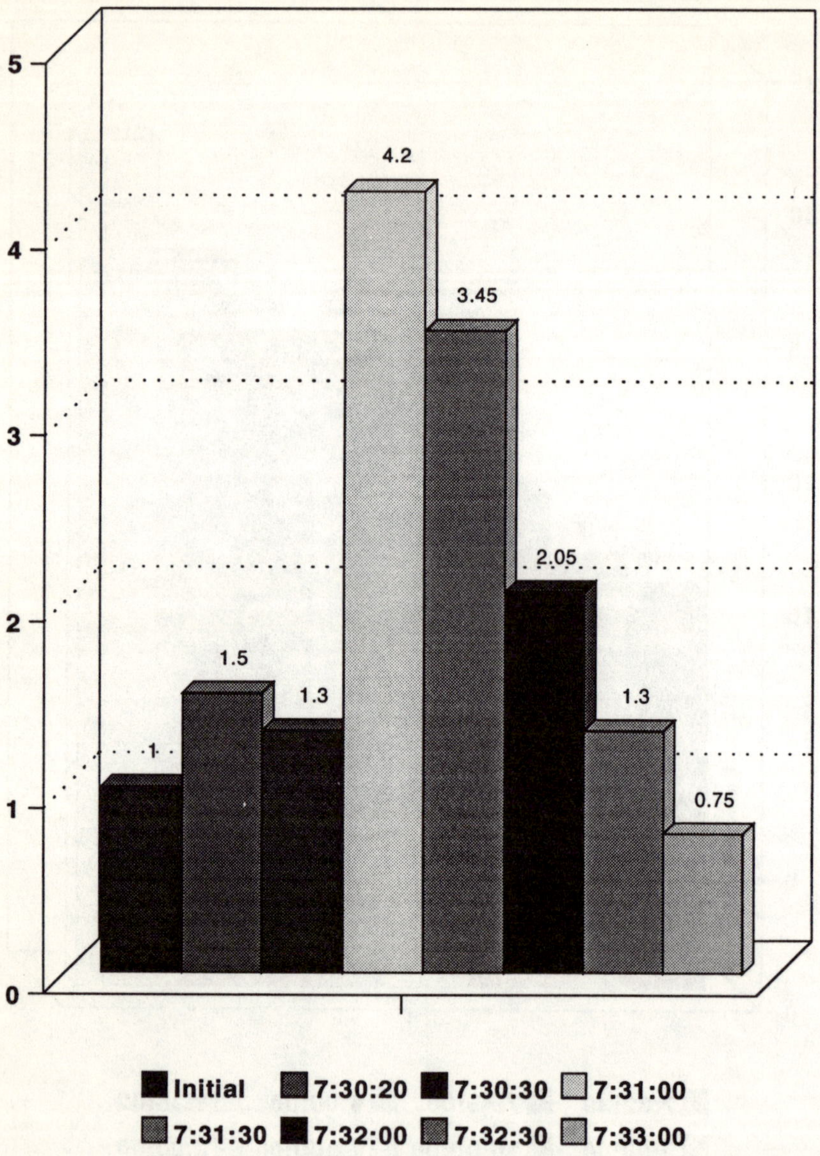


**Figure 7.3** Average absolute incremental change in bond futures prices after the employment report is released: period April 1987 to December 1988, Mid-America Commodity Exchange, in thirty-seconds (excludes April 1988 due to holiday)

than expected. This is illustrated in figures 7.4 and 7.5. Figure 7.4 depicts the average absolute change in bond futures prices within the first four minutes of the release of the report. Notice that bond futures prices were initially down 1/32 and quickly rose to 6/32 within 20 seconds of the report's release. Within two minutes of the report's release bond prices were up one-half point (16/32). This rally proved to be short-lived, however. Market prices fell 5/32 by 30 seconds later and another 5/32 in the next 30 seconds. Four minutes after the report's release bond futures prices were only 1/32 higher than before the report's release.

Figure 7.5 indicates that the decline in bond futures prices began two minutes after the report's release. Bond prices were down 6/32 by 7:45 a.m. (Chicago time) or 15 minutes after the report's release. Of course, it is possible that new negative information entered the marketplace around 7:32 a.m. (Chicago time) and precipitated the decline. Another objection is that the Mid-America Commodity Exchange data are suspect. Perhaps. However, another (more likely?) explanation is that traders collectively changed their interpretation of the meaning of the information in the report, causing the turnabout in bond futures prices on May 6, 1988.

Figure 7.6 presents another illustration of an apparent conflict in the information in the employment report. It depicts the reaction of bond futures prices to the new information contained in the employment report on September 2, 1988. As is readily apparent, there was an initial negative response to the employment report. The market was down by 5/32 within the first 20 seconds of the report's release. By the end of the first minute of trading bond futures were up by 7/32 and were up by 23/32 at the end of the first two and a half minutes of trading after the report's release. Once again, the question that arises is why the sudden reversal in the interpretation of the employment report. Is it explained by crazy traders on the floor of the futures exchanges in Chicago, the arrival of new information, the uncertainty traders face in knowing how the market, as a whole, will interpret the new information in an economic report, or something else entirely?

Yet another illustration of the market's reaction to the employment report when there is conflicting information is provided in figure 7.7. This depicts the response of bond futures prices to the December 2, 1988, employment report which had a higher than

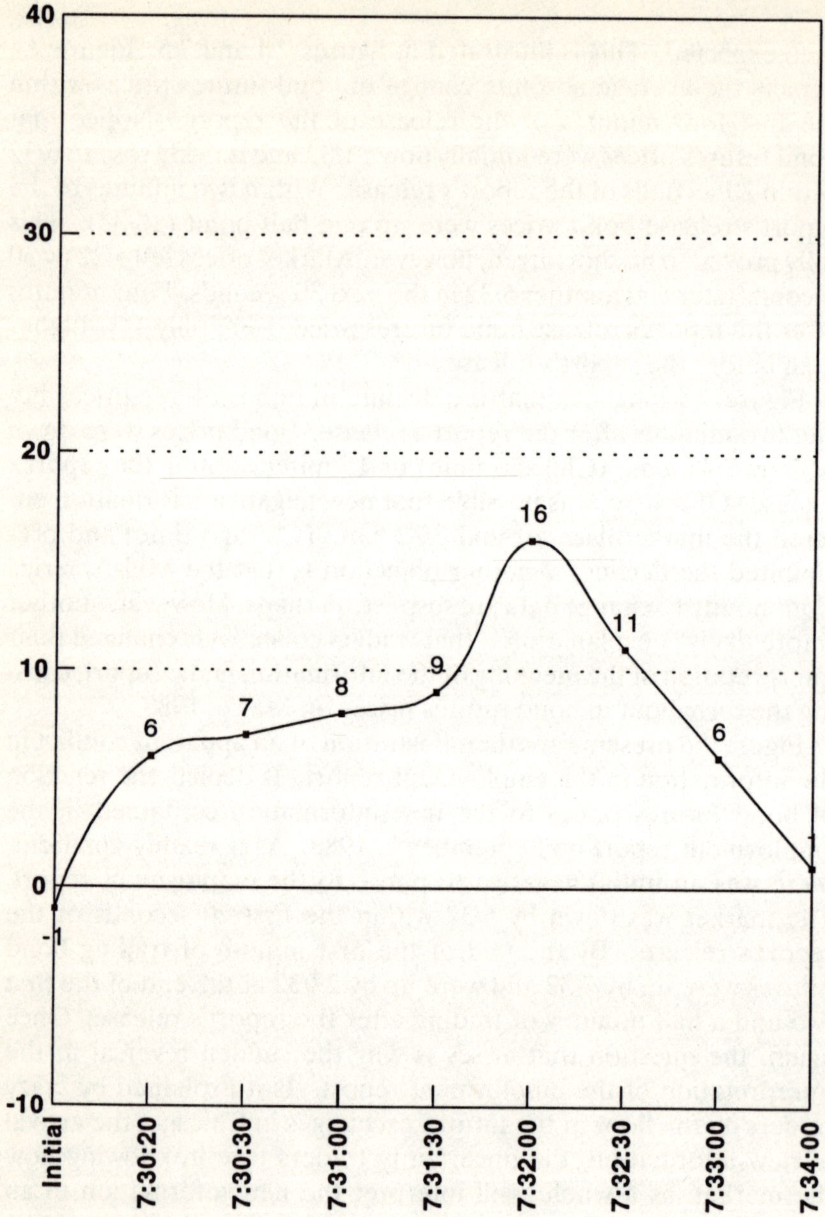


**Figure 7.4** Information conflict – employment report lower than expected unemployment rate and nonfarm payrolls: market reaction to release of the May 6, 1988, report (in thirty-seconds)

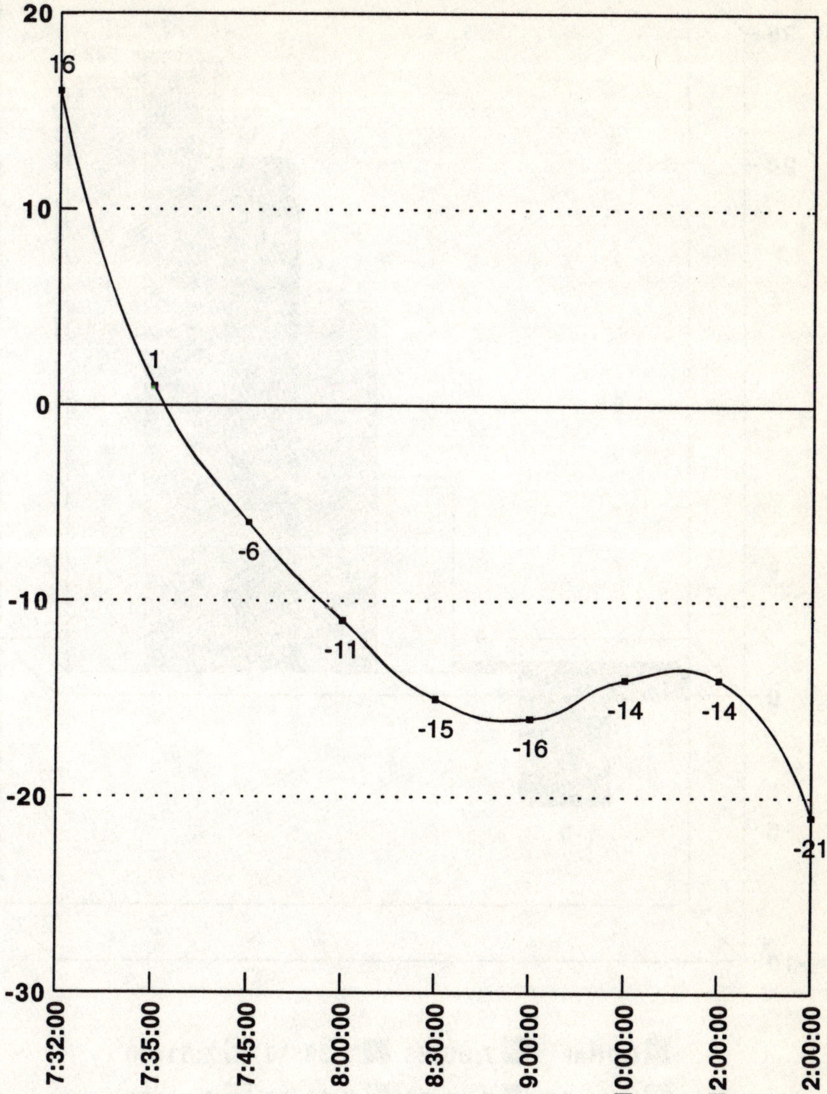


**Figure 7.5** Information conflict – employment report change in bond futures prices: market reaction to release of the May 6, 1988, report (in thirty-seconds)

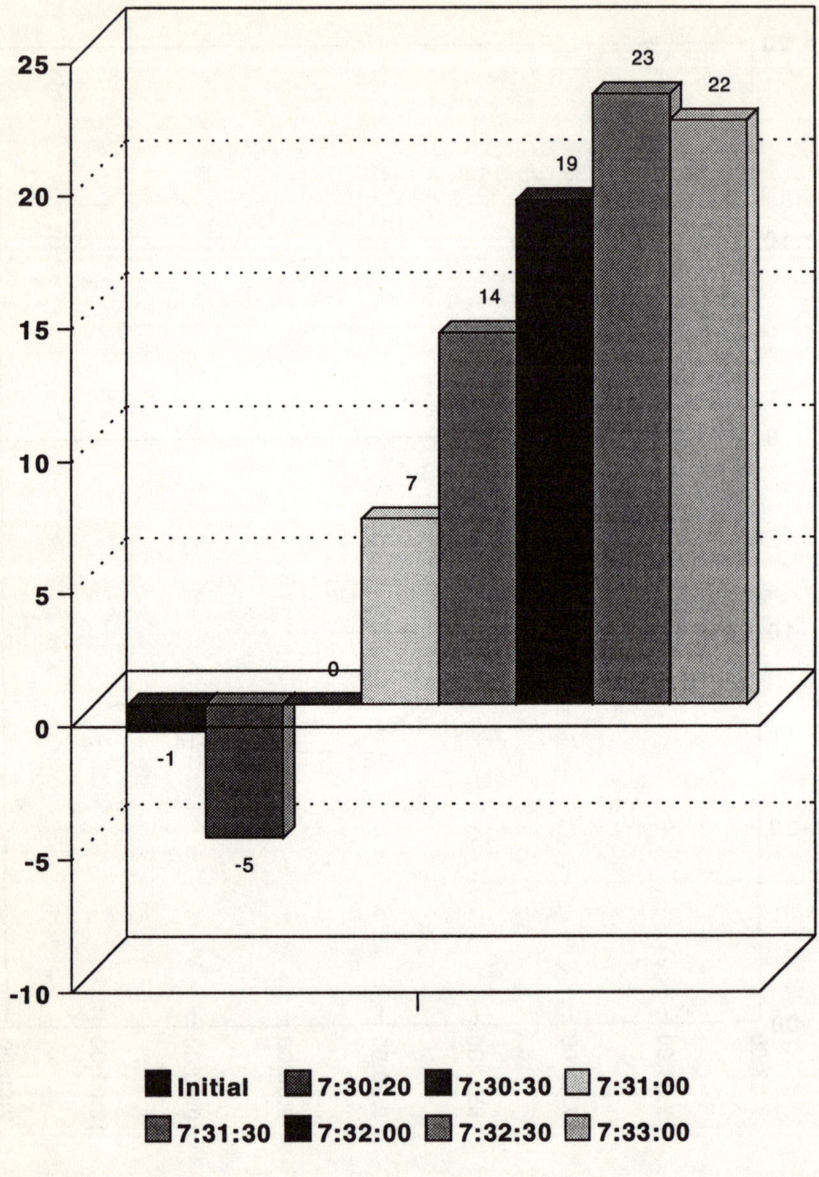


**Figure 7.6** Information conflict – employment report change in initial interpretation: market reaction to the September 2, 1988, report (in thirty-seconds)

expected unemployment rate and nonfarm payrolls. The initial reaction was a 1/32 drop in bond futures prices (and this may only have reflected the bid–offer spread). Thirty seconds after the release the market was unchanged. Over the next 30 seconds bond futures prices were down 8/32 and within the next minute bond futures prices were down another one-half point. On the surface the reaction of bond futures prices to the release of the employment report appears baffling. It is possible that a more detailed search may uncover other factors which explain the seemingly bizarre behavior of futures prices. For instance, apparent anomalies are sometimes explained by revisions to past data.[12] If so, it would be interesting to compare the reaction of various interest rate futures contracts to the same information to determine whether a similar pattern of price behavior was apparent across markets.

One problem with the above analysis is that it does not take into account potential dispersion in forecasts across individuals. Other things equal, the greater the dispersion is around the expected value of the economic report the greater is the information content of any deviation from consensus expectation. This suggests that the forecast errors should be standardized with respect to some measure of the dispersion among the individual forecasts.

Data on individual forecasts were obtained for 1988 from a large institutional investor which surveyed a number of primary government securities dealers with respect to their forecasts of selected economic reports. The average forecast from that survey corresponded well with the median forecast of other surveys of the expected value of the economic report. Standard deviations of the individual forecasts were calculated. The actual forecast errors of nonfarm payrolls and the unemployment rate were standardized by the standard deviation of each forecast for each release date.

Figure 7.8 shows the relationship between standardized forecast errors of nonfarm payrolls and the market's reaction two minutes after the release of the economic report (i.e. at 7:32 a.m., Chicago time). Notice that the size of the forecast error is not necessarily related to the the size of the market's response in prices. Note also that the the sign of the forecast error in nonfarm payrolls is not always in the opposite direction to the change in bond prices. This may reflect days when there is a conflict between the forecast errors for the unemployment rate and nonfarm payrolls. The question

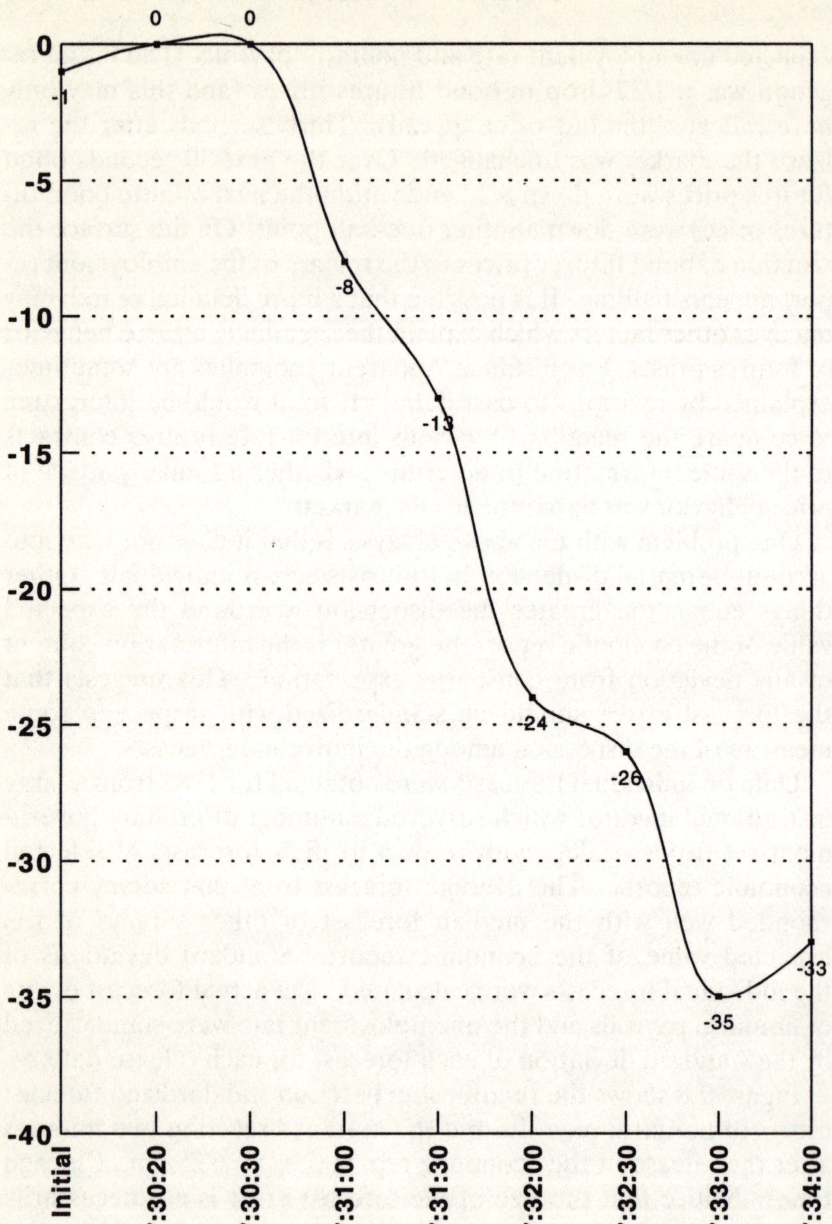


**Figure 7.7** Information conflict – employment report higher than expected unemployment rate and nonfarm payrolls: market reaction to release of the December 2, 1988, report (in thirty-seconds)

naturally arises as to whether the results in figure 7.8 are sensitive to how long one waits after the report is released to assess the reaction. However, similar results (not presented) were obtained when the market's reactions by 8:00 a.m. and 2:00 p.m. (Chicago time) were examined instead.

Similarly, figure 7.9 depicts the standardized forecast errors for the unemployment rate. Again, there is only at best a weak relationship between the size of the forecast error and the change in bond futures prices. Indeed, there appears to be a very crude U-shape. Both large negative and postive forecast errors appear to exert a *positive* impact on bond futures prices. There was one case where there was a zero forecast error and it is associated with a positive change in bond futures prices. Caution in interpreting these data is advisable. Keep in mind that the unemployment rate might rise in a weakening economy or in a growing economy (if formerly discouraged workers join the labor force). Remember also that the unemployment rate report and nonfarm payrolls are released simultaneously. It is important to keep in mind that valid statistical inferences cannot be drawn from the small samples presented here. However, the results are suggestive of the need for further research in this area.

## 6 Merchandise Trade Balance

As noted at the outset of this chapter, the perceived importance of the merchandise trade balance report has declined somewhat in recent years. During 1987–8, the monthly merchandise trade balance report frequently exerted tremendous influence on bond prices. It was noted in chapter 1 that the commonly accepted interpretation of the trade balance report changed 180 degrees between 1986 and 1987. Prior to 1987, a larger than expected trade deficit (in absolute value terms) was seen as a sign of a weakening economy because exports (viewed as a proxy for output) were down relative to imports. A weakening economy was thought to presage lower future interest rates. Conversely, a smaller than expected trade deficit (in absolute value terms) was viewed as indicating a stronger economy because exports were up relative to imports. A strengthening economy was thought to presage higher interest rates

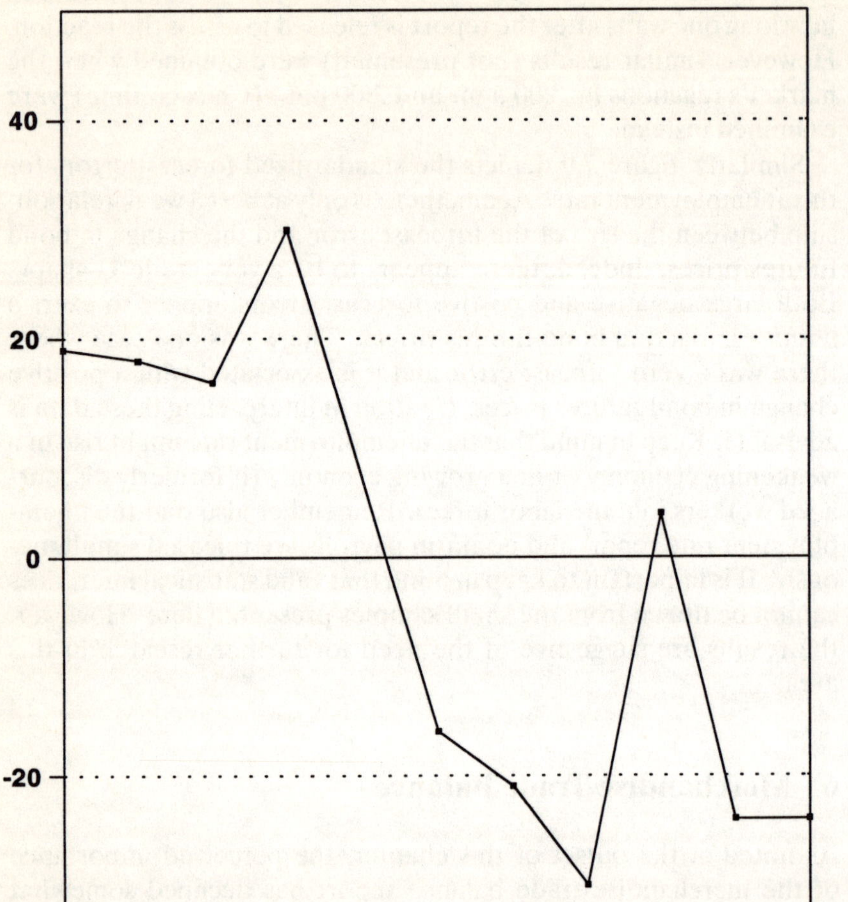


**Figure 7.8** Selected standardized forecast errors of nonfarm payroll growth during 1988 and associated change in bond futures prices (in thirty-seconds): ■, 7:32:00

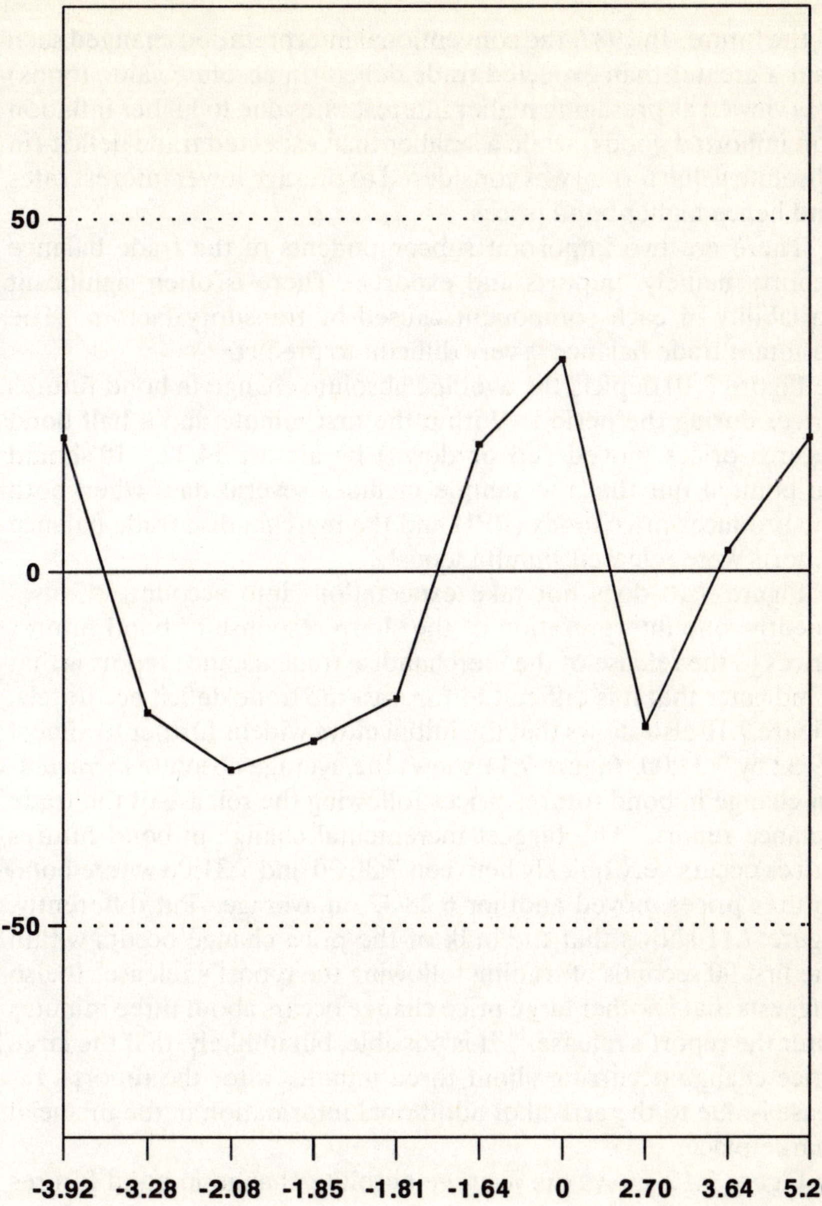


**Figure 7.9** Selected standardized forecast errors for unemployment rate during 1988 and associated change in bond futures prices (in thirty-seconds): ■, 7:32:00

in the future. In 1987, the conventional interpretation changed such that a greater than expected trade deficit (in absolute value terms) was viewed as presaging higher interest rates due to higher inflation (on imported goods) while a smaller than expected trade deficit (in absolute value terms) was considered to presage lower interest rates and hence higher bond prices.

There are two important subcomponents of the trade balance report: namely, imports and exports. There is often significant variability in each component caused by transitory factors. The resultant trade balance is very difficult to predict.

Figure 7.10 depicts the average absolute change in bond futures prices during the period. Within the first minute and a half bond futures prices moved (up or down) by almost 14/32. It should be pointed out that the sample includes several days when both the producer price index (PPI) and the merchandise trade balance reports were released simultaneously.

Figure 7.10 does not take expectations into account. Consequently, one interpretation of the sharp response of bond futures prices to the release of the merchandise trade balance report is that it indicates that it is difficult to forecast the trade deficit accurately. Figure 7.10 also shows that the initial move widens further to almost 19/32 by 7:34:00. Figure 7.11 shows the average absolute *incremental* change in bond futures prices following the release of the trade balance report. The biggest incremental change in bond futures prices occurs very quickly between 7:30:30 and 7:31:00 where bond futures prices moved another 6.28/32 on average. Put differently, figure 7.11 shows that the bulk of the price change occurs within the first 90 seconds of trading following the report's release. It also suggests that another large price change occurs about three minutes after the report's release.[13] It is possible, but unlikely, that the large price change occurring about three minutes after the report's release is due to the arrival of additional information in the financial marketplace.

Figure 7.12 shows the average absolute change in bond futures prices following the release of the trade report from 7:32:30 to 2:00:00 (Chicago time). This should not be misconstrued as suggesting that the price change 7:30:00 a.m. to 2:00:00 p.m. is entirely due to some delayed reaction to the release of the trade report. Nor does this author believe that figure 7.12 suggests that there is an

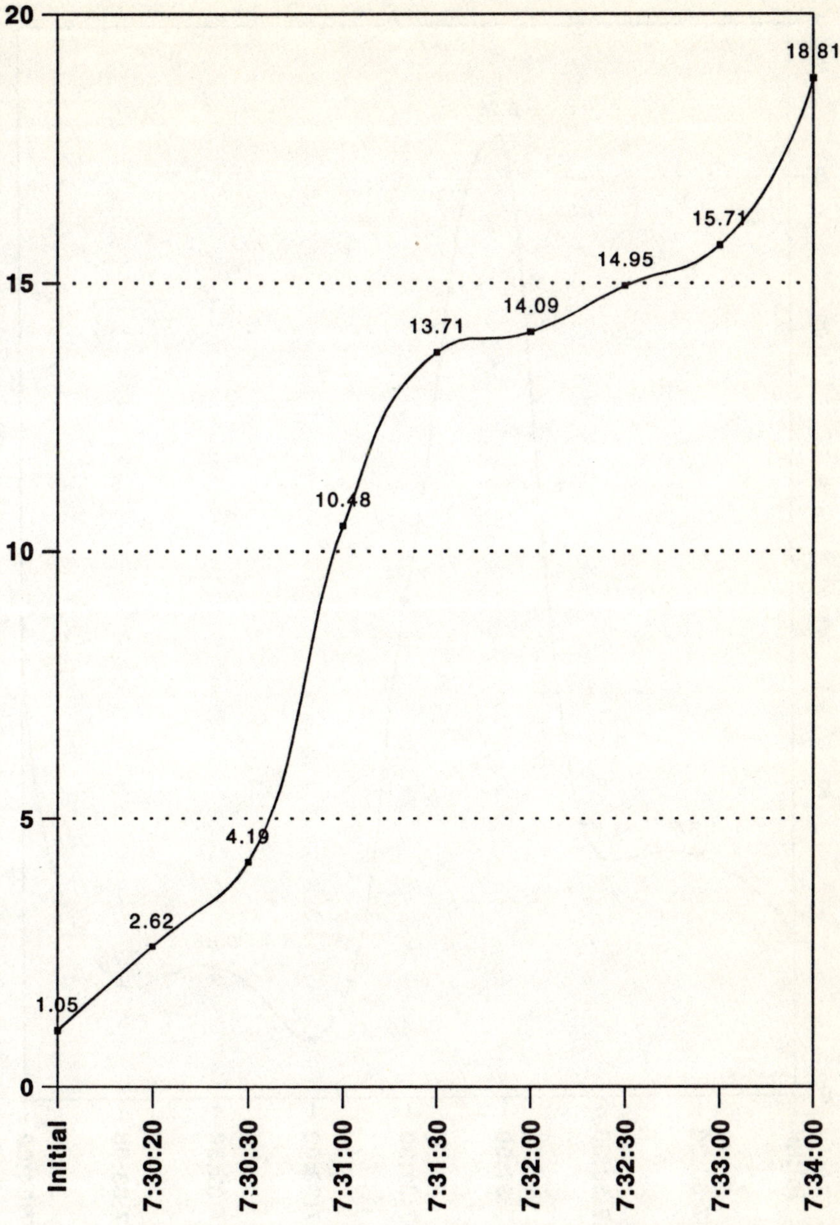


**Figure 7.10** Average absolute change in bond futures prices after the merchandise trade balance report is released (in thirty-seconds)

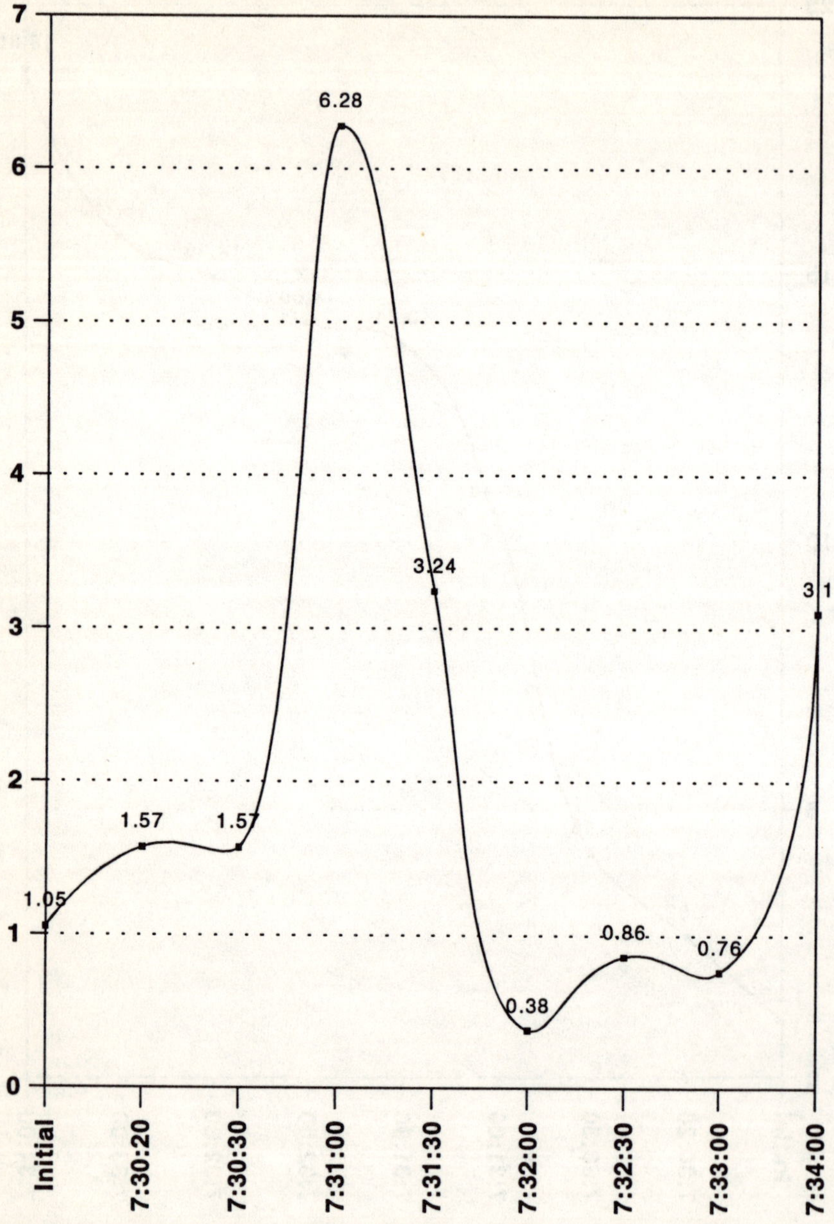


**Figure 7.11** Average absolute incremental change in bond futures prices after the trade balance report is released (in thirty-seconds)

apparent profit opportunity in buying or selling (depending upon the initial reaction in the market) bond futures contracts following the release of the trade report and offsetting the futures position by the close of trading. Rather, figure 7.12 suggests that the change in bond futures prices following the release of the trade report might persist at least through the end of the trading day.

One example of a seemingly delayed response to the trade deficit report occurred on April 14, 1987. At the time that this report was released bond futures trading on the Chicago Board of Trade opened at 8:00:00 a.m. As figure 7.13 makes clear, bond futures prices on the Mid-America Commodity Exchange were essentially unchanged during the first minute of trading (down 1/32). This was followed by a short rally over the next 30 seconds (up 4/32) which, in turn, was followed by a small break (down 6/32) over the next two minutes. A small rally followed over the succeeding two minutes (up 1/32). (The price changes reported represent the change in price compared with the price prevailing prior to the release of the trade balance report.) Fifteen minutes after the report's release bond futures prices were down 12/32 and bonds futures opened on the Chicago Board of Trade one point (32/32) below where bond futures traded on the Mid-America Commodity Exchange before the trade balance report's release. Within seven minutes of the Chicago Board of Trade's opening of the bond futures pit, bond futures prices were down almost two and a third points (down 74/32). This break was followed by a substantial rally as figure 7.13 makes clear. The financial press attributed the break to the release of the trade report.[14] If so, the delayed reaction is puzzling. Of course, it is possible that a closer examination of the days's events will find another apparently transitory information factor which explains the significant change in bond futures prices that day.

As already noted, the above figures depict the reaction of bond futures prices to the release of the trade report without taking expectations into account. Figures 7.14 and 7.15 attempt to rectify that deficiency. Figure 7.14 shows the average change in bond futures prices when the reported trade deficit differed from the consensus expectation. As expected, a smaller than expected trade deficit corresponded to higher bond prices on average during this period. Conversely, a larger than expected trade deficit corresponded to lower bond prices during this period. It is possible that this

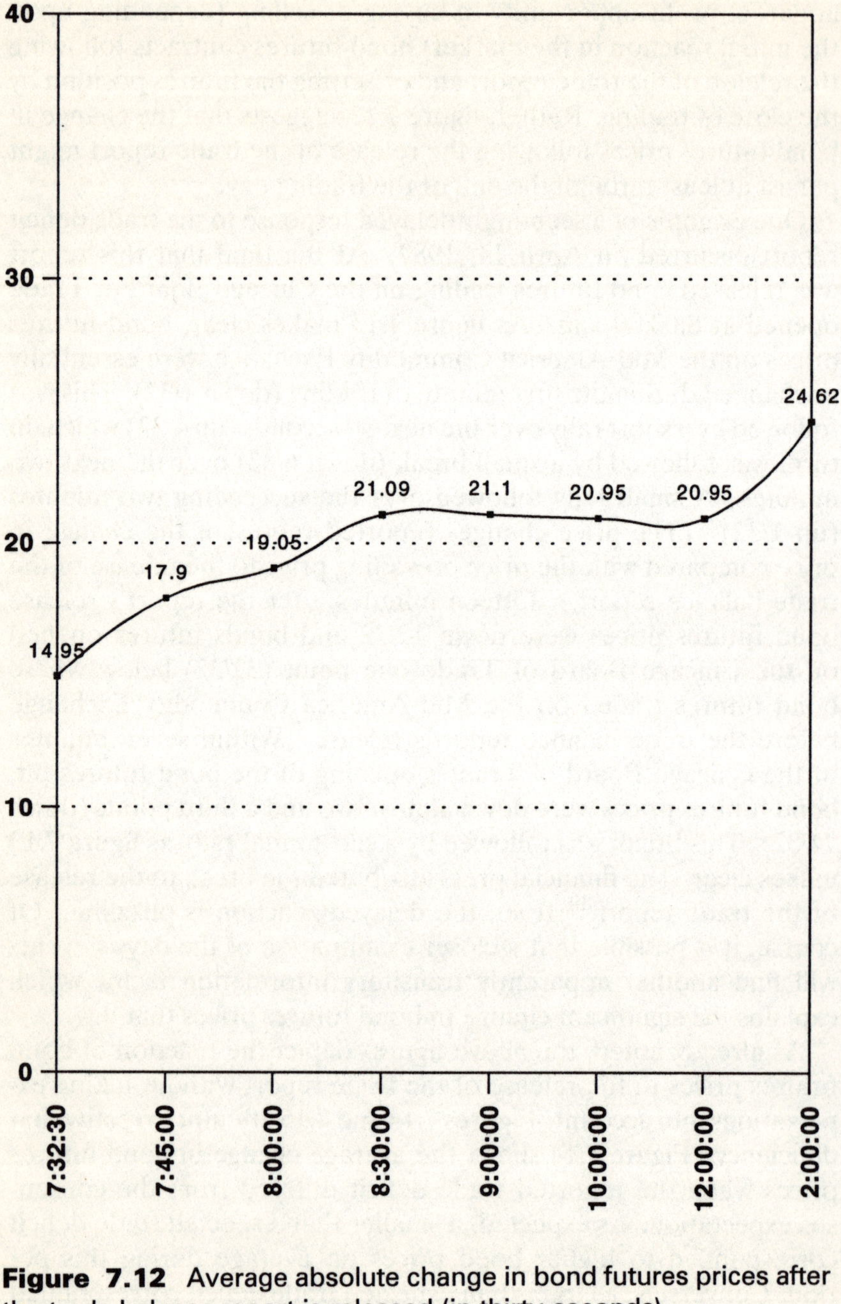


**Figure 7.12** Average absolute change in bond futures prices after the trade balance report is released (in thirty-seconds)

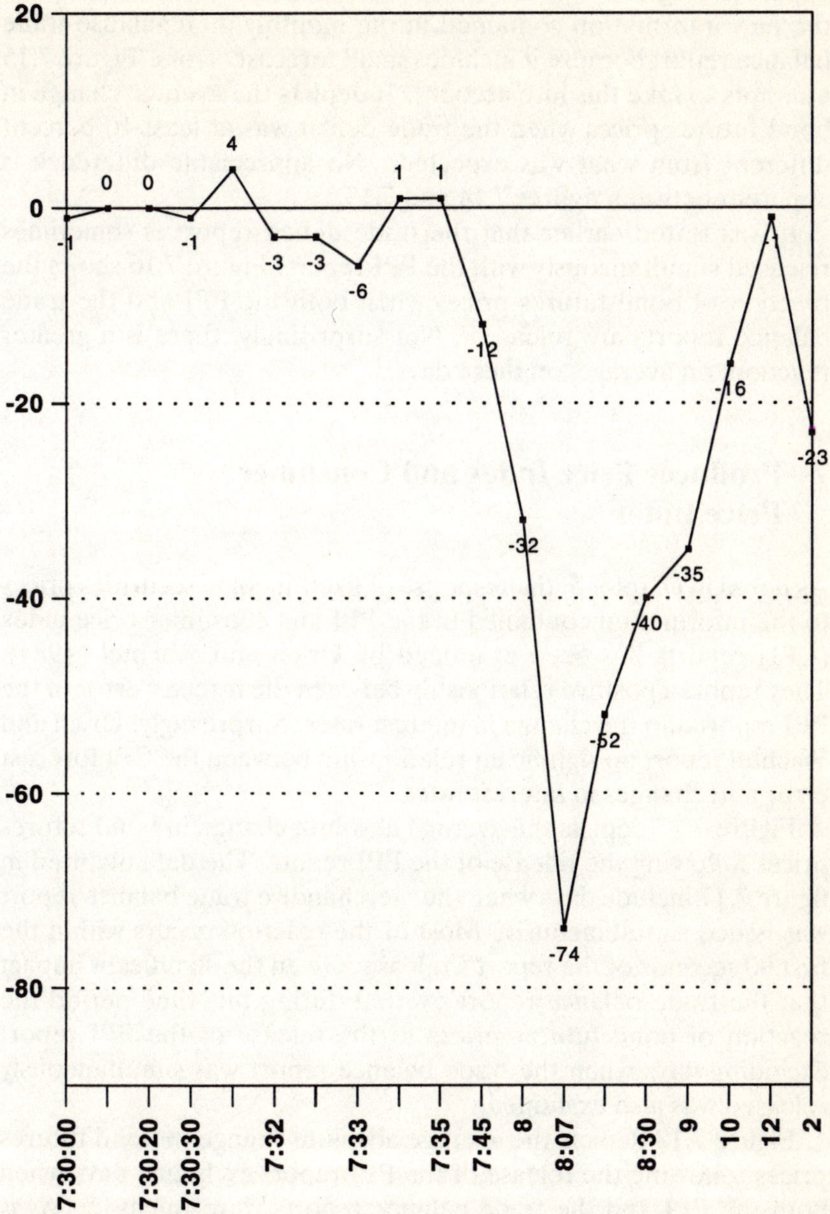


**Figure 7.13** Bond futures market reaction to release of the merchandise trade report (in thirty-seconds): ■, April 14, 1987

approach might understate the reaction of bond futures prices to the new information contained in the monthly merchandise trade balance report because it includes small forecast errors. Figure 7.15 attempts to take this into account. It depicts the average change in bond futures prices when the trade deficit was at least 10 percent different from what was expected. No appreciable difference is apparent between figures 7.14 and 7.15.

It was stated earlier that the trade deficit report is sometimes released simultaneously with the PPI report. Figure 7.16 shows the reaction of bond futures prices when both the PPI and the trade balance reports are released. Not surprisingly, there is a greater reaction, on average, on these days.

## 7 Producer Price Index and Consumer Price Index

As noted in chapter 5, the response of fixed-income securities prices to the information contained in the PPI and consumer price index (CPI) reports has been examined by Urich and Wachtel (1984). They report a positive relationship between the forecast error of the PPI report and the change in interest rates. Surprisingly, Urich and Wachtel report no significant relationship between the CPI forecast error and changes in interest rates.

Figure 7.17 depicts the average absolute change in bond futures prices following the release of the PPI report. The data pictured in figure 7.17 include days when the merchandise trade balance report was issued simultaneously. Most of the reaction occurs within the first 90 seconds of the report's release. Given the significant impact that the trade balance report exerted during this time period the reaction of bond futures prices to the release of the PPI report excluding days when the trade balance report was simultaneously released was also examined.

Figure 7.18 depicts the average absolute change in bond futures prices following the release of the PPI report excluding days when both the PPI and the trade balance reports were released. As is readily apparent, most of the price change is obtained within 90 seconds of the report's release. However, the average size of the

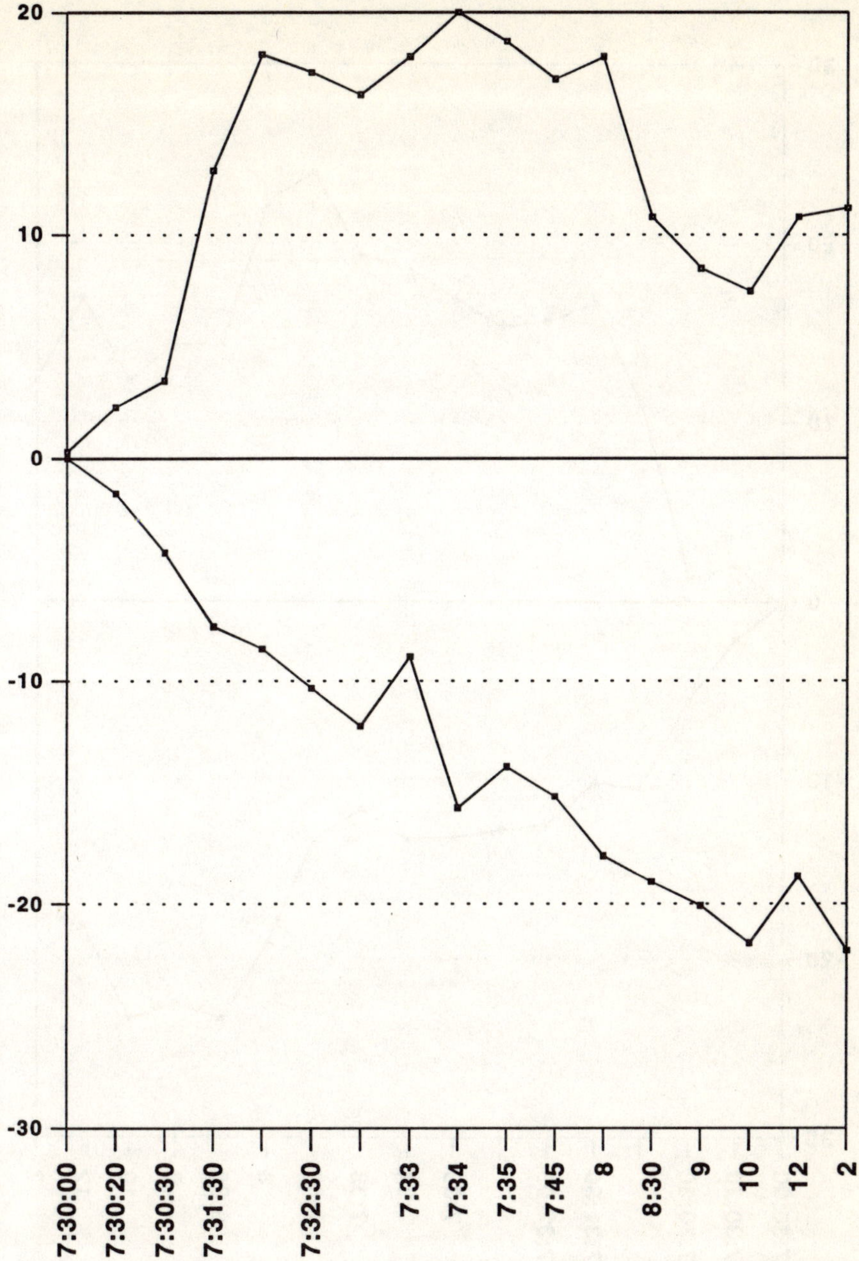


**Figure 7.14** Average change in bond futures prices when the reported trade deficit differs from the consensus expectation (in thirty-seconds): ■, trade deficit larger; □, consensus expectation larger

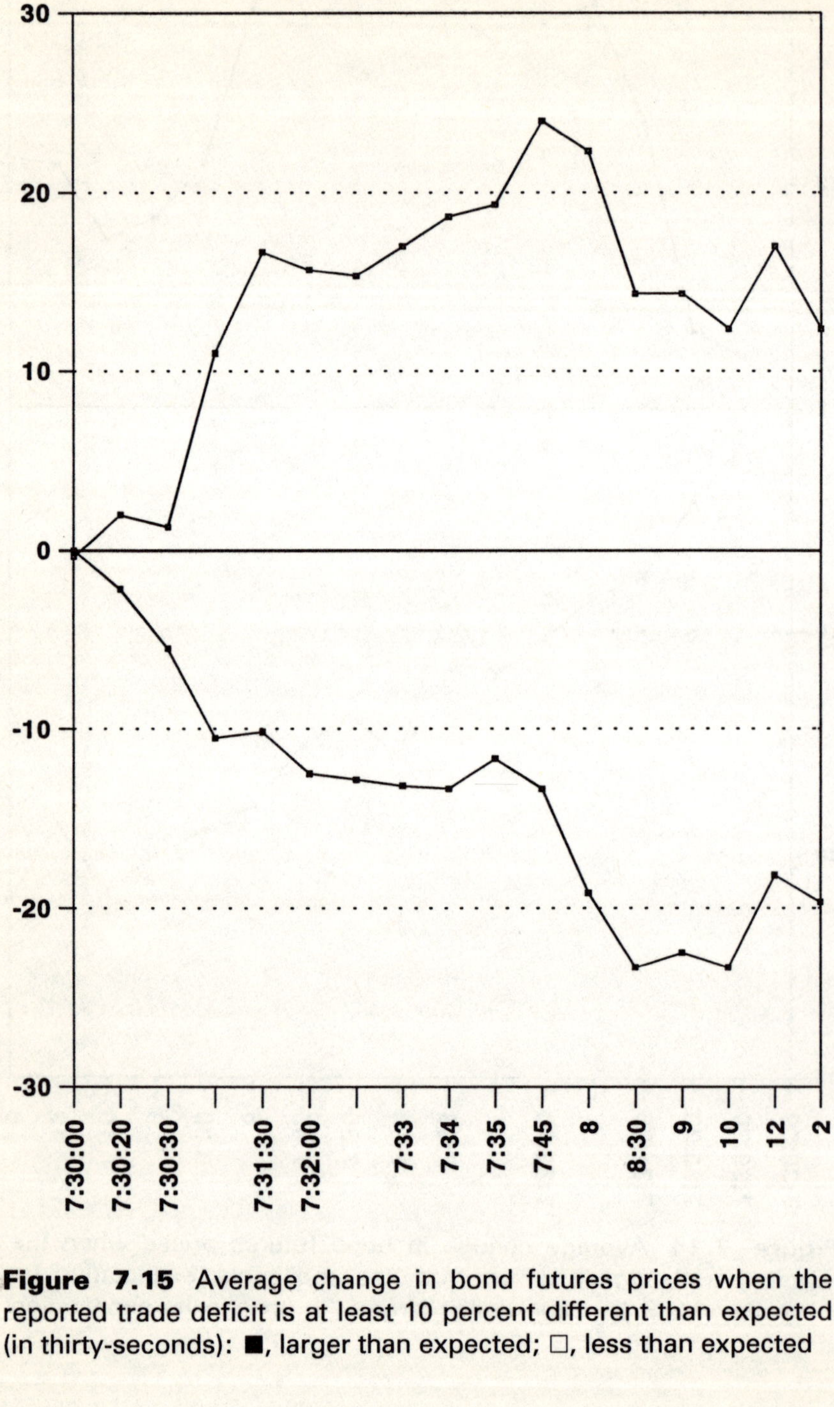


**Figure 7.15** Average change in bond futures prices when the reported trade deficit is at least 10 percent different than expected (in thirty-seconds): ■, larger than expected; □, less than expected

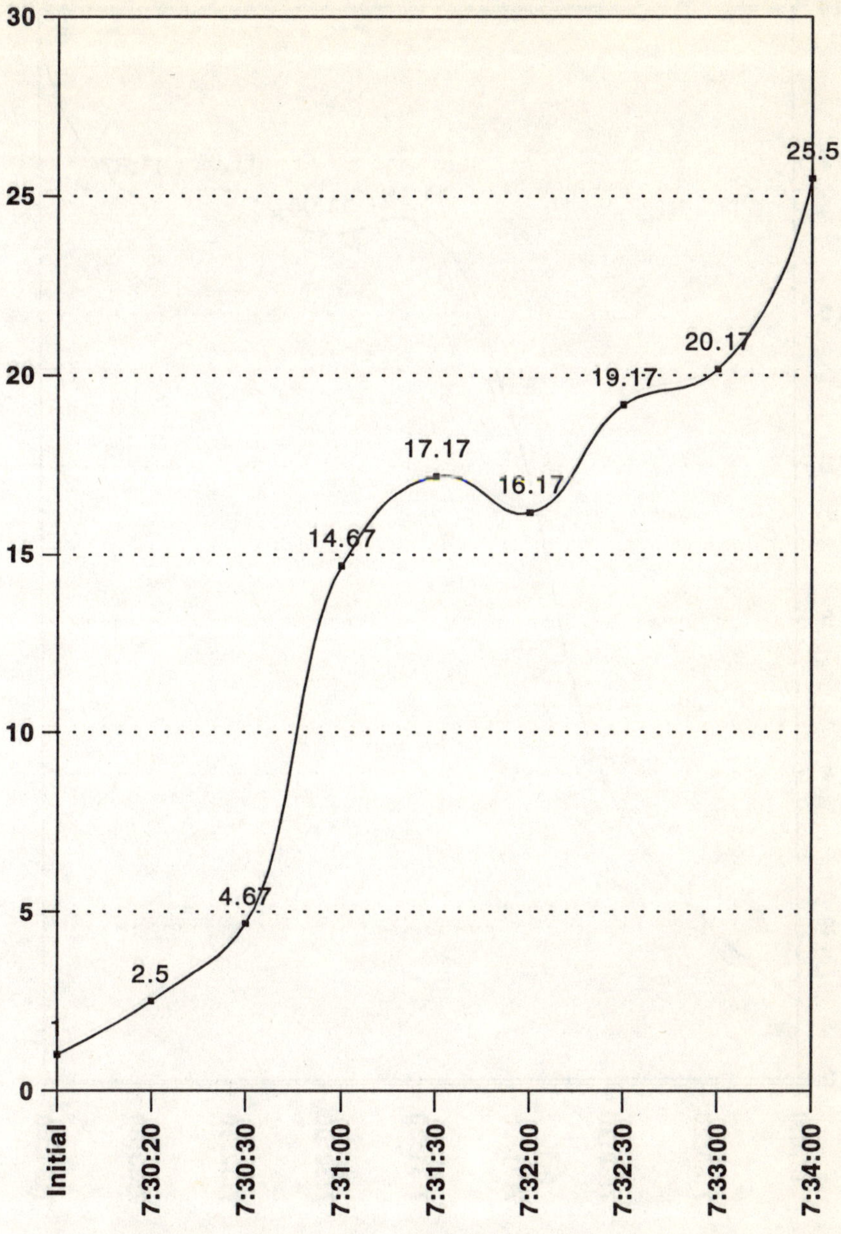


**Figure 7.16** Average absolute change in bond futures prices after the producer price index and trade balance reports are released (in thirty-seconds)

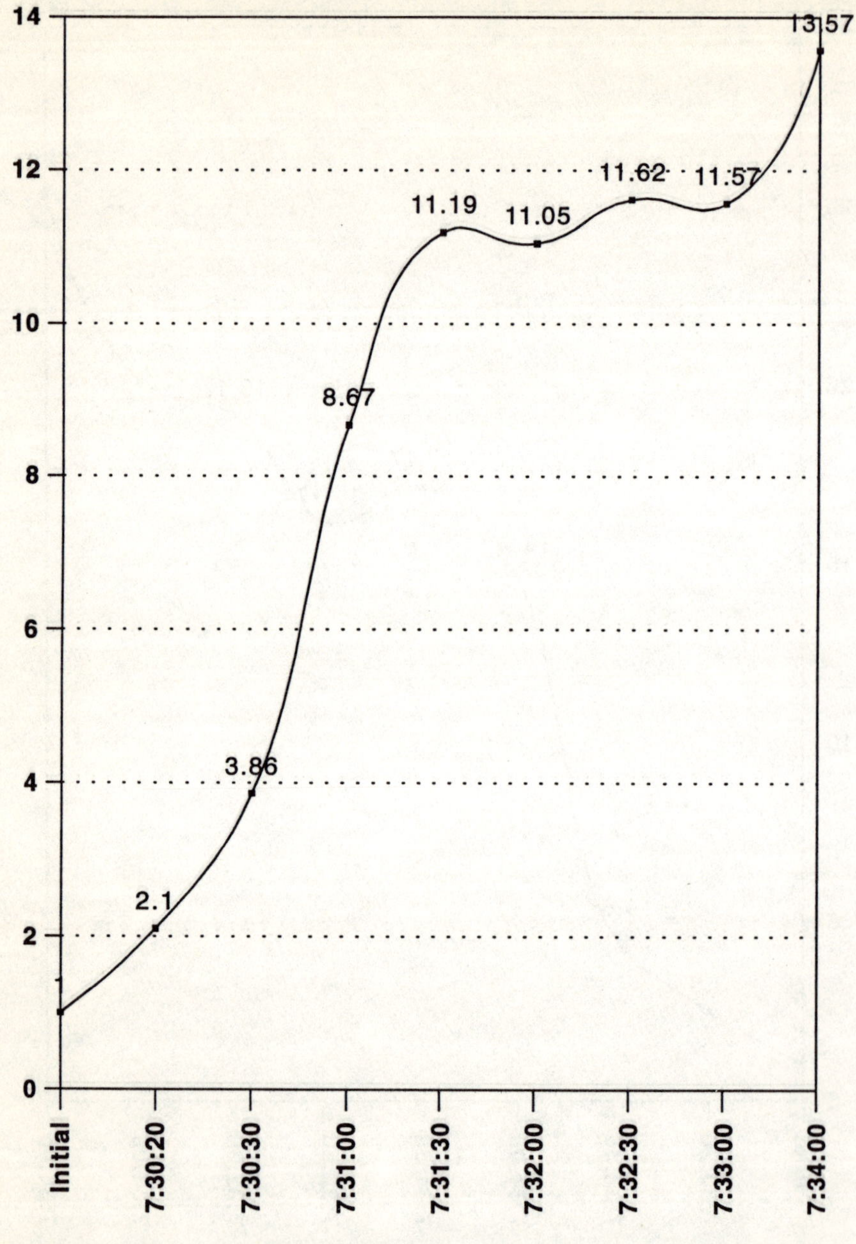


**Figure 7.17** Average absolute change in bond futures prices after the producer price index report is released (in thirty-seconds). The producer price index report includes days when the trade balance report is simultaneously released

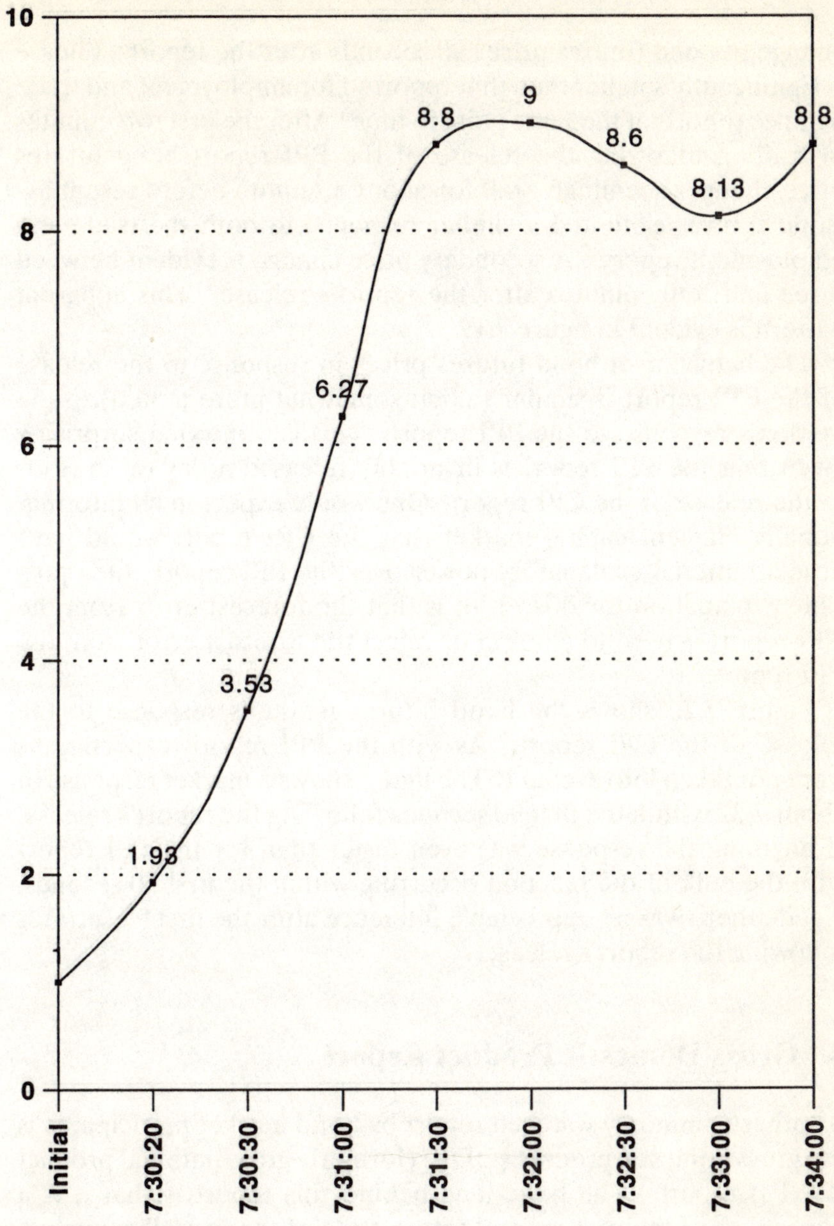


**Figure 7.18** Average absolute change in bond futures prices after the producer price index report is released (in thirty-seconds). The producer price index report excludes days when the trade balance report is released

change in bond futures prices 90 seconds after the report's release is significantly smaller than that reported for employment and trade balance reports at the same point in time. After the first two minutes of trading following the release of the PPI report bond futures price changes seemingly stall for about a minute before resuming. Bond futures exhibited a similar response to both the trade and employment reports. A secondary price change is evident between three and four minutes after the report's release. This apparent pattern is evident in figure 7.19.

The behavior of bond futures prices in response to the release of the CPI report is similar (albeit somewhat more muted) to the market's response to the PPI report. This is somewhat surprising given that the PPI report is invariably released a day or so prior to the release of the CPI report. One would expect in an informationally efficient capital market that the CPI report would have little additional explanatory power over the PPI report. One possible explanation for this result is that the forecast error from the CPI report is used to confirm or reject the forecast error from the PPI report.

Figure 7.20 shows the bond futures market's response to the release of the CPI report. As with the PPI report, expectations were not taken into account. The figure shows a market response of about 7/32 within the first 90 seconds following the report's release. If anything the response was even faster than for the PPI report with the bulk of the reaction occurring within the first 60 seconds. Again, there was no appreciable influence after the first 90 seconds following the report's release.

## 8 Gross Domestic Product Report

Another commonly watched report by bond market participants is the gross domestic product (GDP) (formerly gross national product (GNP)) report. The basic idea behind this report is that it is a barometer of the present and future state of the overall economy. Many market participants believe that the level of interest rates varies directly with the business cycle. Thus, evidence that the economy is weakening is interpreted as indicating lower interest rates in the future due to reduced demand for funds or expectations

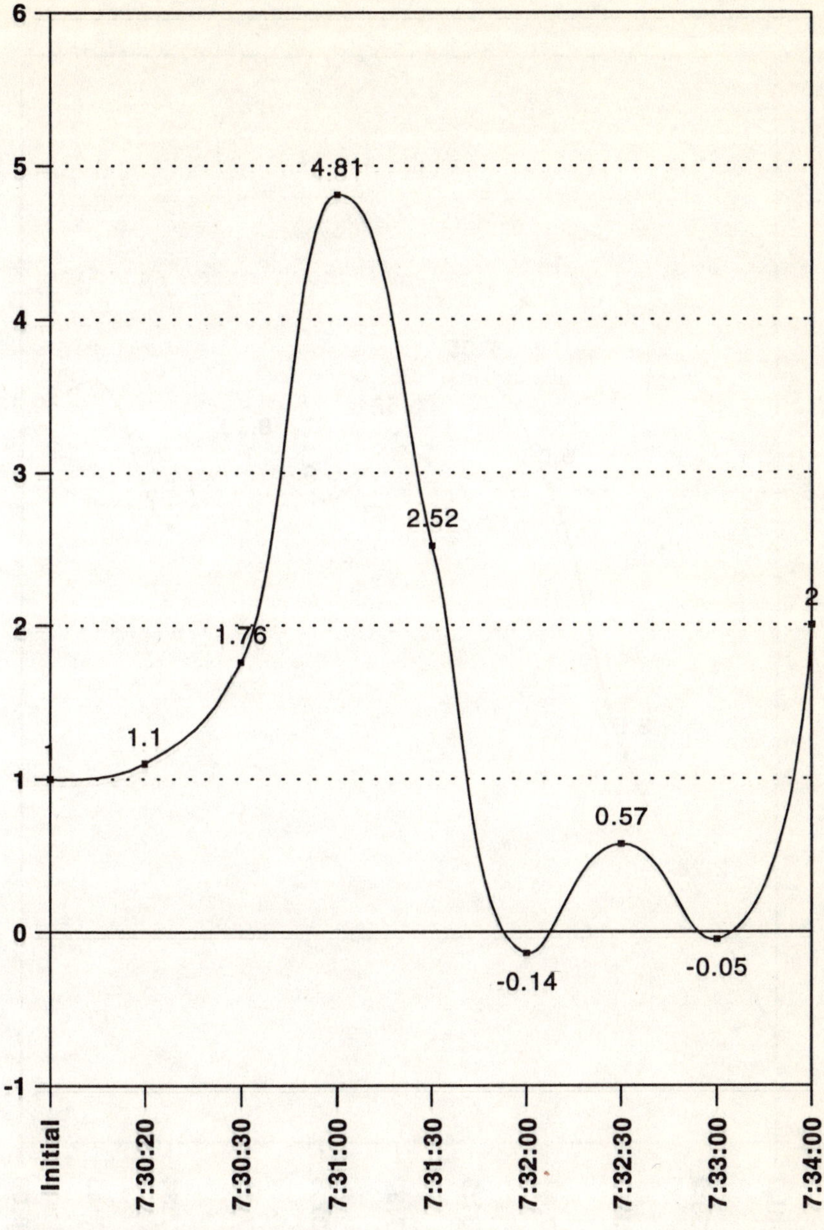


**Figure 7.19** Average absolute incremental change in bond futures prices after the producer price index report is released (in thirty-seconds)

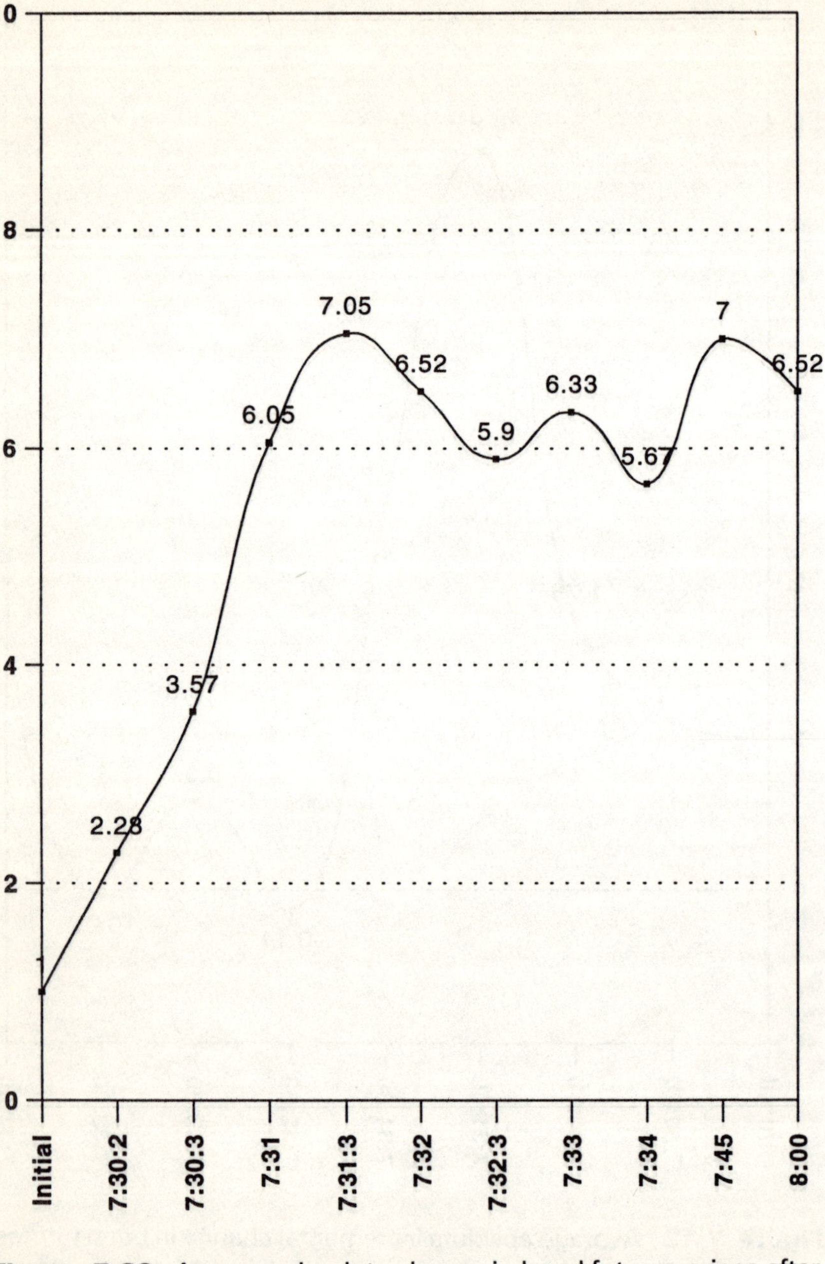


**Figure 7.20** Average absolute change in bond futures prices after the consumer price index report is released (in thirty-seconds)

of additional monetary easing by the Fed. The converse would be true for a rapidly growing economy. As was seen above, similar reasoning underlies the reaction of bond futures prices to forecast errors in the employment report.

Figure 7.21 depicts the average absolute change in bond futures prices after the GNP report is released. It suggests that there is minimal information in the report beyond what is already expected (and hence presumably incorporated into speculative prices). The majority of the price change occurs within the first minute of trading after the report's release where bond future prices changed on average by almost 6/32.

## 9 Retail Sales

The basic rationale underlying interest in the retail sales report is the same as that for the GDP report: namely, as a proxy for the strength of the economy and as an indicator of Fed monetary policy. Thus, a lower than expected retail sales figure would be interpreted as indicating a weak economy and possible Fed easing and hence higher bond prices. Figure 7.22 depicts the average change in bond futures prices after the retail sales report is released. As before, expectations are not taken into account. It is apparent that most of the reaction to the report comes very early (i.e. within the first 90 seconds) and the size of the price change is similar to that reported for the GNP and CPI reports. There is some indication of further increases in bond prices 15 minutes and 30 minutes after the report's release. It is likely that the apparent delayed increase in prices can be explained by the arrival of other information rather than as indicating an apparent profit opportunity.

## 10 Durable Goods

Finally, the durable goods report is occasionally closely followed by bond market participants. Durable goods represent consumer purchases of automobiles, refrigerators, stoves, etc. Not surprisingly, the argument behind the influence of forecast errors in the

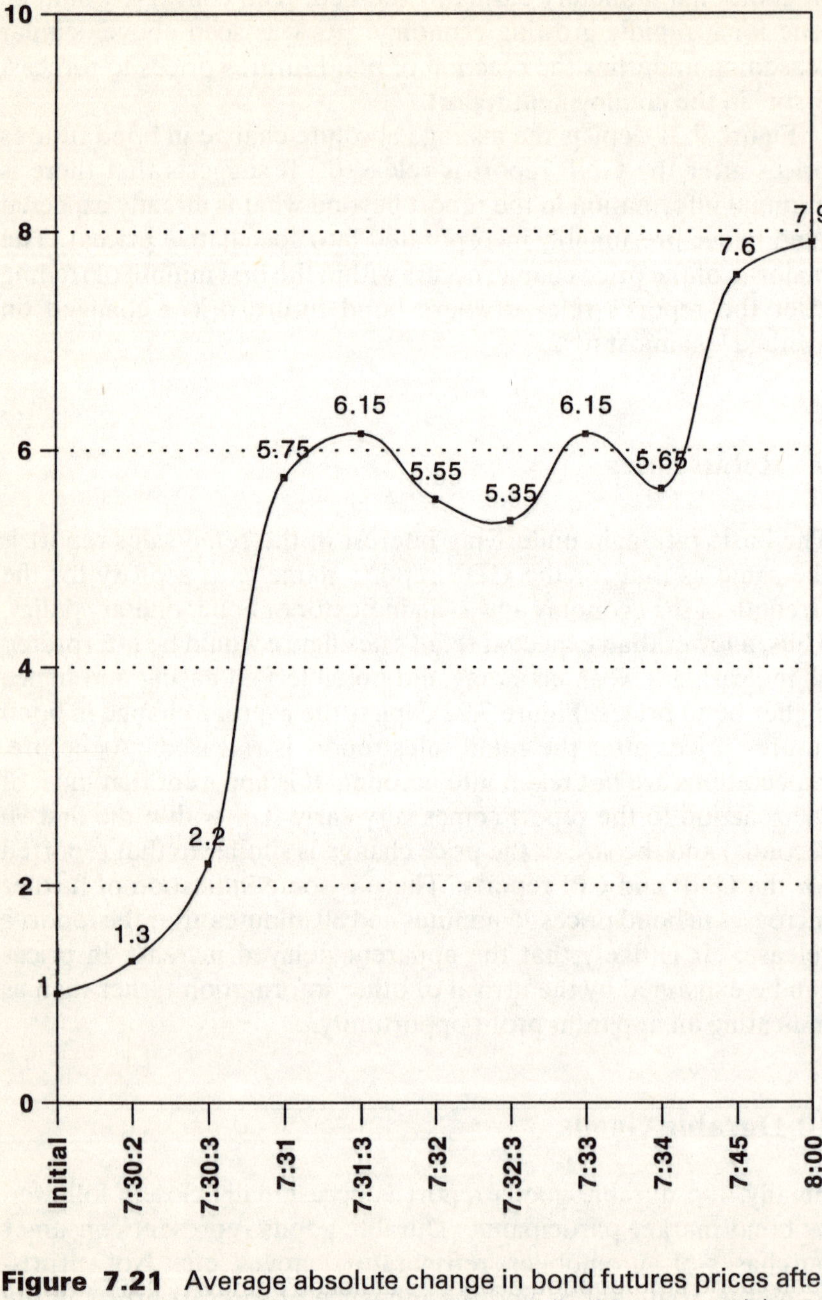


**Figure 7.21** Average absolute change in bond futures prices after the gross national product report is released (in thirty-seconds)

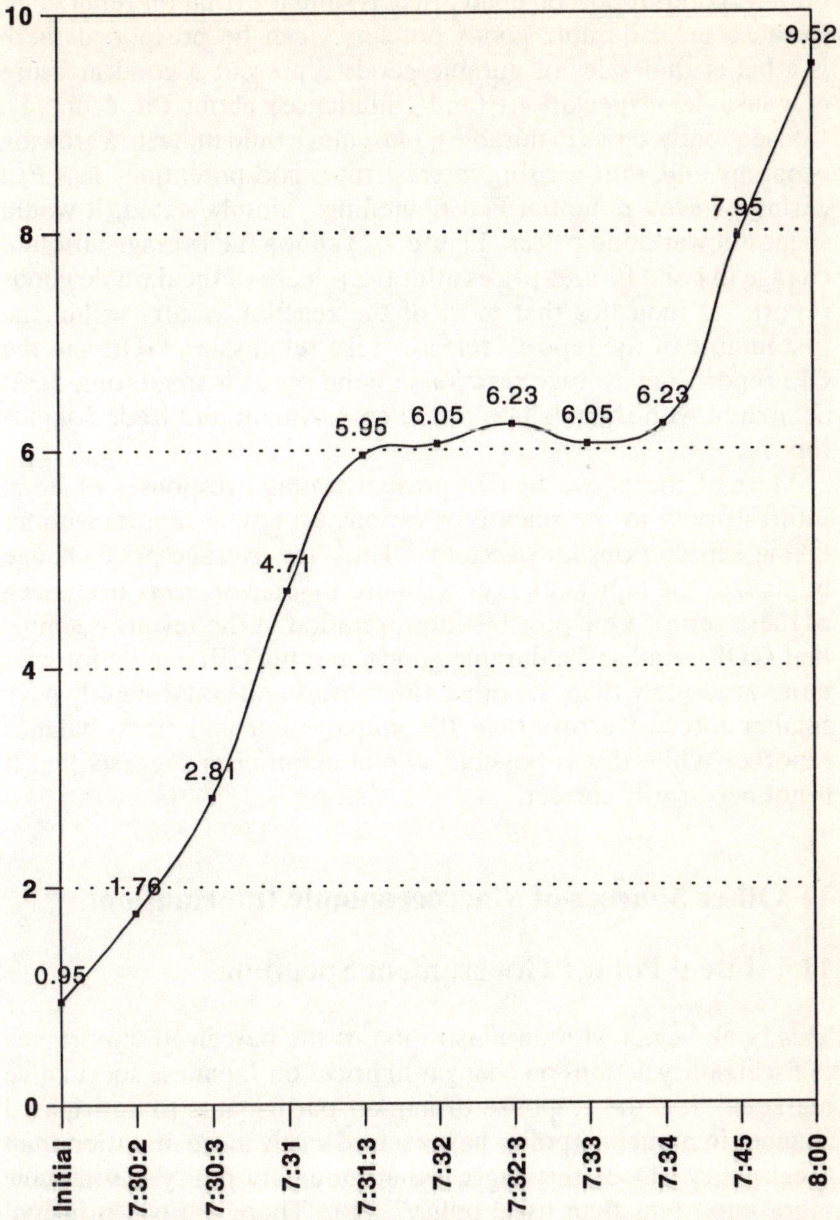


**Figure 7.22** Average absolute change in bond futures prices after the retail sales report is released (in thirty-seconds)

durable goods report on bond prices is similar to that for retail sales. Because most durable goods purchases can be postponed there is a belief that sales of durable goods represent a good measure of consumer expectations (and confidence) about the economy. Consequently, a rise in durable goods sales would indicate a growing economy and with it rising interest rates and potentially less Fed easing or even potential Fed tightening. Simply stated, it would suggest lower bond prices. Figure 7.23 shows the average absolute change in bond futures prices after the release of the durable goods report. It indicates that most of the reaction occurs within the first minute of the report's release. Like retail sales, GDP, and the CPI reports the average reaction in bond prices is small (only 5/32) compared with the reaction to the employment and trade balance reports.

Most of the above figures present average responses of bond futures prices to the release of various economic reports without taking expectations into account. Thus, the average price change minimizes the typical market response to *forecast errors* from each of these series. One possible interpretation of the results is simply that GDP, retail sales, durable goods, and the CPI can be forecast more accurately than the other time series and consequently have smaller forecast errors than the employment and trade balance reports. While this is possible, casual empiricism suggests that it is not necessarily correct.

## 11 Other Sources of Macroeconomic Information

### 11.1 Fiscal Policy: Government Spending

This book began with an illustration of the perceived importance of fiscal policy actions on changes in prices on Japanese speculative markets. Yet, the response of market participants to anticipated changes in monetary policy has received vastly more attention than fiscal policy. Does this suggest that monetary policy is somehow more important than fiscal policy? No. There are two principal reasons for this state of affairs. First, fiscal policy actions occur less frequently than monetary policy actions. Given that speculative markets are open and are looking for direction all the time

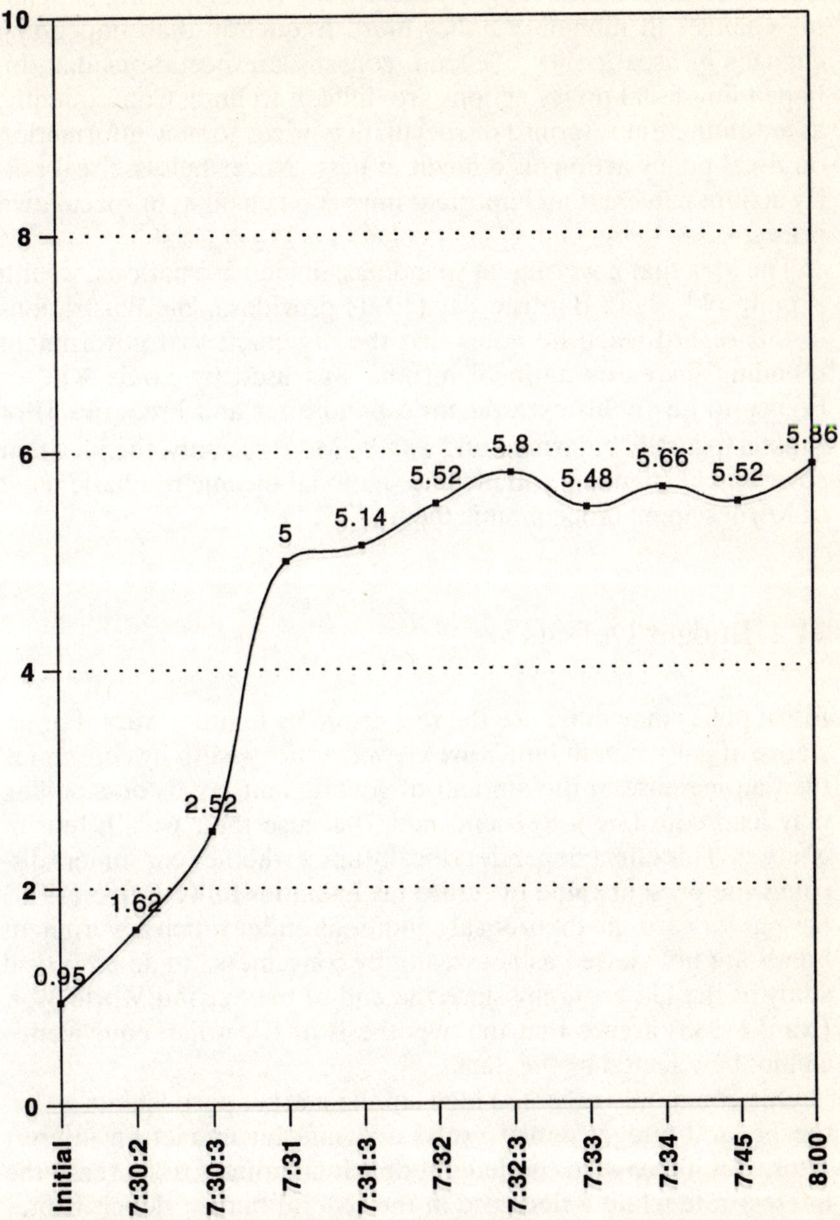


**Figure 7.23** Average absolute change in bond futures prices after the durable goods report is released (in thirty-seconds)

this means that market participants will be contemplating impending changes in monetary policy more frequently than impending changes in fiscal policy. Second, consensus expectations data on impending fiscal policy actions are difficult to find. Consequently, ascertaining the response of speculative prices to new information on fiscal policy actions is difficult at best. Nevertheless, fiscal policy actions can exert an important impact on changes in speculative prices.

The idea that government spending can increase national wealth is quite old. Jean Baptiste Say (1971) provides some illustrations in this regard when he notes that the argument that government spending increases national income was used by Louis XIV of France to justify his extravagant expenditures and Frederick II of Prussia to justify his armies and wars.[15] More recently, the idea that government spending can increase national income is a basic tenet of Keynesian macroeconomic theory.[16]

## 11.2 Budget Deficits

Fiscal policy may influence the real economy in other ways. For instance, if government bonds are viewed as net wealth by consumers then an increase in the amount of government bonds outstanding may lead consumers to spend more because their wealth has increased. This effect depends critically upon whether consumers discount the present value of future tax liabilities fully. Barro (1974) has put forward the theoretical conditions under which government bonds are not viewed as net wealth by consumers. In an empirical study of the US economy since the end of the Second World War, Evans (1988) argues that the hypothesis of Ricardian equivalence cannot be rejected by the data.

One commonly accepted idea among market participants is that the Federal budget deficit exerts a significant impact on interest rates. An increase in the federal deficit is thought to increase the interest rate while a decrease in the federal budget deficit is presumed to reduce interest rates. Despite the fact that this notion is widely believed there is little empirical evidence to support it. In an interesting empirical study, Evans (1987a) concludes: "This paper has found no evidence that interest rates are related to current, past, and expected future budget deficits as conventional macroeconomics posits" (p. 50). Evans (1987b) reaches similar conclusions in a study of the influence of budget deficits on interest rates in other nations.

Those who argue that budget deficits increase interest rates sometimes argue that (during periods of dollar strength) the dollar is strong *vis-à-vis* other currencies because of the high interest rates it induces in the United States. Not surprisingly, given the above results for budget deficits and interest rates, Evans (1986) concludes that high budget deficits were not the cause of a high dollar in the past.

There are a number of relevant issues that often get obscured in discussions of the US Federal government budget deficit in the financial and popular press. These include a failure to differentiate between capital and regular expenditures; a failure to take into account changes in the purchasing power of money or population growth when comparing deficits over time; the use of arbitrary accounting rules which often cause the reported deficit to differ considerably from the actual deficit; and a failure to express the deficit as a percentage of real GNP.

A related issue concerns the source of the present deficit. It has become fashionable to blame recent and prospective budget deficits on the Reagan tax rate cuts of 1981 and 1986. Yet, it is not meaningful to argue that somehow an extra dollar of tax revenues not received due to a tax rate cut increases the deficit more than an extra dollar spent. Put simply, deficits may arise from excessive spending or insufficient tax revenues. Indeed, Canto, Joines, and Webb (1986) argue that the Kennedy and Reagan tax rate cuts did much to stimulate economic activity and with it tax revenues. That is, the tax base and tax rates are related.

Changes in tax policy are another important element of fiscal policy. An increase in income tax rates should cause the before-tax interest rate to increase in order to maintain the same after-tax return. However, many market participants view an increase in tax rates as favorable for the bond market since it is perceived as reducing the federal deficit and hence lowering interest rates. An alternative explanation may also be attached; namely, economic theory suggests that an increase in tax rates should slow down the rate of growth in the economy and hence reduce interest rates if interest rates vary with the economy.

Tax policy also exerts an impact on employment in that it affects the incentives to work in an open market economy. High tax rates stimulate less efficient household production rather than market production as Canto and Webb (1987) point out. It also affects the desire to work overtime or take vacations etc. Another hidden impact is the effect that changes in tax rates have on labor force participation rates for married women with children needing child care. High tax rates reduce the incentive for the primary child care provider (usually the wife/mother) to enter the market labor force. Conversely, economic theory would predict that a reduction in income tax rates would result in an increase in the labor force participation rates of married women with children requiring day care. Simply put, couples filing joint returns would view the marginal income that the wife brings in as taxed at the (potentially) higher tax rate of the husband. This means that the cost of having the wife work has been cut or the reward to both spouses working increased.

This has an important implication for the analysis of employment data, namely, that one cannot treat the labor force participation rate as a constant. Like the tax base, the labor force participation rate is sensitive to changes in the tax rate also. This, in turn, implies that the unemployment rate may be a misleading indicator of what is happening in the economy since a tax rate cut which stimulates economic growth will also affect the labor force participation rates of selected groups. Indeed, it suggests that the nonfarm payrolls number may be a far better indication of the true employment conditions in the economy than the unemployment rate.

In addition to fiscal policy actions, other sources of macroeconomic information are considered relevant to participants in speculative markets. These include debt management and exchange rate policies.

## 11.3 Debt Management Policy

Another potentially important source of macroeconomic information is changes in the debt management policy of the Treasury.

There have been periods when the Treasury or the Federal Reserve have attempted to control some sector of the yield curve. For instance, during the Second World War and immediately following until the Treasury–Federal Reserve accord of 1951 the Federal Reserve followed a policy of pegging short-term interest rates. The objective was to keep short-term interest rates artificially low. During the 1960s the Federal Reserve pursued a policy of trying to influence interest rates in a policy called "operation twist." As the name suggests, the policy amounted to an attempt to twist the yield curve in order to encourage investment spending. There is little evidence that the Federal Reserve was successful in this regard.

Rumors of imminent changes in Treasury debt management policy often exert a substantial influence on bond prices and hence interest rates. In essence, there is a belief among many participants that a change in the supply of Treasury bonds will affect the price of Treasury bonds. Put differently, there is a belief that there is a downward-sloping demand curve for Treasury securities. There is some casual empirical evidence to support a transitory effect on interest rates. For instance, Treasury bond prices appeared to rally in response to the Clinton Administration's decision to eliminate further issuance of seven year Treasury notes and reduce the amount of long bonds it issues. Evidence of a debt management effect on interest rates would conflict with the evidence that Scholes (1972) reports showing a general absence of price pressure effects on stock prices.

## 11.4 Exchange Rate Policies

Government exchange rate policies can influence interest rates and other speculative prices. The European currency crisis of September 1992 provides some examples in this regard. For example, Sweden, which had effectively pegged its currency to the Deutschemark in anticipation of admission into the European Community (and European Monetary Union), was forced to raise its short-term interest rates to astronomical levels in an ultimately unsuccessful attempt to maintain its exchange rate.[17] When Sweden finally gave up the fight to fix the exchange rate for its currency there was an instant decline in its value and a sharp increase in stock prices. The UK had a similar experience after Black Wednesday (September 16, 1992). The withdrawal of the pound sterling from the exchange rate mechanism set off a significant rally in British stocks and gilts and a precipitous decline in the value of the pound sterling relative to the dollar.

Interest rate policy can also influence exchange rates. Germany is a classic example in this regard. The pursuit of a high interest rate policy by the Deutsche Bundesbank without apparent regard for the exchange rate consequences is widely blamed for precipitating the September 1992 currency crisis. The basic rationale for the high interest rate policy was to curb the potential for inflation following unification of Germany.

The experience of September 1992 in the currency markets suggests some lessons for traders and policymakers alike. First, world financial markets are closely linked.[18] Second, it is difficult and extremely costly for central banks to fight the market and win.[19]

## 12 Anecdotal Evidence on the Market's Reaction to Other Sources of Macroeconomic Information

Comments by political leaders and government officials often exert an impact on security prices. The comments of government officials of interest to this book are those which indicate a change in government economic policy. Unlike government economic reports which are regularly scheduled the comments by government officials are irregular both in their timing and in their content. Moreover, much of the information may have been previously released in the form of "trial balloons." Nevertheless, the comments of government officials and political leaders sometimes represent an important source of macroeconomic information to market participants.

One example in this regard is the market's response to the imposition of wage and price controls on Sunday, August 15, 1971, by President Nixon. The Dow Jones Industrial Average rose a then record 32+ points (or 3.84 percent) on then record trading volume of over 31 million shares on Monday, August 16 (the first trading day following the announcement).[20] Bond prices also rose sharply.[21] Analyzing the market's response to the President's address is difficult because President Nixon announced a number of different policy actions. In addition to wage and price controls, the President imposed a 10 percent surcharge on imports and proposed restoration of the investment tax credit (10 percent) and elimination of some excise taxes. There was also a monetary element to the President's address, namely the suspension of the dollar into gold by foreign central banks and the *de facto* devaluation of the US dollar. This raises the question of what the stock market was primarily responding to (i.e. the devaluation, proposed tax changes, or the imposition of wage and price controls).

Another more recent example is President Clinton's address to the American people on Monday evening, February 15, 1993. The initial response by bond market participants was very positive. Bond futures prices were still higher when the US stock index futures market opened on Tuesday morning. Stock index futures opened lower and proceeded to fall further later in the morning.[22]

The differential reaction of the fixed-income and equity markets to President Clinton's remarks can be easily reconciled. The economic consequence of the imposition of higher taxes is a US economy that will grow less quickly than before. This will reduce the present values of the future cash flows of companies which stock market participants have to assess each day. It also makes another economic slowdown more likely which bond market participants interpret as positive for long bond positions.

President's Clinton's aforementioned speech was followed by the State of the Union address on the evening of Wednesday, February 17, 1993. The apparent market reaction to President Clinton's State of the Union address on Thursday is interesting in its own right. Bonds rallied but stocks (taken as a whole) were largely unchanged.[23] If there was new information in the State of the Union address why was there not a more negative reaction in stock prices on Thursday if the reaction on Tuesday was correct? If there was no new information in the State of the Union address then why did bonds rally? Did the President's State of the Union address contain information only of interest to bond market participants? Could trading noise explain the two reactions in speculative prices?

The response of speculative prices to macroeconomic information can be illustrated by their response to a political event which had potential macroeconomic implications (in terms of the level and composition of government spending), namely the ouster of Soviet President Mikhail Gorbachev. When news broke that President Gorbachev was ousted during an unsuccessful coup attempt in August 1991 financial markets around the world reacted sharply. The first reaction to the news occurred in Australasia where most financial markets were open when the news came out. Initially, the US dollar rose sharply especially against the Deutschemark, stock prices fell and the US Treasury long bond fell almost one full point in reaction. As markets opened elsewhere in the world, stock prices continued to fall while the dollar rose. However, the US Treasury long bond *rose* until shortly before the Chicago Board of Trade officially opened. The supposed reason for the subsequent rally in the long bond was a "flight to quality."

Although it is possible that other news arrived in the market which would positively affect Treasury bond prices Gorbachev's ouster was the *dominant* news item during this period. Moreover, the initial reaction in other speculative prices was largely reinforced during the period. Given that the coup looked as if it would succeed in the early hours what is puzzling is the initial reaction in US Treasury bond prices to the news. That is, why did Treasury bonds initially fall rather than rise in response to the news of the ouster if there was a flight to quality?

## Appendix 7.1

## The Household Survey: A Closer Look

The household survey samples the civilian noninstitutional population in an attempt to assess the size and composition of the labor force, as well as the characteristics of those individuals not participating in it. Those in the labor force are further divided into those who are employed and those who are unemployed during the survey period. Individuals are questioned with respect to their employment status during the calendar week which includes the twelfth day of the month. From these surveys are derived labor force participation rates. The survey excludes individuals under the age of 16 or those who are in prisons or mental institutions. Members of the military stationed in the United States are included.

The inferences of the household survey are based on a *potential* sample of 60,000 occupied households. The survey is conducted by the Bureau of the Census and consists of direct interviews.[24] Because only five out of six of the households that the Census Bureau visits are occupied a larger sample is necessary in order to have approximately 60,000 occupied households in the sample. Another problem is that even the occupied houses may not result in completed interviews. Indeed, approximately 4–5 percent of those households visited are unavailable to participate in the survey for a variety of reasons.[25] Respondents are surveyed with respect to their employment status for the survey period (i.e. the calendar week in which the twelfth day of the month falls). Information on full and part-time workers is also collected,[26] and information on why individuals work part-time rather than full-time is compiled.

There is an overlap in the monthly survey from one month to the next. Approximately three out of four households are in the sample for adjacent months. Similarly, approximately one half of the sample is the same from the same month a year earlier.

It should be emphasized that some very specific meanings are assigned to a variety of terms that often take on other meanings in everyday language. These terms include household; employed persons; unemployed persons; labor force; labor force participation rates; overall unemployment rate.

For instance, the definition of an employee is relatively broad. It includes anyone during the survey period who worked as an employee; was self-employed; worked more than 15 hours on an unpaid basis in a family business; was a member of the US armed forces stationed in the United States. It also includes individuals who were employed but were on leave (with or without pay) from work during the survey period. In those cases where an individual has more than one position the individual is counted as employed only once and classified according to his primary position. Homemakers are not considered to be employed nor are those who work as volunteers at religious or charitable organizations. Thus, an individual who has a part-time job working three hours per week and desires full-time employment would be considered employed, while an individual who volunteers 40 hours each week of his time to a charitable organization would not.

In order to be considered unemployed for statistical purposes, an individual must not fit one of the categories mentioned above; be available for work; and actually have sought work during the four weeks preceding the survey week. The exceptions to the rule that the unemployed must seek work are individuals who were laid off and are awaiting recall or those individuals who plan to start a new job within 30 days of the survey week.

To make matters more confusing there is more than one unemployment rate. The overall unemployment rate refers to the ratio of the number of unemployed to the total civilian noninstitutional population. The civilian unemployment rate, in contrast, differs from the overall unemployment rate in that members of the armed forces stationed in the United States are excluded from the labor force.

As previously noted, the household survey provides a wealth of information about employment and earnings patterns across a number of demographic groups.[27] This includes information on race, gender, and marital status among other items. Information is also collected on occupation, industry, and class of worker. The class of worker category is further subdivided into private and public sector positions. Similar information is also provided for individuals who are not in the labor force for a variety of reasons such as they are retired, ill, students, or discouraged. Discouraged workers are individuals who would like to be employed but believe that they are unable to locate desired employment.

A number of changes have been made in the survey over the years such that there is not strict comparability over time. For instance, these changes include an increase in the lowest age in the household from 14 to 16. While these changes are of much interest to labor economists and others using data from these time series they are not of much use to most bond market participants or short-term forecasters of economic variables and are not discussed here.

The question naturally arises as to the reliability of the survey data. It is important to emphasize that the survey data are sample data and, as such, are subject to the same problems as other sample data. One error is sampling error. Sampling error arises when the characteristics of the sample differ from the characteristics of the population. The Department of Labor calculates standard errors associated with various components of the monthly employment and earnings report. It should be pointed out that the standard errors reported by the Department of Labor are generalized rather than specific standard errors. That is, they are approximate rather than exact standard errors.

The other major source of error in the estimates is nonsampling error. Nonsampling errors arise from a number of factors and basically fall into two categories: (1) erroneous information provided by survey respondents (due to misinterpretations of survey questions, failure to recall relevant information, or unwillingness to provide the information requested); and (2) recording, processing, estimation errors and undercoverage of sample households and members thereof (i.e. errors by the census workers or the Department of Labor).

## Seasonal Adjustment

It should be emphasized that the survey data are sample data from which inferences concerning the overall employment picture in the United States are drawn. Thus it is not surprising that seasonal patterns in employment and earnings exist. For instance, additional employees may be hired during the Christmas season in order to deal with increased demand for goods by customers. Similarly, the ranks of the labor force may swell during the summer months as students and recent graduates look for work. Given that these changes in the labor force are well known it makes sense to seasonally adjust the data.

Adjusting the time series for any seasonal influences has the advantage of making it easier to discern cyclical and secular trends. However, the method employed may not completely eliminate seasonality. The Labor Department uses the X-11 ARIMA method to seasonally adjust the data. This has been in use since 1980 and is an extension of the X-11 method.

## Notes

1 Macroeconomic theory is relevant when changes in speculative prices are the output variables from macroeconomic models.

2 Similar information on other economic reports is excluded for brevity.

3 Some private economic reports, such as the survey of purchasing managers, are considered very important.

4 Leaks of the information content of government economic reports are extremely rare.

5 Zarnowitz and Lambros (1992) discuss the importance of taking the dispersion of individual forecasts into account. Among other things, they indicate that the directional impact of an increase in uncertainty on changes in speculative prices may be ambiguous in some cases. For instance, Zarnowitz and Lambros state:

> A rise in uncertainty about inflation, other things equal, can either reduce or increase interest rates, depending on whether it depresses real investment more than real savings or vice versa.
> (p. 518)

6 Jeffreys (1973) argues:

> The use of the expression "exact science" and the scarcity of statements in popular works on physics about imperfection of agreement between physical laws and observation led most philosophers into thinking that exact agreement is attained. ... Exact agreement between physical laws was never attained; Plato knew this, and Laplace had a practical technique for dealing with it.
> (p. 63)

7 The Chicago Board of Trade's (CBT) US Treasury bond futures contract is the dominant bond futures contract. Unfortunately, data on the CBT bond futures contract were not available for the sample period. This is because the CBT bond futures pit used to open for trading at 8:00 a.m. Chicago time (9:00 a.m. Washington DC time) or after most government economic reports were released. The CBT switched to a 7:20 a.m. (Chicago time) opening in early November 1988. Trading in the bond futures contract traded on the Mid-America Commodity Exchange opened at 7:20 a.m. (Chicago time) throughout the length of the sample period used in this study. (The Mid-America bond futures contract has a notional value of $50,000 while the CBT bond futures contract has a notional value of $100,000. Otherwise, the two contracts are identical.) CBT time and sales data were used

for measuring changes in bond futures prices after 8:00 a.m. Chicago time.

8 The front month usually refers to the nearby futures contract. On US financial futures markets, at least, the front month contract is often the most actively traded futures contract. Because interest in the nearby futures contract wanes as it approaches expiration, the "front month" contract is rolled over before the nearby contract gets too close to expiration. The timing of the rollover varies across exchanges.

9 Occasionally the bond market is closed on the Friday that the employment report is released. This occurs when Good Friday coincides with the release of the employment report.

10 Differences between the two surveys are explained in the report accompanying the news release. For instance, the May 1990 Employment and Earnings Report states:

> Data from these two sources [i.e. household and establishment surveys] differ from each other because of differences in definitions and coverage, sources of information, methods of collection, and estimating procedures. Sampling variability and response errors are additional reasons for discrepancies.
>
> (p. 153)

11 In years past, the attention of bond market participants centered primarily on the unemployment rate component of the employment report. At present, the primary attention of bond market participants centers on the nonfarm payrolls component of the employment report.

12 Consider, for instance, the reaction of market participants to the release of the employment report on Friday, April 2, 1993, as reported in the April 5, 1993, issue of *Barron's*:

> The bulk of the week's selloff [in bonds] came Friday in reaction to what appeared to be a bullish (for bonds, at least) employment report for March. Prices spiked higher seconds after news that non-farm payrolls fell by 22,000 persons last month – a stark contrast to the expected gain of about 100,000. But the market did an abrupt U-turn after it turned out that, also contrary to market expectations, the previous months' data were revised upward rather than downward. ...
>
> (p. 62)

13 This seems to suggest that there is a potential profit opportunity of buying (if bond futures prices initially rose) or selling (if bond futures prices initially fell) around 7:33:00 (Chicago time) and then offsetting the position about a minute later. This would result in a two-tick profit,

on average, after taking into account the bid–offer spread. No attempt was made to test this hypothesis, however.

14 The *Wall Street Journal* of Wednesday, April 15, 1987, reported:

> Bond prices took a wild rollercoaster ride yesterday.... Early in the day, actively traded U.S. Treasury bonds plunged in frenzied trading after the Commerce Department reported an unexpected surge in the nation's merchandise trade deficit for February....
>
> (p. 57)

15 Say (1971) states:

> Madame de Maintenon mentions in a letter to the Cardinal de Noailles, that when she one day urged Louis XIV to be more liberal in charitable donations, he replied, that royalty dispenses charity by its profuse expenditure; a truly alarming dogma, and one that shows the ruin of France to have been reduced to principle. False principles are more fatal than intentional misconduct because they are followed up with erroneous notions of self-interest, and are long persevered in without remorse or reserve....
>
> Frederick II of Prussia, ... writes thus to D'Alembert, in justification of his wars: "My numerous armies promote the circulation of money, and disburse impartially amongst the provinces the taxes paid by the people to the state." Again I repeat, this is not the fact; the taxes paid to the government by the subject are not refunded by its expenditure.
>
> (pp. 415–16)

16 Barro (1981) advances and tests a theoretical model which posits differential output responses for temporary and permanent government spending. He reports evidence that suggests a positive relationship between output and government purchases that is less than unity.In another article (which used UK data over an almost 200 year period), Barro (1987) presents evidence of a positive relationship between the current interest rate and lagged values of temporary increases in government spending.

17 During the period when the Swedish Riksbank attempted to maintain its currency's exchange rate short-term interest rates rose to over 500 percent at one point.

18 There is reason to believe that Federal Reserve foreign exchange market interventions are unlikely to exert more than a transitory effect on exchange rates. The reason for this, as noted in chapter 6, is that the

Federal Reserve sterilizes any monetary intervention it conducts on behalf of the Treasury. That is, the Fed attempts to offset any impact of an exchange rate action on the domestic money supply.

19 The Banque de France was one of the few central banks which successfully defended its currency during the currency crisis of September 1992. The battle to defend the French franc resumed in 1993. The *Financial Times* of Friday, July 23, 1993, reported that the Banque de France spent DM 10 billion on Thursday, July 22, 1993, alone in an attempt to defend the foreign exchange value of its currency (p. 1).

20 Brown (1991) states:

> The most important market news of the year came in mid-August when President Nixon announced a freeze on wage[s] and prices for three months and closed the gold window.... For bullion prices it was a nonevent.... The Dow gained a record 32.93 points on record volume of 31.7 million shares. But second thoughts soon cast doubts on the program's prospects and the market fell back sharply to a new low, below 800, in November.
>
> (p. 93)

21 The *Wall Street Journal* of Tuesday, August 17, 1971, reported that: "seasoned utility and industrial company [bonds] were up an average of $2\frac{1}{2}$ points" (p. 24).

22 On Wednesday, February 17, 1993, the *Financial Times* reported:

> US stock markets fell sharply yesterday as investors took fright at US President Bill Clinton's plans to raise taxes on a broader range of investors than expected.
>
> The Dow Jones Industrial Average fell more than 75 points in the first 90 minutes of business in heavy selling, .... In contrast, the bond markets welcomed Mr. Clinton's tough talk on deficit reduction. ... [When asked to explain the market's reaction to his speech President Clinton said] "The bond market's a better indicator, and that response has been very positive."...
>
> (p. 1)

23 On Friday, February 19, 1993, the *Wall Street Journal* reported:

> Bond prices surged as investors bet that President Clinton's economic plan will either thrust the economy back into a recession or significantly reduce the U.S. budget deficit. Stock prices and the dollar ended mixed as a result of confusion about the effect of the plan....
>
> (p. C1)

24 The establishment or payroll survey uses mail questionnaires to obtain information for the employment and earnings report. Over 300,000 establishments are examined.

25 Noninterviews arise due to a variety of factors including the refusal of the household respondent to respond to the survey. Census employees also report finding almost 16 percent of the housing units they call on in a given month vacant. Noninterviews may also arise because the interviewer does not conduct the interview. There is reason to suspect that the noninterview rate in crime-ridden inner-city neighborhoods may be higher than in other areas.

26 Full-time employment is considered a position at which an individual works 35 or more hours each week.

27 It should be noted that the number of hours worked differ from the number of hours workers are paid for because of holidays, vacations, and sick leave etc.

## References

Barro, R. J. 1974: "Are Government Bonds Net Wealth?," *Journal of Political Economy*, 82, 1095–1117.

Barro, R. J. 1981: "Output Effects of Government Purchases," *Journal of Political Economy*, 82, 1086–1121.

Barro, R. J. 1987: "Government Spending, Interest Rates, Prices, and Budget Deficits in the United Kingdom, 1701–1918," *Journal of Monetary Economics*, 20, 221–47.

*Barron's*, selected issues.

Bates, J. M., and C. W. J. Granger 1969: "The Combination of Forecasts," *Operations Research Quarterly*, 20, 451–68.

Brown, J. D. 1991: *101 Years on Wall Street: An Investor's Almanac*, Englewood Cliffs, NJ: Prentice-Hall.

Canto, V. A., and R. I. Webb 1987: "The Effect of State Fiscal Policy on State Relative Economic Performance," *Southern Economic Journal*, 54 (1), July, 186–202.

Canto, V. A., D. H. Joines, and R. I. Webb 1986: "The Revenue Effects of the Kennedy and Reagan Tax Cuts: Some Time Series Evidence," *Journal of Business and Economic Statistics*, 4 (3), 281–8.

Clark, T. A., D. H. Joines, and G. M. Phillips 1988: "Social Security Payments, Money Supply Announcements, and Interest Rates," *Journal of Monetary Economics*, 22, 257–78.

Evans, P. 1986: "Is the Dollar High Because of Large Budget Deficits?," *Journal of Monetary Economics*, 18, November, 227–49.

Evans, P. 1987a: "Interest Rates and Expected Future Budget Deficits in the United States," *Journal of Political Economy*, 95 (1), 34–58.

Evans, P. 1987b: "Do Budget Deficits Raise Nominal Interest Rates? Evidence from Six Countries," *Journal of Monetary Economics*, 20, September, 281–300.

Evans, P. 1988: "Are Consumers Ricardian? Evidence for the United States," *Journal of Political Economy*, 96 (5), 983–1004.

*Financial Times*, selected issues.

Ito, T. 1990: "Foreign Exchange Rate Expectations: MicroSurvey Data," *American Economic Review*, 80 (3), June, 434–49.

Jeffreys, H., Sir 1973: *Scientific Inference*, 3rd edn, Cambridge: Cambridge University Press.

Palm, F. C., and A. Zellner 1992: "To Combine or Not to Combine? Issues of Combining Forecasts," *Journal of Forecasting*, 11, 687–701.

Say, J.-B. 1971: *A Treatise on Political Economy or the Production, Distribution and Consumption of Wealth*, New York: Augustus M. Kelley.

Scholes, M. 1972: "The Market for Securities: Substitution Versus Price Pressure and the Effects of Information on Share Prices," *Journal of Business*, 45 (2), April, 179–211.

Urich, T., and P. Wachtel 1984: "The Effects of Inflation and Money Supply Announcements on Interest Rates," *Journal of Finance*, 39 (4), September, 1177–88.

US Department of Labor 1990: *Employment and Earnings*, Washington, DC: U.S. Government Printing Office, May.

*Wall Street Journal*, selected issues.

Webb, R. I., and D. G. Smith 1994: "The Effect of Market Opening and Closing on the Volatility of CME Eurodollar Futures Prices," *Journal of Futures Markets*, February, forthcoming.

Zarnowitz, V. 1992: "The Accuracy of Individual and Group Forecasts," in V. Zarnowitz (ed.), *Business Cycles: Theory, History, Indicators, and Forecasting*, Chicago, IL: University of Chicago Press, pp. 444–61; *Journal of Forecasting*, 3, January–March (1984), 11–26.

Zarnowitz, V., and L. A. Lambros 1992: "Consensus and Uncertainty in Economic Prediction," in V. Zarnowitz (ed.), *Business Cycles: Theory, History, Indicators, and Forecasting*, Chicago, IL: University of Chicago Press, pp. 492–518; reprinted from *Journal of Political Economy,* 95 (3) (1987), 591–621.

# 8

# Conclusions

> All our empirical data are sensations. The test of a scientific law is its capacity to account for sensations already recorded and its interest lies in its capacity to predict new ones.
>
> (Sir Harold Jeffreys, *Scientific Inference*)

The manner by which new information is incorporated into speculative prices is fascinating even though it is not completely understood at present. In this book we considered the behavior of changes in speculative prices in response to the arrival of new macroeconomic information. Particular attention was directed to the reaction of speculative prices to the presumed information content of periodic government economic reports.

The reaction of speculative prices to the arrival of new macroeconomic information is interesting because it involves issues of interest to macroeconomic and financial economic theorists, traders, and economic policymakers alike. Among other things, it provides an opportunity to assess the macroeconomic beliefs of traders; the potential validity of various macroeconomic theories; the informational efficiency of speculative markets; the influence of noise on speculative prices; and the process by which new information is incorporated into speculative prices.

The reaction of speculative prices to the arrival of new macroeconomic information is sometimes quite puzzling. Extreme examples in this regard include changes in the apparent importance of weekly money supply announcements in speculative markets (i.e. from extremely important in years past to unimportant today) and changes in the interpretation traders assign to the information in the merchandise trade balance report (i.e. the sign changed).

To be sure, explanations for these phenomena consistent with informational market efficiency may exist. For instance, it is possible that the recent lack of response of speculative prices to forecast errors in the weekly money supply announcements is the result of the Fed's adoption of contemporary reserve accounting in February 1984. As Joines (1991) argues, the shift from lagged reserve accounting to contemporary reserve accounting may have decreased the information content of the money supply announcements (and hence their relevance for bond market participants).

While this explanation is plausible, it does not explain the continued influence of the money supply announcements beyond February 1984.[1] Moreover, puzzles remain in the response of speculative prices to weekly money supply announcements even if this explanation is correct.[2] For instance, why should long-term bond prices react so much to the preliminary data contained in weekly money supply announcements?

Monetary theory suggests that the central bank has, at best, short-run control over the nominal money stock. However, whether the central bank actually exercises such control remains controversial.[3] There is considerable evidence in the empirical economics literature that the money supply is endogenously determined (see for example Sims, 1980).[4] This is especially true for small open economies as Zarnowitz (1992) observes.[5] Yet, there appear to be significant announcement effects associated with discount rate changes and, in years past, weekly money supply announcements. As Smirlock and Yawitz (1985) note, the existence of announcement effects for discount rate changes when the money supply is endogenously determined is difficult to reconcile with informational market efficiency.[6] Similar comments apply to other monetary policy announcements when the money supply is endogenously determined. The hypothesis that speculative prices respond to noise rather than information in the short run offers one way of reconciling these contradictory empirical results.

There is considerable evidence in the economics literature that budget deficits (past, current, or expected future) do not influence interest rates or exchange rates (see for example Evans, 1986, 1987).

Yet, casual empiricism suggests that fixed-income market participants often react as if they do.[7] The hypothesis that speculative prices often react to noise rather than information in the short run may explain these apparently contradictory results as well.

Conventional wisdom on Wall Street holds that the level of interest rates varies inversely with the strength of the economy. Indeed, this belief lies at the heart of many of the macroeconomic relationships that traders appear to believe in. For instance, lower than expected retail sales, durable goods sales, or new job creation are all perceived as indicating economic weakness and hence lower interest rates. The reason why economic weakness results in lower interest rates is that the demand for credit is presumed to fall relative to the supply of credit which, in turn, causes the price of credit (i.e. the interest rate) to fall.[8] This may result from lower demand for credit or increased supply of credit due to monetary easing. Yet, there is little empirical evidence in the economics literature to support the assertion that *real* interest rates vary with the strength of the economy. Other observers contend that the level of nominal interest rates varies with the strength of the economy because inflation varies with the strength of the economy. To be sure, there is some evidence that nominal interest rates vary with the strength of the economy. However, even this is problematic in that it suggests that, holding the money supply constant, the price level increases (decreases) as output increases (decreases). This is inconsistent with the commonsensical idea that inflation can be described as "too much money chasing too few goods."

The response of market prices to the arrival of macroeconomic information raises a number of questions many of the answers to which remain elusive. These include such questions as the following. Do economic reports with preliminary data contain noise or relevant macroeconomic information? Is the reaction of speculative prices consistent with received macroeconomic theory? Do speculative prices overreact to macroeconomic information? Does the reaction in speculative prices vary according to the amount of dispersion in individual forecasts? Is the reaction in speculative prices consistent over time in both direction and magnitude? Is the reaction in speculative prices consistent across similar financial markets (e.g. bond futures and Eurodollar futures) where one expects the same directional response (if not magnitude)? How important are revised data in economic reports? To what extent does the composition of the economic report matter in assessing its "true" information content?

The largely anecdotal evidence discussed in this book suggests that noise or noninformational factors play an important role in explaining the behavior of changes in speculative prices. To be sure, speculative prices usually respond quickly to the presumed information content of economic reports as one would expect in an informationally efficient capital market. It is also possible that the market is informationally efficient but relevant macroeconomic information is mismeasured (e.g. due to incorrect consensus expectations); ignored (e.g. revisions); or does not take into account stochastic economic policy actions. However, a closer examination of the reaction of speculative prices to new macroeconomic information (as well as the relevance of the presumed information itself) suggests potential inconsistencies with market efficiency.

To the extent that noise or noninformational factors are important, an examination of the immediate response of speculative prices to the arrival of macroeconomic information may give an incorrect picture of the relevant relationship between economic variables. This has important implications for economic policymakers whose policy actions may be influenced by such responses.

If speculative prices react to noise rather than information how inefficient are speculative markets? Black (1986) argues that speculative markets are "reasonably efficient" despite the influence of noise on changes in speculative prices. Others appear to suggest that speculative markets are grossly inefficient for various reasons, some unrelated to the existence of noise (see for example Modigliani and Cohn, 1979).

At present, the noise models of Black (1986) and DeLong et al. (1990a, b) appear to offer the most promise for a systematic explanantion of the observed behavior of changes in speculative prices in response to the arrival of new macroeconomic information. These theories may also explain why the perceived importance of various economic reports changes over time. However, even these models may require further modifications as more systematic evidence is obtained on these phenomena.

One possible starting point in the search for potential models to explain the market's reaction to macroeconomic information is to consider the time series behavior of changes in speculative prices. After all, changes in speculative prices are essentially the output variables from the unknown correct model (i.e. a "black box") of financial markets. The observed simplicity of the times series models that many changes in speculative prices follow imposes sharp limits on possible *linear* models of asset pricing in either an informationally efficient or informationally *inefficient* capital market, as well as on the joint times series processes of the potential input variables.[9]

From a trading perspective, however, it matters little whether the reaction of changes in speculative prices to the arrival of new macroeconomic information conforms to accepted macroeconomic or financial economic theory. It matters little whether traders are rational or consistent in their interpretations of macroeconomic information over time. Rather, from a trading perspective it only matters that forecast errors from economic reports and other sources of macroeconomic information sometimes precipitate large changes in speculative prices. As long as this is the case, financial traders will be interested in the influence of macroeconomic information on changes in speculative prices and continue to wager vast sums of money on the outcome of economic reports and other sources of macroeconomic information.

## Notes

1 For example, the *Wall Street Journal* of Friday, April 13, 1984, reported:

> A huge drop in the nation's money supply, coupled with a government report of a steep decline in retail sales, sent bond prices surging yesterday. The basic money supply known as $M_1$ plunged $5 billion in the week ending April 2,.... The larger than expected drop brought the measure close to the low end of the Fed's target range.... Prices of actively traded Treasury bonds spurted almost a point yesterday....
>
> (p. A3)

Or, consider the following article in the Friday, May 11, 1984, the *Wall Street Journal* which reported:

> The bond markets suffered a sharp setback yesterday as prices tumbled and investors shunned the Treasury's $4.75 billion auction of 30 year bonds. The market's woes were intensified

by a steeper than anticipated $2.4 billion jump in the money supply....

(p. A3)

2 Upon closer inspection, the evidence on the influence of unexpected changes in the discount rate or money supply on changes in interest rates appears to be inconsistent. As noted earlier, a number of studies report a positive relationship between unexpected changes in the money supply and interest rates after October 1979. Similarly, other studies report a positive relationship between unexpected discount rate changes and interest rates. Yet, monetary theory suggests that a discount rate change exerts its influence on interest rates by changing the money supply in the *opposite* direction.

3 If the Federal Reserve controls the money supply then one would expect to see evidence of that control in the behavior of the monetary base. However, as noted previously, Cornell (1983) and Joines (1991) report a general absence of relationship between unanticipated changes in the monetary base and changes in interest rates. These results are consistent with Zellner's and Palm's (1975) finding that the log of the monetary base follows a random walk.

4 On a practical level, the Federal Reserve's notorious inability to forecast accurately the level of the nominal money supply over short time intervals is consistent with an endogenously determined money supply. Evans (1978) presents evidence that suggests that the German money supply was endogenously determined during the German hyperinflation of the 1920s.

5 Zarnowitz (1992) states:

> The potential for an autonomous [i.e. exogenous] monetary policy is generally overestimated by analysts who concentrate on the United States, the only large market economy in which balance-of-payments considerations could long be treated as secondary even under fixed exchange rates. For any small open economy under this regime, the nominal money supply depends on changes in the available foreign exchange reserves; it must tend to be consistent with prices and incomes that will balance the country's international payments and hence cannot be determined independently by domestic authorities....
>
> (p. 49)

6 Smirlock and Yawitz distinguish between "technical" (i.e. expected) discount rate changes which are endogenously determined and "non-technical" (i.e. unexpected) discount rate changes which convey new information to market participants. They report evidence that only the

latter discount rate changes have significant announcement effects associated with them and that the quick reaction in speculative prices to these announcements is consistent with an informationally efficient capital market.

7 This reaction may be explained in part by the fact that fiscal (and monetary) policymakers appear to believe that such a relationship exists.

8 Essentially, this is nothing more than the loanable funds theory of interest rates.

9 Webb (1985) essentially makes this argument. There is little reason to believe that nonlinear models may explain observed economic relationships better. Indeed, the Jeffreys–Winch simplicity postulate suggests that simpler models are preferred to more complex models.

## References

Black, F. 1986: "Noise," *Journal of Finance*, 42 (3), July, 529–43.

Cornell, B. 1983: "Money Supply Announcements and Interest Rates: Another View," *Journal of Business*, 56 (1), 1–23.

DeLong, B. J., A. Shleifer, L. H. Summers, and R. J. Waldman 1990a: "Noise Trader Risk in Financial Markets," *Journal of Political Economy*, 98 (4), 703–38.

DeLong, B. J., A. Shleifer, L. H. Summers, and R. J. Waldman 1990b: "Positive Feedback Investment Strategies and Destabilizing Rational Speculation," *Journal of Finance*, 45 (2), June, 379–96.

Evans, P. 1978: "Time Series and Structural Analysis of the German Hyperinflation," *International Economic Review*, 19, February, 195–210.

Evans, P. 1986: "Is the Dollar High Because of Large Budget Deficits?," *Journal of Monetary Economics*, 18, November, 227–49.

Evans, P. 1987: "Interest Rates and Expected Future Budget Deficits in the United States," *Journal of Political Economy*, 95 (1), 34–58.

Joines, D. H. 1991: "Money Supply Announcements and Real Economic Activity," *Journal of Monetary Economics*, 28, December, 391–410.

Modigliani, F., and R. A. Cohn 1979: "Inflation, Rational Valuation and the Market," *Financial Analysts Journal*, 35 (2), March–April, 24–44.

Sims, C. A. 1980: "Comparison of Interwar and Postwar Business Cycles: Monetarism Reconsidered," *American Economic Review*, 70 (2), 250–7.

Smirlock, M., and J. Yawitz 1985: "Asset Returns, Discount Rate Changes, and Market Efficiency," *Journal of Finance*, 40 (4), September, 1141–58.

Webb, R. I. 1985: "The Behavior of Speculative Prices and the Consistency of Economic Models," *Journal of Econometrics*, 27, 123–30.

Zarnowitz, V. 1992: *Business Cycles: Theory, History, Indicators, and Forecasting*, Chicago, IL: University of Chicago Press.

Zellner, A., and F. Palm 1975: "Time Series and Structural Analysis of Monetary Models of the U.S. Economy," *Sankhya: The Indian Journal of Statistics*, 37, 12–36.

# Index